The Love of a Master

To Dave

love & light

Jesus

A Banks

A reflection on this book

I have completed the reading of your book on "The Love of a Master."

Every sentence in the book shows your intense devotion to your Master. Spiritual Masters operate as ordinary human beings as well as superhuman beings at the same time. To attend on and take care of such a unique person is not easy and presents several challenges. Suddenly he needs something like an ordinary person and suddenly he is Master of All and needs nothing but is fulfilling the needs of others.

Jsu, you did a great job in taking care of J-R! I commend your Seva! You have set an example for others to follow. I send you my love and Great Master's Blessings.

– Ishwar Puri

(Ishwar Puri is the initiate of His beloved Satguru Hazur Baba Sawan Singh Ji, the Great Master.)

The Love of a Master

Rev. Jesus Garcia, D.S.S.

Scott J-R Publishing

Copyright © 2017 Scott J-R Productions. All rights reserved.
Published by Scott J-R Productions
c/o Jesus Garcia, D.S.S.
1626 Montana Ave, Suite 624
Santa Monica, California 90403
http://www.soultranscendence.com
utah7@mac.com
Printed in the United States of America
ISBN - 13: 9780692881262
ISBN - 10: 0692881263

Library of Congress Control Number: 2017910440

Scott J-R Productions, Los Angeles, CA

Cover Design by David Sand and Maria Rajput – DesignerXD, and Scott J-R
Productions
Copyright © 2017 Scott J-R Productions

Excerpts from *The Wayshower Book* by John-Roger, D.S.S.
Copyright © 2011 Movement of Spiritual Inner Awareness

"12 Signs of the Traveler" excerpted from *The Path to Mastership* by John-Roger, D.S.S.
Copyright © 1976 and 1982, Peace Theological Seminary and College of Philosophy®

Previously unpublished excerpts by John-Roger, D.S.S. from archives/database
Copyright © 2017 Movement of Spiritual Inner Awareness

"Abu Ben" poem by James Henry Leigh Hunt (1784–1859)

"Zenobia: Real Life Warrior Princess" Copyright © 1997 Glenn Barnett

"Pheidippides and the Marathon" Copyright © 2017 Glenn Barnett

Article excerpts from *The New Day Herald* by David Sand
Copyright © 2017 Movement of Spiritual Inner Awareness

Photos by Laurie Lerner, Copyright © 1988 Laurie Lerner

Photos by Betty Bennett and David Sand
Copyright © 2017 Movement of Spiritual Inner Awareness

Photos by Jesus Garcia, Copyright © 2017 Scott J-R Productions

Photos of Sawan Singh by Ram Nath Mehta (taken 1903-1948)

Dedication

For my friend and Wayshower and Great Master, Dr. John-Roger.

Table of Contents

J-R: You know, with friends, you do reality checks all the time. <u>Like, Zeus is one of my best friends</u>. God! If he's awake, he's asleep. Do I do reality checks on you often?

Zeus: *Yeah.*

J-R: He'll tell me something. I'll say, "Let me see that." He will get up to bring it to me and I'll look at it and I go, "Damn you, it's pretty good. This guy's reporting real accurately." Then, one day he tells me something and I say, "Let me see it." He says, "I don't have it. It's just what I got." I'm starting to trust that a lot. But I never give everything over to it, 'cause that might be the time where I trusted a lot and there was wrongness in it that I could have caught. So, I go up to the point that I also trust; then, I start to check. And I say, "You check and I'll check." We check back. Got the same information.

– JOHN-ROGER, D.S.S. (1991, WINDERMERE
RANCH DURING PAT TRAININGS)

"Pauli Sanderson and Zeus and I went out the other day on a horse for about an hour and 10 or 15 minutes, we never ran—I think we did a little bit just for the hell of it, but we just went on trails looking at erosion patterns. We had a great time 'cause we were talking about this and about that and how neat this is—I doubt if we'll do anything that we talked about, but damn, it was sure fun to socialize."

– John-Roger, D.S.S. (1992, Board Meeting at Miracielo, Santa Barbara)

"*Now, tonight I want to show you a technique of the Sound Current. These things, like anything else in the world, have to be practiced so they feel familiar to you. So we're not going to be listening to what we call the physical sound here. We're going to be listening to the audible stream, the Sound Current. And, to do this, we're going to connect up to it by just chanting the Sound Current tone, and then after we've chanted it for about five minutes, we sit and listen. Now, **part of this exercise that can help you is that you place your attention on the Tisra Til, or the seat of the Soul**. The Basic Self of our own consciousness that resides primarily in the negative world will resist the Spiritual thrust. Be prepared for it. And when you start moving the Sound Current into it, it'll do everything in the world to stop you. But I do know that not one Soul's going to be lost. And that means there'll be chances and chances and chances. However, if you can do it this time, why not, right?*"

— JOHN-ROGER, D.S.S.

Introduction

MY NAME IS JESUS GARCIA; my teacher and spiritual guide is John-Roger, who is also known as J-R. J-R called me "Zeus." I'm writing this book to give an inside look at life with a spiritual master and "spiritual warrior," to share my experiences, and to put things in context, so people who did not know J-R physically, as I did, might have a better understanding of who he was and where he came from.

I'm also writing this book to explore the things I learned both from him and about myself in the process of being with him practically 24 hours a day, seven days a week for 26 years. For many of those years, I was John-Roger's right-hand man and the only time I was away for any length of time was when I was producing, directing or acting in films.

Many of the things I'll talk about are not only learnings for me, but might be valuable lessons for others. I'm aware that everyone he touched already has their own inner experience with him, so mine are just a few out of many examples from around the world. Of course, I'm really writing this book for myself to best capture my experiences with J-R. I wanted to complete what he recommended to me years ago at Windermere Ranch.

I remember J-R once telling me to take photos, make an album. He said that all this is going to go by fast. He was right. That's why

I find myself wanting to write while it's still fresh and I remember how I saw things. I apologize if I leave out people's names or if I see it one way and not your way. I know that I love you, and I hope you know that, too. I'm writing so I won't ever forget that.

It's now 2014, and by the time I finish this, it will be 2017. J-R will have been gone for around three years. He definitely was right; I was with him for 26 years and life came and went in what seems like no time. To have lived that life and to be so grateful—and to be aware of it—is a blessing.

John-Roger came into this world for a brief period of eighty years and touched millions. How grateful I am that I met up with this man who held the office we call the Mystical Traveler and also that of the Preceptor, a Consciousness that shows up on earth only about every 25,000 (!) years. I was pulled into his orbit, and I just loved it.

I hope what I write touches your heart and awakens some of the things inside of you that John-Roger's presence awakened in me.

$\mathcal{P}rologue$

JOHN-ROGER PASSED INTO SPIRIT AT 2:49 am on October 22, 2014. It was the end of a life that had profoundly altered me and had defined my own life.

The hardest thing for me at that moment was watching and listening as J-R breathed his last breath, and realizing that he truly was gone. That fact was driven home as one person said, "That's it for the Preceptor. He's gone."

Many people lost a teacher and guide, but I lost so much more. I lost a friend.

I had always thought that in the end it was going to be only Nathaniel Sharratt and me with J-R. We were the ones who had been taking care of him every day for many years. However, when J-R passed away at the hospital, there were several people present. Besides (and, thankfully, beside) me and Nathaniel, those present were John Morton, Paul Kaye, Vincent Dupont and Mark Lurie. Those last three are the men who run the MSIA organization and are collectively known as the Presidency. The way we all were positioned around J-R as he passed came about because of a sort of vision I had gotten from Spirit.

J-R would send me internal pictures, through dreams or spiritual exercises, and I would check them out in the world. In this particular picture, I had seen John Morton at J-R's head, the MSIA presidency on J-R's right, Nathaniel on J-R's left, and me at his feet.

When J-R later chose those very people to be at the hospital, it was a confirmation of the vision I had received. So I told the others about what I had seen and they agreed that it was an appropriate formation for us when the time came. The main purpose for that vision was for all of us to be surrounding J-R's body, what I considered to be the body of the Christ, in a specific way. A symbolic anchor to continue the harmony we experienced a month before in Israel on J-R's 80ᵗʰ birthday.

I know that many reading this may not agree with that description, but my experience was that J-R embodied the spirit of what people call the Christ.

J-R was a unique person. Part of his uniqueness was that he was very sensitive to the "energy" of others, especially his "students." So he generally did not share publicly how he was feeling or what was going on with him, especially when he was in the hospital, because people would worry. Then he'd have to deal with the fear and concern energy coming from them when he had enough to deal with to just keep breathing in and out. So those of us gathered in the hospital were pretty much the only people who knew what was really going on.

Because of our respective positions of responsibility and authority in the MSIA organization, over time, and especially as J-R spent less and less consciousness in his body and more time meditating in the Spirit, we had had our times of disagreements. I can tell you that none of that was present as we ministered to J-R. There was only love in the room. We were in harmony, inside and with each other, as he passed.

I thought to be there at the time of his passing was the most beautiful thing and the most personally wrenching thing I've ever seen. Being at his feet meant a lot to me. It was a completion of sorts because there was a time when I was going through a very deep experience during an aura balance in Las Vegas and he was at *my* feet. I felt that being in this almost primal location was a way to show my appreciation for him being at my very foundation and holding me all those years. I was going to hold him now.

I thought the placement of those present was so important. It had to do with the energetics of what I was aware of and what I've seen in the spirit. For many years J-R drilled it into us to have him cremated within 3 days, and Nat and I had always protected his body when he was meditating or sick. This wasn't any different.

I knew that J-R's soul would slip out the crown chakra, and that's what John Morton had covered. Some years earlier, John had accepted a spiritual mantle and anchored the Mystical Traveler consciousness. J-R used to joke that he had to be nice to John because one day John would be taking care of him. I learned later that, traditionally, the new Traveler was the one to help the old Traveler on his way. So I believed it was appropriate that John was at J-R's head as part of that responsibility.

I knew that my job was basically to make sure that nothing manipulated J-R or entered him through the soles of his feet. The others protected him from the sides. I knew that my intention and that of the others present was that no kind of negative power would slip past us and get to J-R.

J-R had warned us over the years of energies or entities that might be attracted in possessing spiritually a powerful being like J-R when he physically leaves the planet. We were all there to protect J-R through this process.

We did that. And we did it in full cooperation with each other and with the love and fellowship we had in Israel. It was a Christ action, all of us together.

"The sparkle of the soul, the essence, was everywhere. His cheeks were red."

– Jesus Garcia, D.S.S.

CHAPTER 1

A New Chapter in My Life Begins

I REMEMBER SEEING J-R GO and sending so much Light, holding for him. In the midst of that, I also was aware that there was going to be a new job for me to do. When J-R made plans for his departure from this level, he had arranged for me, and Nathaniel if I was unable to do it, to have power of attorney for him and to stand in for him when he could no longer make his own medical choices. It was a pretty challenging assignment and, I can say with all humility, that I did it with excellence.

I don't know if anyone can imagine what it was like in the days when J-R was declining. J-R was very private about himself, especially when he was really sick. To protect him from the energy of the fears and concerns of others, even those closest to him, I couldn't really let my hair down with anyone. My friend Nathaniel Sharratt was the one person who was in it with me and the one person with whom I could share my feelings about it. Thank God for you, Nat.

After everybody left the hospital room, my job was to just be there with Nat until they took J-R's body. Then we would arrange for it to be cremated. J-R had been very clear that he wanted his body cremated, preferably within 3 days. With today's laws, it took a week and during that time, Nat and I were very vigilant in keeping J-R's body secure and holding for him until he transcended.

When we looked at J-R's body, the whole procedure just seemed crude—and it is crude in a way. But we had arranged for one of the cremation services to handle that process, and they did it very respectfully.

Oddly, after his death, J-R's body looked the healthiest it had looked in a long time. I could not believe it, and neither could Nathaniel. I'd heard stories of Paramahansa Yogananda and how his body was preserved after he died. I can believe it because J-R looked preserved. He looked great. He looked healthier than when he was alive during his last six months. The sparkle of the soul, the essence, was everywhere. His cheeks were red. Maybe that's an indication of just how much J-R was carrying for all of us, maybe for the planet, before he was able to let it all go.

Later, Nat and I watched his body go in at the crematorium. I couldn't cry for my friend at that time. I didn't have that luxury. I needed to be together to handle all the details following his death. But I am crying now as I remember it. It was hard. Now, eight months after my friend and teacher, whom I liken to the Christ, has passed, everything is cracking. I think I've been resting, and I think that J-R left us with something beautiful. But, for me, I'm experiencing the loss maybe even more intensely now.

Oddly, there is also a resurrection inside of me because, relative to everything, if I put flesh and blood on it, I think the return of Jesus is very similar to the return of J-R. Initially, I felt him so far away, and then at times, I feel him in his house, where I continue to live for now. I feel the presence of the Holy Ghost is comforting me. And now, after all these years of devoting my full time and attention to J-R, I have Nicole as I am writing this, and she is a comfort. She helps keep me more peaceful so I can be open to experiencing J-R's presence.

There's nothing more amazing than feeling this inner loneliness, and, at the same time, being visited by J-R. Most often he comes to me through dreams. When it happens, there's a presence, a feeling as if he's holding me. Other times it's as if he's sitting next to me when I'm driving his car.

I definitely feel now like I'm finally mourning and grieving. For years, I drove J-R around in his car. Or maybe I should say cars. There were a number of them over the years.

When I first started on staff, I wanted to drive J-R. I would see John Morton driving J-R and I wanted that job. One of the first cars I drove was a brown Lincoln and on the license plate it said TRAVELER. There was also a blue Lincoln that had two gas tanks—a product of the 1970s gas crisis. (J-R knew how to work around.) I would drive the double-tank Lincoln and, as the first tank would go dry, I would reach down and flip the switch to activate the second tank. Then the succession of Lexuses arrived and once we had a Range Rover.

I'm mentioning cars because driving was my life. I remember the struggle staying awake while J-R would check the SAT tapes and CDs and the other NOW production media they had recorded of him presenting a seminar. I would speed in order to scare myself into staying awake. And the times J-R fell asleep in the car, quietly snoring away, I carefully avoided potholes. It was a real skill to master a way of driving where J-R could leave his body to do the work. Crazy times.

Now I frequently have dreams of driving him in his 2008 Lexus. In the past when I had those dreams, John would be driving the brown Lincoln or a Jeep and I would be in the back seat. (I hated that. Having a competitive side to my personality, I wanted to be the driver.) Now, I find myself in the front seat, as a metaphor, driving the Master.

I had a dream in June 2015 where I was trying to find which direction I was to go. I didn't know whether to go left or right. In that dream, I couldn't go anywhere. I looked toward J-R, and it seemed like he was telling me to cry. All I was doing in the car was grieving. It was like J-R telling me I couldn't go on until I handled my grieving.

"The things that get me are what Uta Hagen referred to in her book, A Challenge for the Actor, *as 'inner objects.' She says that something happens in the psyche such that it remembers an event in relationship to some object, and that object, when touched or seen, can kick off the memory again."*

– JESUS GARCIA, D.S.S.

"(Regarding grieving,) I know that lying around doesn't help. I tried it. And after lying around, J-R's still gone and I still have to wash my dishes."

– JESUS GARCIA, D.S.S.

CHAPTER 2

Reflections on Death and Loss

TODAY, AS I'M WRITING THIS, Vice President Joe Biden's son, Beau, passed away and they held a funeral service. I think there's nothing worse than a parent burying their child. I never could understand that kind of grief before. You might have compassion, but you really can't understand the depth of the experience until you've had a similar experience.

When I was 23, I lost a half-brother, Carlos. I saw how that affected my mom. I did not understand that then. But now I have lost my grandmother and John-Roger in the same year. I think I got a pretty substantial dose of empathy. With those experiences under my belt, my heart goes out to people who lose family members and really close friends. I can understand their grief now. I find now that it's hard to tell someone things will get better. I've read about the steps of grieving and all the psychological material on the process. I think intellectually, yes, I get it; things get better in time. But at the moment, that's no comfort.

I know, too, that most people who lose someone really close to them have to suck it up and get back to their lives, get back to work. I don't know how they do that. Luckily I haven't had to do that. I have great respect and compassion for any person who does. But maybe being forced to confront the new reality helps. I don't know. I don't think there's any one answer that's right for everyone. I can only speak for me. I know that lying around doesn't help. I tried it. And after lying around, J-R's still gone and I still have to wash my dishes.

But for now, I currently live in the same house where I've been since 1988: John-Roger's house. It doesn't bother me to be here. I love the photos, the comfort of the familiarity, and that is really healing. It's not spooky or creepy at all.

The things that get me are what Uta Hagen referred to in her book, *A Challenge for the Actor*, as "inner objects." She says that something happens in the psyche such that it remembers an event in relationship to some object, and that object, when touched or seen, can kick off the memory again. Nothing has become so apparent, so clear about what an inner object meant than when I accidentally touched John-Roger's wheelchair the other day. That set it off. I touched the handle of his wheelchair and everything flooded through me, everything came out. I couldn't believe it. You never know what will set you off. These things are not bad. They're not judgmental events. They're just kind of daily life, like the smell of his clothes. Just things that I love. I mention that here in case the awareness might help someone.

"He was a man, take him for all in all.
I shall not look upon his like again."

– William Shakespeare (*Hamlet*)

"I believe it would be ideal if we all had halls of self-awareness where we could go to and be self-realized and walk around in that state in the world. I think we'd have a much better world."

– JESUS GARCIA, D.S.S.

CHAPTER 3

Starting to Study Myself

BY THE TIME THIS BOOK is published it will be three years after J-R's death and I will have completed my studies in Spiritual Psychology with Drs. Ron and Mary Hulnick at the University of Santa Monica, which was founded by John-Roger. There is learning using techniques brought forward by John-Roger, Carl Jung, Erik Erikson, Carl Rogers, Fritz Perls, and many others. While it's really an expansion on more academic psychology, it's interesting how we can combine psychological techniques and skills with intuition, which is the spiritual part, and really ferment that, get that growing. The course starts with the awakening to and study of the soul in an academic/scientific/grounded kind of way. It's really cool.

I come to these studies from the spiritual side of it, through my work with John-Roger in the Movement of Spiritual Inner Awareness (MSIA), and Peace Theological Seminary and College of Philosophy (PTS). These schools are all, to me, what I had dreamed of years ago in some faraway cosmic place before I was born. I do have a memory of a pre-birth meeting with some "beings," and I was shown how I was to come down here and follow my path.

Now I'm on my path, part of which was to serve J-R and get me connected to the Sound Current and into the mystery schools where I was to learn awareness.

I believe it would be ideal if we all had halls of self-awareness where we could consciously go to and be self-realized and walk around in that state in the world. I think we'd have a much better world.

Self-awareness is my main pursuit now; that and being aware of what's all around me, through me, in front of me. And then to serve God and the Lord, and to be here and to be of service. (By the way, God, if I can also be an actor, that would be great.)

Before I got involved in any of these spiritual studies, I was in acting classes with people like Stella Adler, Uta Hagen, Howard Fine, Peggy Fury, and John Abbott. They all bottom-lined it: It's all moment-to-moment. Being in the moment causes self-awareness. In these classes, we learned not to be self-conscious in our work as an actor or an artist but to be self-aware. Howard Fine said to me while I was shooting *Spiritual Warriors* that acting is revealing, not concealing. That's my path. That's what it's all about in acting—and in life.

CASSIUS: *Forever and forever farewell, Brutus.*
If we do meet again, we'll smile indeed.
If not, 'tis true this parting was well made.

BRUTUS: *Why then, lead on. Oh,*
that a man might know
The end of this day's business ere it come!
But it sufficeth that the day will end,
And then the end is known.—Come, ho! Away!

– William Shakespeare (Julius Caesar)

"I find myself asking all sorts of crazy stuff, like 'Why?' But then I realize I needed the break."

– JESUS GARCIA, D.S.S.

CHAPTER 4

The Back Seat, Crawl-Into-A-Foxhole Mentality

IF NOTHING ELSE, IN THIS book you're going to get the really blunt, up-front, in-your-face, honest sense of my devotion. I don't want this to come across as bragging, I just want to share my story as honestly as I can. I loved it. I got high on devotion. And with J-R's passing, I find myself reflecting on my own life.

One of the realizations I had today was about my stepfather beating my mother. When I was a kid, my stepfather would beat my mother relentlessly. I would try to intervene, but good luck with that since he was a powerful big guy and I was a scrawny little kid. Often it would happen in the car and after a futile attempt to get him to stop, I would just crawl into the footwell of the back seat. I would just cower there, helpless, waiting for it to be over. I am feeling that futility and hopelessness today, at over 50 years old.

In the midst of this, I had an awareness about people getting upset with me. As soon as I feel anything that's confrontational, I just want to collapse and crawl into a foxhole. Or, in my case, into a back seat footwell. It's like a nice little bunker for the back seat people.

I'm kind of familiar with the back seat, crawl-into-a-foxhole mentality. Whenever I'm in a situation where I hear any kind of arguing or hurting or yelling, I tend to want to go hide. When I am in meetings where there's conflict, I tend to tense up and prepare for the worst. What I'm aware of is how J-R would stretch me by putting me in leadership positions so I could learn to stand in it. Some part of me would collapse and J-R would encourage me to hold strong. Taking chances by stepping out of my comfort zone and asking for what I wanted—like asking people for roles in a movie—was part of it, too. I was always auditioning to be strong. He would push me to hold strong in my integrity without hurting myself or others. How to stand up for myself and not have againstness.

This collapsing is something that I need to forgive in myself. J-R always said we're responsible for what happens in our lives; either I allowed it, I promoted it, or I created it.

In secular schools, the perspective is focused more on the physical/material world. In the realm of spiritual psychology, like at the University of Santa Monica, they work on really getting your intention, getting your responsibility and your acceptance down, for any kind of issue. I love that because it really "teaches a man to fish," rather than giving a man a fish. It builds strength and self-reliance. I think it's important to have schools like that; they really teach people to do things for themselves and not get into blame. That's a key.

"Things done well and with a care, exempt themselves from fear."

– WILLIAM SHAKESPEARE *(HENRY VIII)*

"That's all great, but on a personal level, wow, I do miss John-Roger. Even as frail and aging as he was, I still was attached to him being here with us; with me."

– JESUS GARCIA, D.S.S.

CHAPTER 5

Some Thoughts Post J-R

SINCE J-R'S PASSING, IN THE recent days and weeks, my experiences in the Inner Realms have been amazing. I mostly get them in dreams. With all the devotion, with all of the learning I've had from John-Roger, I really excelled at opening to inner experiences. I played the student role very well. I very much liked that.

So what's up for me is realizing that and knowing that I'm stepping into my competence in the ways J-R taught me to do that. And what's really clear to me is how much I really love myself and love others, and how things really changed dramatically for me after his death.

Of course, things didn't only change for me. After J-R passed there was a definite shift in my universe. J-R set it up so he would have a successor to carry on the key parts of his work here on this level, and he trained that successor very well. That's John Morton. However, the presence of John-Roger, and what I experienced in him as the Preceptor consciousness, are gone; that energy, which was so prevalent on the planet, is not here. You can feel its absence—well, I can feel it. But then, if you know Carl Jung's work about the collective unconscious, you know we're all connected. So that would mean J-R in the spirit is connected with us here right now, and therefore we are not separate. Separation's an illusion.

That's all great, but on a personal level, wow, I do miss my friend. Even as frail and aging as he was, I still was attached to him being here with us; with me. I've spoken with others who weren't so physically close to J-R and their perspective is that after J-R left, they were still connected to him. So, clearly it's my own process of loss, and everybody has a connection with John-Roger and John Morton.

John-Roger often told us that Jesus was his boss. In the spiritual line of succession we follow, Jesus and J-R are John's bosses. I feel we are in good hands. I do acknowledge John Morton as the present Traveler anchoring the Traveler energy on this earth. It's an amazing time.

Also, being in love with my fiancée, Nicole, is like a gift from J-R. I love her deeply. Ultimately though, what J-R taught me was that it's really about loving myself. So I'm still working at learning to love myself. In the meantime, I love Nicole, and I love—and miss—J-R.

Actually, I think there's something cosmically funny in all of this. As J-R used to say, "If you're going to laugh about something later, laugh now." So I'm laughing.

*"There is nothing either good or bad,
but thinking makes it so."*

– WILLIAM SHAKESPEARE (*HAMLET*)

"J-R shared endless stories about his childhood and family. From those tales, it seemed that his dad and mom were his main teachers."

– JESUS GARCIA, D.S.S.

CHAPTER 6

A Brief History of J-R

MOST OF WHAT I'M GOING to relate here isn't really important in the grand scheme of things. J-R rarely talked about this stuff. But I imagine you'd like a little context since I talk so much about J-R. So here you go.

J-R was born Roger Delano Hinkins on September 24, 1934, right in the middle of the Depression. He was raised in Utah and was considered a part of the "Silent Generation." That was the generation of about 50 million people born between 1925 and 1945. They experienced financial instability and were the ones that fought in WWII and Korea.

His family did not have a lot of money but there was always an abundance of love. Because funds were scarce in those early years, one Christmas the Hinkins kids—two boys and three girls—found only lumps of coal in their Christmas stockings. But after letting Roger, and his brother and sisters, stew for a little while, their dad said he was going to go out, and asked if the kids would bring his shoes. So they scampered off to get their dad's shoes and with the shoes were their gifts.

J-R shared endless stories like that about his childhood and family. From those tales, it seems that his parents were his main teachers and the source of many of his later teachings.

J-R relates that in 1957 he was asked by Spirit to accept the mantle of the Traveler. As he tells it, he turned down the request. Around that time, his brother was in a coal mine accident that severely injured him, literally burning off a large part of his face. J-R quit his job and went so far as to take a job in the hospital where his brother was being cared for so he could be with him.

Then some powerful and life-changing personal events took place in the following several years. J-R does not talk about the specifics, but he has said in seminars that eventually Spirit asked him to take two souls back home to the Soul Realm and he agreed. He said that those two souls were his mother and his father.

J-R also shared with me something that happened during that period of time. He told me there was a young woman he loved and they had a son named Scott. Both were killed as a result of a car accident. I have to say that there are times when you hear something and think, "that's interesting," and times when you hear something and you just know it's true somehow or some way. This story was the latter for me. When J-R and I were writing *The Wayshower* script together, we included that incident in the movie, but it was a very quick scene and I think a lot of people missed it. I'm not telling this here to try and convince anyone of anything. You can believe it or not. These were just things that J-R shared with me that had gone on in his life. It wasn't information for my mind, it was what I experienced when I was talking to him about it.

From his teachings, it's evident that J-R was firmly grounded in the realities and practicalities of the physical world. He knew that to prosper spiritually, you had to take care of the physical level responsibilities. He used to say that life is not a free ride; you need a job if you want to stay here. If you ever went out to eat with J-R, you would see his Depression-era upbringing reflected in his food choices. His tastes were very modest; he was a very simple eater.

Speaking of eating, J-R told me the story of a guru who used to eat a lot. When onlookers would judge him, the guru explained that was how he would eat the karma of his students. J-R has told me he's done the same. Sometimes going to the bathroom was a way for him to clear. But, essentially, J-R was a sponge. That's what Love does.

He took on a lot of karma from people around us. That was the thing about J-R; if someone had cancer, if it was permitted, he took it. If someone was having a rough time breaking up, and he was allowed to, he took it. If someone was defaulting in some area, he took it. I don't think it was easy, but since J-R wasn't attached to the material world, it could pass right through him. Even so, I think it had to take a toll on his body in some way.

Seeing J-R in his role as the Mystical Traveler was always amazing. But one of the things that fascinated me as I was working on *Mystical Traveler*, the documentary of his life, was wondering what J-R was like before he got the spiritual keys that entirely changed his life. I know that he grew up in Utah and his dad labored in the coalmines until he worked his way up into management. I know that J-R had worked his way up to being a manager of a Cornet store and went to college in Utah. He worked at a local prison for a time, then moved to California where he was an avid surfer. He lived in San Francisco and became an insurance investigator at one point, then moved to Los Angeles where he taught school. But outside his family, few people really know about J-R's personal life. And I'm not really sure how much of J-R's personal life even they knew about after he left Utah. (Note: If you'd like to get more of J-R's personal history, he was about as forthcoming as he ever got about his life when we co-wrote the *Mystical Traveler* movie. The movie is filled with subtle and not-so-subtle anecdotes about J-R's life. You might see how many you can catch.)

On one of MSIA's annual trips to San Francisco, Nathaniel, Zoe (GoLightly) Lumiere, Eddie Chow—a Movement friend and resident of the area—and I decided to do some research for *Mystical Traveler*. As the co-director with J-R, I wanted to get a sense of the environment J-R had been in during that period of his life. So we went off in the rain to see if we could verify some of the stories we had heard from J-R about his younger life before he took on the spiritual work.

The story has it that, around the age of 24, he was an insurance fraud investigator for a while during his time in San Francisco. So we went to an address near the Tenderloin District, which J-R had mentioned to me as someplace he once had lived. We actually found the place and at first we were pretty impressed that we had been able to locate it. Then it was more like, "okay, so what?" I found that reconstructing J-R's mundane worldly life was a way to help me understand what he had experienced early on in his journey of seeking God that was embedded in his DNA.

To give you an idea of J-R's feisty side, there's a story he tells about when he lived in San Francisco, from *The Wayshower* book:

"Some of the greatest people in the world have said something like, 'know thyself' and 'to thine own self be true.'

"When I was around twenty, I saw this across the top of a high school in San Francisco: 'To thine own self be true.' I remember stopping the car and thinking, 'Why would they want to put something so confusing on the top of a high school? Why don't they put something like "Health, wealth, and happiness"?' That's universal; everybody wants to be healthy, wealthy, and happy. But 'to thine own self be true' seemed to me such a waste of time.

"Dishonesty forfeits divine aid. But I never knew where I was being dishonest. I knew I couldn't drive the car when it was out of gas, and then I'd get a ticket because I couldn't move my car. Then I thought, 'What difference does it make? They're going to give me a ticket anyway, so I'll just park it even if I'm not out of gas. So go

ahead and ticket it.' It was the same thing in my mind, but, still, something would always say, 'Who are you kidding?'

"I knew that after two years I was going to leave the city and state, and they didn't know where I was going, so those tickets would all be gratis on the city. Well, they gave me a good deal. I think I parked anywhere I wanted to in San Francisco for about two and a half years for fifty cents a day.

"I remember the judge, a beautiful man. He looked at me and said, 'What do you think you're doing?' and I said, 'I think I was getting away with it.'

"He sat there and asked me questions, and I just answered him, but my attitude wasn't too good. It was like, 'What can he do with me, kill me?' And inside me, it was, 'Don't try. Don't do that!'

"The judge said, 'Do you feel sorry about where you've been parking?'

"I said, 'No, I don't feel sorry for where I've been parking. But I'm not going to do it anymore.'

"'Well,' he said, 'that was my next question. Did you learn?'

"I said, 'Oh, sure. It isn't fun to stand here in front of you and this prosecuting attorney.'

"He asked me what I was doing down here, and I just looked him in the eye and laid the whole thing out to him. He said, 'What are you looking for?'

"I said, 'I'm looking for myself.' He asked, 'Have you seen a psychiatrist?'

"When I said yes, he asked, 'What did he say to you?'

"'He said he couldn't find it either.'

"The judge told me to go to a minister, and I told him I'd been to several. I told him the names of all the people I had seen—the professors, the psychologists, the psychiatrist, the ministers. He asked, 'Aren't you ashamed of it?'

"I said, 'I wasn't there for help as if I were sick. I was searching. I'm looking for my own self—the self in "to thine own self be true."'

"He just said, 'Good luck'" And it hit me. He didn't say, 'Good luck.' He said 'God luck.'

"Something inside me started saying, 'Hey, dumdum, listen.' And I also thought, 'I'm not going to listen to all that stuff.' I was starting to find out who the self was, and every time I'd get a little insight into it, it would scare me. I'd think, 'You mean, that's in me? Oh, come on! That's more than I want to look at. I don't think I... oh, no!'"

As an aside, finding the school in San Francisco with that quote, "To thine own self be true," became part of my research for the *Mystical Traveler* movie. I was fascinated following the footsteps of J-R before receiving the Keys and many of his seminars also helped me connect the dots. It was important that I make this film as accurate as possible and it took three years to finish.

In the early days, J-R apparently used amusing acronyms for his "bosses." Folks have told me that J-R said things like, "The bus needs gas." Apparently, BUS meant "The Boys Upstairs" and GAS stood for "The Guardian Angels Society."

There are a million other stories about how J-R was fearless in testing limits and being ruthless with himself in checking things out. Fortunately, you can hear most of them in his seminar recordings. The story about the tickets and the judge are in a CD packet called *The Wayshower* on the disc called *In Search of My True Self*, as well as in the book of the same name.

"*This above all: to thine own self be true,
and it must follow, as the night the day, thou
canst not then be false to any man.*

– WILLIAM SHAKESPEARE (*HAMLET*)

"*I remember the Karmic Board. I was nothingness and I met with some Elders. They were telling me something about mystery schools like I would have to be studying or I was already going to the schools. They laid it all out and I agreed. I was also to decide whether I wanted to be with a strong father or caring father. I chose the strong father—and I believe that's what prepared me to work with John-Roger.*"

– Jesus Garcia, D.S.S.

CHAPTER 7

In the Beginning (at least for me)

A REMEMBRANCE FROM BEFORE BEING born:

> *I remember the Karmic Board. I was nothingness and I met with some Elders. They were telling me something about mystery schools like I would have to be studying or I was already going to the schools. They laid out all of what I would be dealing with in my upcoming incarnation and I agreed to it all. I was also to decide whether I wanted to be with a strong father or caring father. I chose the strong father— and I believe that's what prepared me to work with John-Roger.*

And a memory of being born:

> *I remember standing in line with a bunch of other souls on top of white pillars like we were all on conveyor belts. We were white light being formed into hundreds of human bodies, waiting to enter earth. Then I was born.*

Those two memories set the stage for my life this time. It was kind of like getting a peek at the script of a movie, then comparing that to what I was seeing on the screen. In any case, here's a little bit about me and my life.

I was born with the name Jesus Garcia. My acting name is Jsu Garcia. And J-R eventually would just call me Zeus—because he liked one syllable names—until he passed.

I come from a broken home, so I guess I overcompensated by being in the Movement of Spiritual Inner Awareness and connecting up with John-Roger. I do realize that everyone is my family and I know that I'm loved. However, the Movement takes that to a different level. It's a hell of a family.

I was born in New York and raised in Newark, New Jersey. I lived by the river, close to the Ballantine Beer brewery. I remember, even when I was very young, that I intuitively felt like something was always watching me. I didn't feel danger, just that I was being watched—or watched over. I always felt protected. Maybe that's how I grew up with hookers and thieves and I learned love.

It was this presence that's been with me my whole life. The purple I saw when I was 13 years old felt like a breath next to me. When J-R talks about the etheric level, it's kind of like that. It can be a bit scary, but I have to remember that past that is the Soul. Perhaps I'm close. It's with me today. I'm having the awareness of the story of the guy seeing only one set of footprints in the sand and thinking God had abandoned him when it was actually the footprints of God carrying him.

I also felt that the house I lived in had what I would now call "astral creatures" that I could sense in dark rooms. I imagine that I was very much like any young child, sensing all these creepy things. I was afraid to cross the street because I thought there were witches. It was very much Harry Potter-ish before Harry Potter. But it was real for me—at least in my imagination. It was vivid and often scary.

Everything seemed to be in black-and-white for me in New Jersey in the late 1960s. Part of what made it seem that way was my relationship with the man who was to become my stepfather. Let's call him Jorge, which is not his real name. At the time, he was a sort of surrogate father and was married to my mother. And he was really good to me. But he had some bad habits, among them that he cheated on my mother and would also beat her up pretty severely. I was raised around that, and it was awful. I was angry about it.

But at the same time, I loved this man. For me, he was my father. But how could he treat my mother so badly? One day he and my mom had a big fight right in the middle of the street that involved both of them tugging on me, each pulling me in a different direction. Jorge finally looked at me and demanded, "are you going with me or her?" How is a kid supposed to make a choice like that? But I did have to, and I chose my mother. This was so hurtful until I realized it was for my highest good so I could meet and work with J-R.

This was a benchmark for the rest of my life. I had to be careful and responsible when I found myself in a position to choose. I hated it. However, now I see that there was someone/something inside me that knew better. I acknowledge that part and love that part. It led me to John-Roger. Thank the lord.

Even so, when I think back on it, that was just an awful thing to do a child. I later told my mom that I felt guilty that I rejected Jorge, but going with her was the greatest choice I ever made because that ultimately led me to my spiritual life. I sometimes think that if I had gone with Jorge, that would have led me to jail.

Much later I told my mother that I didn't have to see a psychiatrist to work this all out because when I was with John-Roger, a day of talking to him was like a year in psychotherapy.

At any rate, I made a choice and I went for the loving. Or, at least, I went for what I now believe J-R probably wanted me to have in this lifetime. And I believe that the powers that be—what J-R called "the boys upstairs"—made it happen. I believe these guys helped me choose my mom instead of Jorge, which led me to John-Roger and the spiritual work that I'm so grateful to be involved in.

Now, the fact is, I'm a bastard. I know my friends are grinning and nodding their heads, but what I mean here is that my mother and biological father were not married. People used to call me a bastard, and I would respond that that was true. I didn't add that I was in pretty good company, considering that Alexander Hamilton, Leonardo da Vinci, Oprah Winfrey, Confucius, Steve Jobs and T. E. Lawrence (I could go on and on) were also born out of wedlock.

When I was young, I thought Jorge was my father because that was what I was told. But I was lied to. Or maybe they thought they were protecting me. I don't know. However, at sixteen, I found out who my real father was, so I knew Jorge wasn't my biological dad. That was a pretty big shock at the time, but I was able to move past it pretty quickly.

When I was little, my mother was often away from the house working or doing other things, so it wasn't unusual for me to be dropped off at other people's homes. When we moved to Florida, one of my favorite places to go was my Auntie's house in Orlando. Auntie was a beautiful woman and I loved her. I remember playing with my train set and electric speed car tracks when I was around eight or nine years old, and in the afternoons eating oranges. I loved to climb up orange trees in the Florida humidity and suck on oranges.

I also remember walking maybe about a mile and a half to school each day and seeing a bunch of spiders in their webs along the road. These were not itsy bitsy spiders; they were monster spiders. I guess many people would have been freaked out by them, but, in fact, they're very common in Orlando. They were just part of my daily life. It's funny what you remember, looking back on your childhood.

I have a lot of memories about staying at my aunt's. One night, in a kind of twilight sleep, I saw a man in a white suit. He was sort of angelic; I didn't sense anything negative about him. He just appeared in my room for a while and I was okay with it. I didn't say anything about it, but the next day my aunt said that she could see the person who lived—and had died—in the house. When she said that, I told her about what I had seen and she said that was him. We assumed that the man in the white suit was the ghost of that person, but in fact, Auntie and I were tapping into something that would show up later in my life.

I can't say I had an average childhood. Some things in my young life were pretty unusual. For example, my grandfather, who had divorced my grandmother and moved to Los Angeles, worked for the San Pedro refinery and on the side as a hobby he ran a numbers racket. I remember seeing Grandpa collecting money and pieces of paper when I was a young teenager at the barber shop. Eventually, I put the clues together.

Grandma always played the numbers, too, like a lot of the neighborhood people. Grandma and step-Grandpa lived in the Little Havana section of Miami. That's where I was raised when I wasn't in Orlando.

Sometimes people would dream of numbers to play, or they'd have some superstition running the numbers. Some people played the same numbers time after time. No matter how many times their number didn't come up, they still thought it was going to be a winner sooner or later. Sound familiar?

The people in my environment when I was a child had plenty of other weird ideas, too. We all believed in Christ, of course, and prayed. And there were the saints. Oh my God, there were tons of saints, and that was so confusing. There was Lazarus with the dog and the wounds. There was Mary, and I also remember Elizabeth, John the Baptist's mom. Their pictures were all over the walls in our house, and our neighbors' homes.

There would always be the typical Jesus Christ image, which was a white dude with blue eyes. Being around Latin friends, I've heard people ask, why isn't Jesus Latin? Or why isn't Jesus black? American and European people don't like to recognize he really came from the Middle East; the Bible says he was a Galilean Hebrew Israelite, so scholars believe he would have had a dark, olive-skinned Semitic appearance.

So, the common blue eyes with light brown hair depiction is probably not what Jesus looked like. The King James Bible says: "His head and his hair were white like wool, as white as snow; and his eyes were as a flame of fire;" so maybe he had a perm or a white Afro. Or he could've been just an all-American boy. (Okay, maybe not.)

When I was little, I went to a Holy Roller type church in Orlando. At Sunday school, the priest or minister was yelling "Do you feel the Christ come into your heart?!" He was yelling and everyone around me was yelling back, "Yes! Yes! Yes!" They were crying and they seemed authentic. But I felt left out. I thought, "Wait a minute, why can't Jesus be in me?" I wanted to be loved and accepted so I said yes although I didn't feel Jesus in my heart. Fast forward. I do feel Jesus in my heart now. More than that. I know the Christ is J-R and I have *experienced* the tremendous love and comfort from J-R/Christ and I'm throwing Jesus in there too. This experience is what I was looking for when I was younger; I just didn't know better.

It didn't help that I'd been in an obsessive, confusing and interesting relationship with Jesus Christ for some time. My birth name was Jesus. I was beat up in school and kind of bullied because of my name. School kids would chase me and sing the lyrics from *Jesus Christ; Superstar*, which was popular at the time. "Jesus Christ, superstar, who do you think you really are..." Looking back, I realize that perhaps they were just teasing me in a fun way and I was being oversensitive. I think everything in my life was really a preparation to be stronger, tougher, and yet, more vulnerable. And J-R was right: it gave me so much strength when I went into my own vulnerability.

Another part of my growing up was in Los Angeles. (We got around.) I remember as a young child walking with Grandpa in L.A. to the barbershop to get a haircut. They had those leather chairs like some sort of hardcore dentist chair with the footrest that always managed to hit on my Achilles tendon. My neck and head were never comfortable when I was in the barber chair. I remember the barber would come out like Sweeney Todd, the Demon of Fleet Street, with his straight razor and the leather strop, and the sharpening and the heating of the blade. And the warm shaving cream that he would lather on my face.

Of course I didn't have a beard or anything back then, but they'd use the blade to give us kids a nice straight hairline on the back of our necks. At the end, they would put talcum powder on a big floppy brush and brush off the back of my neck and shoulders. That was kind of cool. To this day, despite the uncomfortable chairs, I love barbershops: the antique-style barbershop chairs where the overhead fans blow the cut hair, and the striped barber's pole turning.

Another person who made a big impression and affected my life was a lady who taught Jesus Christ stories from the Bible when my mother and I first arrived in Los Angeles. I loved her so much! She would gather all the kids around her in the alley behind our apartment near Temple street, and orally teach us the stories of Jesus from the Bible. It was a throwback to the times before recorded history. No books, just stories from her. It was so real—I was there with Jesus Christ, but in the back alleys of L.A. When I asked J-R who she was spiritually, he told me, "she was your angel."

Soon after that experience with her I would begin seeing more and more of the purple light. I remember this was around the same time that Bruce Lee died, the summer of 1973.

That's a taste of my childhood; some of the things that stand out and some of the things that influenced who I became. Then, when I was in my 20s, things started to change.

"But Jesus said, Suffer little children, and forbid them not, to come unto me: for of such is the kingdom of heaven."

– *KING JAMES VERSION*, MATTHEW 19:14

"*If I got really hungry I would raid the Vedanta Center and steal strawberries from the gardens. Sometimes I would even sleep in the Ramakrishna Temple.*"

– Jesus Garcia, D.S.S.

CHAPTER 8

Getting to the Traveler

THE EVENTS THAT WOULD LEAD to my meeting John-Roger all started in 1980, at actress Leigh Taylor-Young's home during a Teen MSIA or Insight meeting. Insight Seminars is a personal growth organization founded by John-Roger that had developed a phenomenal seminar for adults and teenagers. I was a teenager coming of age and scared of the powerful love in that room. I was looking for love and I really didn't know how to go about it. I needed a sense of belonging; I wanted to belong to something. But I didn't know how to let the loving in. It was intense in the room with all those young people expressing with courage and being so open and vulnerable. The room was bright light. I dreamed of being like that, but apparently I had some other experiences to go through before I would find myself opening up to genuine loving.

When I walked into the house, in the foyer was a picture of a man in a white suit, looking very angelic. It stopped me cold because that was the guy I had seen that night so many years before at my Auntie's in Florida. It blew my mind. But I still didn't know who this man was.

I now know that what I had seen at my Auntie's was the Traveler in his radiant form. But, in any case, before I could ask someone about the picture, the event started. There was a lot of sharing from the teens that got pretty personal and deep. I couldn't handle the energy. I was involved in my own problems and I wasn't about to share them in front of a group of strangers. I thought I was wrong to be having the kinds of problems I was dealing with. I was very sensitive about those things and my feelings about them, and I just held it in. Instead of going the personal growth route, I chose drugs to deal with my pain. But I also started to follow my dream of getting into acting, and I began exploring how I could make that happen.

I had always known, even from childhood, that I wanted to be an actor. More than that, I wanted to be a star. I started finding ways of meeting people who knew people in the business. I began to experience the wild life that tended to happen around show biz. There's a big difference between the art of acting and show biz. Show biz and chasing fame hurts. John Lennon wrote a song called "Fame" that David Bowie sang; just listen to that song and you'll understand what I mean. I sometimes fell into the fame trap.

When I was around 16, I struck out on my own and I had to survive. To make money I was kind of a pseudo-carpenter wannabe. At best, I knew how to put up drywall.

I lived in the basement of a mansion in the Hollywood Hills, along with a bunch of unidentified critters I could hear scurrying around in the dark. Truth be told, I didn't want to know what they were.

The owner of the home was a guy named Dr. Julian. His parents lived upstairs and they were really nice to me. They recognized that I was a starving actor and would feed me. The old grandpa would send me peanut butter and jelly sandwiches. I would never forget the kindness of that old man.

Dr. Julian was a great man. Eventually he arranged for his friend Michael Bell to take me under his wing and mentor me until I turned 18. Michael is a voiceover actor and terrific screen actor, and he gave me the opportunity to enter the acting world gracefully.

Around the corner from Dr. Julian's home were the Hindu Vedanta Center and Temple. I didn't have a lot of money...okay, actually I was on the fringes of poverty and homelessness. I lived in a basement. If I got really hungry I would raid the Vedanta Center and steal strawberries from the gardens. Sometimes I would even sleep in the Ramakrishna Temple.

I had no idea what this spiritual group was about until later J-R shared with me about them; however, I would fall asleep in the Temple praying to God for help, to please save me.

J-R did confirm that it was a blessing to be connected to them. I really appreciate the Vedanta Center for all they gave to me, and when I made money in my acting career I donated a fair amount to the Vedanta Center as sort of payback for those blessed strawberries. And I want to thank Ramakrishna for the comfort I found through his organization when I was younger and Dr. Julian, too, for his kindness.

One time, I asked J-R to come for a ride with me to see the Vedanta Center and he came and we blessed the area. To this day, I bless and pray for Dr. Julian and the Vedanta Center. However, in those days, my life as an actor was not terribly glamorous.

Eventually I found the right agent who set me more firmly on track. I started going to acting classes and began studying in earnest. At that time, I was focused on the world and the materialistic things, and I always felt empty, especially when I would try to escape through worldly pursuits. Often, I just felt a void inside, and I didn't know how to fill it.

So, as many do, I continued to turn to the world: fame and drugs. They provided temporary relief at best. Then I started getting acting jobs in movies, which I thought was going to be the ultimate high because it would be the fulfillment of something that I had set forth in my mind to do. That sure didn't turn out to be true. In the middle of achieving what I thought I wanted, I would find myself wondering if this was all there was. I thought…I hoped…there was more to life than this.

As I continued to pursue my goals, I remained frustrated. I had, or was well on the road to having, all the trappings of success in acting and the reality of it didn't match my belief of what it would be like.

For example, I was making movies when I was younger than James Dean had been when he started getting famous. I really thought I was going to become another James Dean. Later, after more accomplishments and appearing in significant roles in some very successful movies, I realized I was good enough to reach or exceed the heights James Dean had reached. Yet it still wasn't enough to fill the hole inside of me. I was still pretty young, and I had my heroes. I wanted to be them. Then I realized I *was* them, just in my own way. I finally realized that I had achieved more at a young age than a lot of actors had—and it wasn't making me happy.

What's worse, when I achieved a goal, I became depressed because I didn't know what I'd do to top it. So I did the only thing I could think of, which was to set higher goals. I wanted to be in TV Guide and I wanted to be in every teen magazine like Scott Baio, an actor I admired at the time. And I accomplished that. But there was still something missing. No matter what goal I set and then hit, it never satiated this hunger and emptiness.

Eventually I stopped and took a good look at my life. I was at the height of my career. I had a great agent, but I was numbing myself and my pain with substances. And I was miserable. I was soul-less. I was searching for something but I didn't know what it was.

At that time in my career, Insight Seminars was still in my periphery. What made it more fun was the amazing energy at the Insight headquarters building in Santa Monica. Though I didn't really understand what was going on there at that time, I remember the energy was booming. It was electric. There was a store where you could buy J-R seminars on cassette tapes, and J-R books and other study materials. There was Baraka health clinic where you could get all kinds of alternative treatments, from chiropractic to acupuncture to other energetic therapies. You could study Spiritual Psychology at Koh-E-Nor University, now called University of Santa Monica. You could sign up for Insight or run into Tony Robbins and firewalk on coals in the back courtyard. WOW. I signed up. I found myself having mind-blowing physical experiences with mind-over-matter things.

Remember for context, at the time I was acting and doing very well. Now, I was about to fly.

I walked on fire at the Sheraton Universal Hotel, where I would later attend decades of workshops with J-R. In one seminar with Tony Robbins, I walked on the hot coals four times, more than what was allowed for the seminar. Tony was irritated and at the same time, impressed. I wanted more. Of course, as soon as I said in my mind, "Oh wow, I'm walking on fire," I got burnt. Tony gave us a pressure point to press and the next day, there were no blisters. He was amazing and an integral part of my life.

I had people around me—acquaintances, not friends—telling me I needed to take one of the Insight Seminars. I blew them off for a while, but eventually I did take the Insight I seminar. While signing up for Insight I and II, I saw a crowd and there in the middle was John-Roger walking towards the exit with an entourage. I was thinking to myself, "wow, John-Roger." It's like I saw Elvis. Insight Seminars became impactful enough that I quit taking drugs. Not long after my first Insight seminar, I met and started dating a girl. I told her that she needed to take Insight, and she did. She liked it and things were going pretty well between us, then I fell off the wagon.

My girlfriend tried to keep me sober, but it was pretty much a losing battle. Even so, I finally got fed up with my behavior and took the Insight II seminar, a more focused and even deeper experience than the Insight I. It was the most incredible seminar I've ever done. It literally changed my life.

Through that seminar I realized—from a very visceral place—that what I really was looking for was love. I wanted to know what love was. I had always thought that love was what happened when the panties came off. But I started to realize it was way more than that. I had heard people talk about unconditional love. What the heck was that? Insight II gave me a taste of it and I wanted more. But my life was set on a new course when, as I was walking out the door after my Insight II graduation, the guy who had facilitated my seminar looked at me and said, "You need to be on Discourses." And I heard him.

After my Insight II, I wanted to conquer the world. The seminar had opened my heart and I wanted to start living the principles I had discovered during the seminar. One of those tenets was being in integrity and keeping my word.

Shortly after graduating from Insight II, I got an opportunity to appear in a Steven Spielberg movie. But to do that, I would have had to break my agreement to appear in a less prestigious film that was to be shot in South America. Because of what I learned in the Insight seminar, I chose to keep my original commitment. An Insight II friend, who knew that I would be away to shoot my next movie, wished me well after our graduation and gave me a bunch of spiritual books to read while I was gone. They were by this John-Roger guy. I devoured those spiritual books during my shoot in Colombia.

Before I left for South America, as I was looking over the books, I saw a picture of the author on the back of one of them. It was the same picture as the one on the mantel of the house where I had gone for the teen gathering years ago; the same guy I had seen in my Auntie's house over ten years ago. Okay, that was weird. I had no idea that what I had seen at my Auntie's was the radiant form of the Master. That's the kind of thing that happens when the Master marks you. Despite my ignorance of what actually was going on, I decided maybe I would take the books with me on location.

So off I went to Colombia, and I remember praying to God that I wanted to have more love, real love in my life. Being in Colombia, and, in those days, around the ever-present temptation of drugs, I fell off the wagon again. But I also met a girl and fell in love with her. There was a lot of emotional pain in me at that time and I was certainly not emotionally the clearest I had ever been. I wanted to experience true love. I actually ended up marrying her six months after we got back to the States.

Meanwhile, I had read all the spiritual books I had taken with me and had somehow mistakenly decided that if I wanted to be spiritual I would have to give up everything. I wasn't ready for that. Of course, later, I would realize that I didn't have to sacrifice everything; I just had to find the discipline within my heart so I wouldn't be *attached* to anything. But I wasn't there yet.

After much playing around in Colombia with my wife-to-be, while also reading the spiritual books I had brought, I decided to come home, and study these discourses and actually get on a more spiritually focused path. The way I saw to do that was to follow my Insight II facilitator's advice and start reading Soul Awareness Discourses; little booklets of John-Roger's key teachings. Discourses were, and still are, the primary study materials of MSIA, the organization J-R founded—an organization that I would come to recognize as a mystery school.

In fact, later, when I reflected back on my pre-lifetime dream, I began to realize that it was not an earthly school I was going to find this life, and, in fact, this was the school I had been preparing for.

Per the instructions that came with these Discourses, I would read only one every month. Each one addressed a principle, like forgiveness, or working with a spiritual energy called the Light, or even mundane things, like procrastination or relationships.

What I didn't realize at the time was that Discourses were not only about the information. J-R had charged them in such a way that they actually connected the reader to the Mystical Traveler Consciousness and the Sound Current, the spiritual energy that J-R anchored and that the Movement folks work with—or that works with them. Reading them is also a preparation for initiation into the Sound Current for those who choose that path. Each Discourse somehow related to the challenge or lesson I was dealing with that month. Soon after I started reading Discourses, I found I was having some incredible experiences.

One had to do with the Discourse itself. On the cover of the Discourse booklets back then was a drawing of a man. He was old and wise looking, exactly what you'd expect a spiritual master to look like. One day, that man actually showed up in my spiritual exercises (MSIA's form of meditation, chanting a sacred name for God).

Another experience was that I actually saw a Lord of one of the non-material realms. This very powerful presence came into me and I knew I was experiencing something out of this world.

Yet another was the purple flower in the center of my inner eye. This flower would pulsate and move and change from big to small. At one point in my Discourse reading, I flashed on when I first saw this flower and the color, and had a realization that J-R, the Traveler, had always been looking out for me. I had never been alone. This purple color is the sign of the Traveler, and, at the time, of John-Roger in particular. In the Seminars I've heard J-R talk about following this light and it's the light that pulls one into the Sound Current. The Traveler is the way-shower to the Heart of God, and one of his calling cards is the purple light.

In the midst of all of this, I discovered that, in addition to books and these Discourses, there were cassette tapes of this John-Roger guy giving talks around the world. (Not as ancient as 8-tracks, but close. Remember, this was before the days of CDs or MP3s.) So I ordered a bunch of them and immersed myself in these teachings. I was just blown away by this man and what he had to say.

It didn't take long before I realized that the tapes tended to take me out of my body. That is, it was as if I was both sitting on my chair and was also somewhere else. It was something like being in a more meditative state. While that was kind of cool, I really wanted to get what was being said. So I would hop in my car, pop a tape in the cassette player and listen while I drove around for hours. Being in the car forced me to stay awake and focused while I absorbed what was on the tapes. I was really saturating myself with this knowledge. It seemed like these things were already inside of me, and yet I needed to awaken to them.

By this time, my girlfriend and I were back in the States and I had decided to marry her. The marriage had its challenges and I was struggling to keep things going. One of the challenges was that my then-wife had been in a relationship with a guy who had started practicing meditation intensely after they had gotten together. He would go off and meditate for hours each day, leaving her to feel essentially abandoned.

When I met her, it was before getting on Discourses; with the partying and drugs, getting involved in spirituality was probably the last thing she expected. However, it was something I was very hungry for. So that's exactly what happened. I'm sure it was déjà vu for her, and that was a problem. There I was, meditating two hours a day, just like her ex. That, and going to all the events, would create separation between us.

I began to realize that I might have to sacrifice one or the other; my spiritual pursuits or my wife—not because that's what you had to do to be spiritual, but because I didn't have the discipline, bandwidth or tools to maintain both. As you can imagine, as immersed in materiality as I was, this was not an easy choice.

I later learned one of the many great J-R quotes that helped bring me understanding: "The freedom I give to you is the freedom I take for me."

"My soul is in the sky."

– WILLIAM SHAKESPEARE
(*A MIDSUMMER NIGHT'S DREAM*)

"I realized I needed to change some really basic things about my approach to life. I decided to commit to my spiritual studies 100%. Then I had my first face-to-face encounter with John-Roger."

– JESUS GARCIA, D.S.S.

CHAPTER 9

The Training Begins

IN TRYING TO SUSTAIN MY relationship with my then-wife, I took a number of workshops that the various organizations founded by John-Roger were offering. In 1987 or 1988, we went together to see J-R at a San Diego seminar he was giving. It was amazing because it was there that I saw J-R on stage and heard in my mind that he was my friend. "I know him." I had no idea how I knew that...but I knew it.

On his way up to the stage, he had walked by us and stopped at the couple in front of us. He asked if they were planning on having kids because, he said, there's no reason to be married if you're not going to have kids. I looked at my then-wife and I remembered I had told her I didn't want kids. Uh-oh. I remember walking out to the parking lot with her and getting into the car. As I entered the freeway, beside me was a brown Lincoln—the driver was John Morton and John-Roger was in the back seat, reading. I stared and never let go. I dreamt that one day I would be driving them, especially John-Roger.

At some point after that, John-Roger, with Drs. Ron and Mary Hulnick, offered an event called The Relationship Workshop, which was adapted from John-Roger's book, *Relationships: Love, Marriage, and Spirit*. It was facilitated by the Hulnicks; I had heard they were phenomenal, so I jumped at the chance to take it.

The workshop was fantastic. It dealt with unconditional loving and enhancing the relationship with yourself. I figured that was what I needed to do in order to save my marriage. I thought I would learn in the workshop about how to fix my wife. What I learned was that it was really about me, not her. If anything needed to change, it was me. That's where it started. Of course, that was easier said than done.

In the workshop, I also found out that I didn't need to lean on my wife or smother her, but I could support her. I tried and tried to encourage my wife to work with me on the things I had learned, but this was not her way of doing things. At some point, I realized I needed to give her the freedom to be who she was and to do what she needed to do.

I realized I needed to change some really basic things about my approach to life so I decided to commit to my spiritual studies 100%. Then, during that workshop, I had my first face-to-face encounter with John-Roger.

A key feature of these events was that people could talk about their issues or concerns with the facilitators in front of the group. We could learn a lot about our own situations by hearing about how others dealt with their issues. But sharing like this with John-Roger was on a whole different level. It was as if he could see deeply into the hearts of people who shared.

I had matured enough that my resistance to sharing my stuff in front of a group was not as powerful as it had been in my teens. I had taken enough seminars and acting classes to see that this kind of sharing was really beneficial—both for the person sharing and the people listening. So when the time for sharing arrived, I couldn't wait to have my moment with J-R.

I was in the first row, and on his way to the stage, J-R stopped and leaned over and asked me my name. I said it was Jesus Garcia and he said, "No, Spirit's telling me something else." I thought for a second and said my stage name: Nick Corri. J-R nodded and said, "That's it."

I just lit up to think that I had somehow been recognized. It was a different recognition and I experienced J-R checking with Spirit, he knew me from there: my ego had it that he'd recognized me from my films.

Then J-R was on the stage and they were picking two or three people to share with him. I raised my hand along with maybe 30 or 40 other people and, much to my surprise, I was called on.

I stood up and J-R looked at me, and, as had happened in San Diego, in that moment I recognized, in a very deep place, that I knew John-Roger from a long time ago. It's hard to explain, but there are people that we know throughout lifetimes. J-R was one of those people for me.

One of the things I asked J-R that day was if could still be an actor and do the spiritual work with him. J-R said yes. And he's helped me over the years to both be successful as an actor and also to let go of my need to do that.

I do remember that I got really high from that sharing with John-Roger. On some level I knew I had done more than meet the man. I may not have had the vocabulary, but I knew something had happened that day. I came to realize that I had met a real spiritual warrior, the Mystical Traveler.

Another thing that came out in my sharing that day was that I told John-Roger I wanted to work with him. In those days he had a small staff of people who worked closely with him and I wanted to be one of them. I came right out and said I wanted to do what John Morton does; I want to be like John Morton. What I was really saying was, "I want to be your friend and devote myself to you and your work."

He told me to talk to John. So I made an appointment with John for an interview. Later that night as people were exiting the event in the parking lot, I saw what seemed like J-R and John Morton in the brown Lincoln. I waved at a figure on the passenger side—the car stopped, the car window rolled down, and I locked eyes with J-R. It seemed like he didn't remember me, so I introduced myself again, "I'm Nick the actor." He agreed and said, "I know, we saw you in your movie, *Gotcha*." I couldn't believe he recognized me from the movies.

I definitely wanted a way to get closer to J-R, but how? Meanwhile, a good friend, Marla Ludwig, told me the way to get to get to J-R was to start with yard work at Mandeville. So I began doing volunteer work in the yard at the Mandeville Canyon house where J-R lived.

On the day of my appointment with John, he met me outside at the pool in the back. I remember that he was wearing shorts with white socks to the knees. Clearly he was an athlete and I knew a lot of people admired John. In the time I had with John, I saw how he inspired everybody to really go for it and to stay in shape.

The interview itself was really pretty cool. I just kept saying "sure" while he talked. And all I kept thinking of was living with the Boss.

John had not received the keys to the Traveler Consciousness yet and I was just ignoring his warning that working with J-R wasn't glamorous. I thanked him and insisted that he tell J-R that I want to work with him. I came every day until one day while I was working on the PVC piping in the volleyball court, J-R came out holding two popsicles and handed me one. I was floored. I couldn't believe he was standing there with me. The experience of that was amazing. I was hooked.

I loved the way he was. There was a deep connection that was all soul and felt like God was looking at his son.

"Are you sure
That we are awake? It seems to me
That yet we sleep, we dream."

– WILLIAM SHAKESPEARE
(A MIDSUMMER NIGHT'S DREAM)

*"Interestingly, John-Roger, who is based in L.A.,
happened to be giving seminars and doing other
spiritual work in New York at the same time I was
there. (A cosmic coincidence?) So I managed to get
a note to him and invited him come to the film
set and visit me. To my total surprise, he showed
up with his assistant, and I was blown away."*

– JESUS GARCIA, D.S.S.

CHAPTER 10

Traveling with the Traveler

THE NEXT THING THAT HAPPENED was that I started to hear about annual trips that John-Roger had been leading to the Middle East and
Holy Land. Called PAT IV trips, they were like month-long spiritual
retreats/pilgrimages. PAT stood for Peace Awareness Training and
there were a series of three (PAT I, PAT II, and PAT III) that were
done in a retreat setting for about 5 or 6 days. Taking those trainings
first were a requirement in order to lay the foundation for the PAT
IV. In all, there were seven PAT IV trips from 1984 to 1990.

On that year's trip, there were going to be about 150 people flying
to Aswan, Egypt, cruising along the Nile, doing meditation, visiting
temples and doing the PAT interactive processes while on the boat.
They would also be touring the Promised Land: Israel. Explorations
of the old city and staying at a kibbutz called Nof Ginosar were on
the schedule, too.

I had to go. But I hadn't done the prerequisite PATs I – III, which
were several hundred dollars each, and I didn't exactly have the
thousand or so dollars required to reserve my space on the PAT IV.
I didn't care. Somehow, I was going.

As I started having deeper and deeper experiences with J-R,
I found myself making changes in my life. For one thing, I had
dropped everything in order to get clean and sober. Unfortunately,

when getting clean becomes the goal in life, friends for whom getting high was an integral part of life start to drop away. As that happened, I saw that they were somehow enabling me in my drug use. I'm not blaming them, but I took responsibility and broke off relationships with the people in that crowd who were still left. My wife helped, and we went forward.

So I was staying sober and watching my career kind of change. I wouldn't say it went down. It was more that it was a lower priority for me than my soul and my spiritual progression. Taking care of myself (in relation to my Self) became my number one priority. I was beginning to see that what I was hungering for was Spirit. All those years of not learning about who I am, where I came from, what life was all about, kept me distracted from my real passion. Sure, I was learning how to pay the rent, make money, be a successful actor. But I was so immersed in being a movie star that I forgot to live life. I had put the brakes on that and I felt I was at my wit's end and didn't know why.

Being married was beautiful at first, and then all the Catholic guilt appeared. My belief was that I had to succeed in this marriage because, after all, I was Catholic and there is no other option. I was trapped in the false belief that Catholics aren't allowed to divorce. However, as time went on, I started to see all many issues with my lack and low self-esteem, and it seemed like they started to show up in our marriage. That's what I was projecting, at least.

In the process, we forgot to love ourselves and be our true selves in the relationship. We were just too busy playing some role we needed to play that was impossible to fulfill, spelled "Karma."

In the midst of all this, I was getting deeper into the Traveler's teachings. I was in my second year of reading the *Soul Awareness Discourses*, and when the opportunity to complete the set of aura balances showed up, I sped to Las Vegas at the very last minute to get my aura balance number 3, which was another prerequisite for going on the PAT IV trip.

To explain more about this process, here is what John-Roger wrote in his 3-book set, *Fulfilling Your Spiritual Promise*: "Aura balances are done in person by people specifically trained to do them, and they are a technique for clearing the aura (or energy field) that surrounds your physical body. In MSIA we offer a series of three aura balances: the first works in the physical aura; the second, in the emotional aura; the third, in the mental/spiritual aura. Each aura balance helps to clear imbalances in the aura and to strengthen the consciousness so it can better handle everyday stress, tension, and emotional changes. Aura balances can also help bring the mind, body, and emotions into a greater creative flow. A balanced aura can assist you in having a more accurate perception of yourself and the world and being more available to the presence of Spirit in your life."

That third aura balance I had went really deep, and at one point I noticed J-R come into the room. He went to my feet and stood there touching my toes and the pads of my feet. I can't begin to describe for you just how profound that was. John-Roger was holding for me while the person doing the balance completed what he was doing.

That was the first of the two "bookends" that completed many years later when I stood at his feet and held for him as he took his last breaths on this earth.

Not long after that experience in Vegas, I scored a great job on a Merchant Ivory movie called *Slaves of New York*. So away my wife and I went to New York. We got a nice little loft and we were having a pretty good time. Then, what I can only call miracles started to happen for me.

Interestingly, John-Roger, who is based in L.A., happened to be giving seminars and doing other spiritual work in New York at the same time I was there. (A cosmic coincidence?) So I managed to get a note to him and invited him to come to the film set and visit me. To my total surprise, he showed up with his new assistant, and I was blown away.

That visit had a big impact on me, and not just because he came. Seeing him with his brand-new assistant hit me really hard. I almost freaked out because I thought this guy had been hired and had taken *my* place on J-R's staff. I remember doing my scene while thinking that I could be that guy and wondering what I was doing in front of the camera instead of standing with J-R.

That really underscored for me that I wanted to be that person. I *had* to be that person. I think that was a key awareness that started a real karmic shift in my life. I also think that if the movie I was shooting had been successful, my life would have taken a really different turn. I suspect I would not have gone on my first PAT IV trip and would not have ended up on staff. But the film bombed and my life soared.

Looking back, it seemed like J-R and the powers that be worked it out that I somehow would get the money for the PAT IV trip to Israel. You can imagine that the price of a month of travel in the Middle East and plane flights and such add up. The overall cost was several thousand dollars. I sure didn't have that kind of money. I was making payments toward the trip, but still…

By the time J-R left the movie set, I had really connected with him. It was amazing and I felt like I was in love. Not a romantic love—it was like re-connecting with my absolutely best friend from many lifetimes. It was a real full-immersion experience of a spiritual love that was pure, like the love of a mother for a child. I believe it was the product of eons of reincarnations, of simply "knowing" the countless times we had been together.

J-R has talked about the soul impulse and how, when that happens, it can become a convergent moment for change. So at times I could have a Sound Current experience, a breeze or a thunder or rain, and it could completely set a different course in my life. That's what this was like.

A couple of nights after J-R had been on the set, I was invited to a party. It would have been good for my career to be there and hang out with those people so I decided to go. Andy Warhol had just died, and a lot of the Warhol crowd in that whole underground New York artist scene were going to show up. It was in Tribeca.

Tribeca was on the verge of exploding, but at the time was pretty much run down. There were lots of huge, industrial lofts and that's where I would hang out with these artists and actors and creative types. On this particular night, I was taking a taxi with a bunch of people on the way to the party. These parties were pretty wild with lots of drinking and plenty of drugs.

All of a sudden, I got a hit that I wanted to talk to J-R. It didn't exactly bowl me over, but somewhere inside I had the sense that I was a door and opportunity was knocking.

It was in that moment that I made a choice that would affect the rest of my life. That's a dramatic statement, I know, but it's absolutely true. I chose to go toward J-R and not toward the party and the life that would entail. I was studying Discourses at that point and I wasn't doing drugs, I was being pulled towards J-R. Love is the pull towards the Sound Current. J-R was the Sound Current; I just didn't know how to articulate it back then.

I looked out the cab window and saw we were in front of the Sheraton Hotel, which happened to be the hotel where J-R was staying. Without a second thought, I told the cabbie to stop, and I got out of the taxi while the other passengers looked on somewhere between shock and puzzlement. I paid the driver and walked up to a telephone booth. I dropped in a couple of quarters and called J-R's hotel room—and he answered! It was amazing. We ended up talking for hours; I was outside in the booth and he was literally up above me in his hotel room.

I was in the acting world, but I was looking at this other life—this spiritual life of being with John-Roger. I saw that that was what I really wanted. But I didn't know how to make that happen. I didn't think I could be part of that life. J-R already had plenty of people working with him. Still, we talked. And there's something amazing that happens when the student sees the teacher or the master or the way-shower. It's like I finally found what I'd been looking for almost all my life and deep inside of me I knew it. From then on, I was J-R's man. J-R would always say, "The willingness to do, gives the ability to do." Once I made that my intention, the methods manifested.

Interestingly, not too long after the events in New York, I was in Miami. I went to a John-Roger home seminar and there was a rumor that J-R had passed the keys to the Traveler Consciousness to John Morton. I freaked out, thinking I had lost my chance to be with the great master John-Roger. I thought that meant that J-R would be retiring.

Although I was happy for John, I was deeply connected to J-R. I called him crying and he said, "Don't worry, I got you. I'm your Traveler." I would learn later that a Master marks his initiates, and I was marked by John-Roger.

I was relieved. But I wanted not only to be connected to John-Roger but to also be on his staff. So that became my big challenge; figuring out how to get onto J-R's personal staff.

The first thing I did was let him know that I wanted to go on the PAT IV trip, even though I didn't have the prerequisites handled—which is to have completed the PAT I, II, and III retreats—and I surely didn't have the money. But not too long after that, Gisèle Bersot's daughter had the same issue; one day she came up to me and said that she was going on the PAT IV. When I asked her how she did this, she replied, smiling, "I wrote to John-Roger and asked him.

He said 'Yes.'" Duh! As the famous Bible quote goes, "You receive not because you ask not" (*James 4:2*). I asked and he approved me. That was a lesson I would never forget. Regarding the money issue, I will always be grateful to Ozzie Delgadillo (who recently passed away) for fronting me the initial $1,000 deposit so I could get on the list. One month later, I paid him back in full.

A while later, I finished shooting the movie and got my final check. That did it! I paid for the balance of my trip and I gave my wife a bunch of money. But there was more I had to handle and it had to do with our marriage. I had to explore this new world. She actually agreed that I should go, albeit reluctantly, and said she'd stay in New York. So away I went to my first PAT IV trip.

At the start of that trip, I was on the flight to Israel. J-R was in first class and pretty much the rest of us who had taken that particular flight were in coach. After we were in the air, J-R left the front cabin and walked back to coach to visit with us. Though there were a number of people in the section who were going on the PAT IV trip, I was feeling pretty left out and not part of the group. They seemed like they knew each other pretty well and I didn't know them at all. But J-R walked right over to me. Once again it felt like I was with an old best friend I hadn't seen in a while, but we were picking up right where we had left off.

After J-R went back to his seat, I kept thinking about what I wanted. The more I thought, the more I felt compelled to move on what I was experiencing inside. So I took a deep breath, went up to first class and, standing in the aisle, started to talk with him. I didn't know what was going on, but soon I found myself almost collapsed on the floor with my head on J-R's lap, sobbing. It felt like I cried for hours and like I was washing away lifetimes of karma. I don't know if that's what was happening, but that's about as close as I can come to describing it.

J-R just held for me while things I didn't even know had been inside of me came out. That was another milestone on my journey of reconnecting with J-R, who, I was to learn, I had been friends with many, many times before.

Now my life with him was starting again.

Two years later, on the PAT IV in 1990 (who knew that would be the last one?), I was inspired by staff member Michael Feder and really respected the way he managed the trip. It was a crazy time. Saddam Hussein had just taken over Kuwait and, because of the turmoil in the region, there were long lines of buses trying to cross the Red Sea. When Michael would work with J-R, I saw miracles. We encountered a line of trucks and buses at least a mile long, but somehow Michael was able to get us three busses together right in front of the line. I admired Michael's leadership and John Morton's devotion for John-Roger. Those were the two qualities I adopted as I moved into my new life.

"Love all, trust a few, do wrong to none."

– WILLIAM SHAKESPEARE
(*ALL'S WELL THAT ENDS WELL*)

"*To add even more icing to the cake, on the train to Leningrad, I was initiated into the Sound Current of God. It was an amazing experience. I would say that all my aura balances, ordinations and initiations have been on trains or exotic, adventurous locations and places I've never thought of going to. I definitely will never forget any of my travels, especially this one.*"

– JESUS GARCIA, D.S.S.

CHAPTER 11

Moving Along My Spiritual Path

IN MSIA, AFTER READING TWO years of Discourses, a student can apply for initiation into the Sound Current. What that means is that the student has prepared himself or herself and developed the inner support to learn the next phase of spiritual study, which is chanting a sacred tone, or name for God, that is spiritually charged just for them.

That was just about where I was in my studies when I took the PAT trip, sort of on the edge of this next step. But, of course, I had no way of knowing if I was ready to receive this level of initiation, I could only apply for it.

I want to emphasize how powerful Discourses are. They are compact booklets and the information in them can sometimes seem pretty simple. However, over the years and after having completed the twelve years of Discourses, I can testify, as a knowing, not a thinking, that they are not about the words. They are a portal into the Mystical Traveler Consciousness that is both inside us all and also in what I'd call the outer realms of Spirit. They are a door through which people can enter what we call the Sound Current of God.

Maybe I'm projecting, but I sure didn't catch on to what I had in my hands when I was initially reading the Discourses. However, especially in the three or four years before J-R passed, I found the Discourses were the catalyst for some pretty profound Sound Current experiences that became mile markers on the path to where I was going and indicators of what was to come. Since I had developed a real love for tracking and keeping track of things—something I learned from John-Roger—I was becoming more consciously aware of these experiences.

But back to the story. The first leg of the PAT trip was Amsterdam. We spent the night there and then flew into Cairo, Egypt. Next was an overnight train ride to Aswan. When we reached Aswan in the morning, we boarded the boat that would take us up the Nile and headed towards Alexandria. It was the most biblical, beautiful experience I've ever had in my entire life.

While we were on this pilgrimage, we had to read or already have read three books: Herman Hesse's *Journey to the East*, *Initiation* by Elisabeth Haich and, of course, the MSIA Discourses. The thing about Discourses is that often the topic they discuss that month somehow ends up being exactly what life brings forward to deal with. That's the magic of Discourses. You read the information, then Spirit brings you the lesson so you can integrate the teaching. So the trip was extra interesting.

I loved the trip. We went to every temple along that stretch of the Nile. I immediately latched onto John-Roger and went everywhere he went.

I still desperately wanted to be on J-R's staff but had no idea how to make that happen. But I just kept showing up and doing whatever needed to be done. That's when I would understand intention first, then methods would appear from Spirit. Things were such a blur, but I do remember that at some point on the trip, I was told that I was now on J-R's staff.

Actually, I didn't know all of what that really meant, but I didn't care. I was with J-R. One thing I found out it did mean was that I was able to do things with John Morton and the other staff guys. I got to hang out and watch how J-R worked with the staff, and how he shared, and it was beautiful.

During my first PAT IV in 1988, I began learning that J-R was a voracious reader. On occasion, I would see him reading a book and the next night in a seminar he would reference something from it. Things inspired J-R, he was a seeker. He once told me, "Seek ye first the kingdom of heaven and all else will be given to you. Remember it says 'seek', it doesn't say 'find.'" I got it. Just seek. Trying to find it can be frustrating, but seeking is great. I became a seeker, too.

On the 1990 PAT IV, J-R, one of his other staff guys, and I would spend hours in his cabin reading the Anne Rice "Vampire Chronicles" and "The Mummy" books. I was not a fast reader, so sometimes I would get the books after the other guys had read them. While this may not be a big deal to you, it actually assisted me when I ran into Tom Cruise some years later. (That story comes later on.)

I was getting used to unofficially being on staff as we entered the Promised Land. Israel was gorgeous. I had some very profound experiences being there and found myself on the fast track to learning how to function in this new position. The trip was amazing and, at the same time, it went by in a blur. Before I knew it, we were getting ready to leave the Promised Land.

As the PAT IV trip was ending, John-Roger and some other people were heading to a Peace trip in Germany and Russia by train through Eastern Europe. I was not prepared to be away from J-R. I wanted to go on this extended trip to be with him. So I asked if he'd take me with him. He looked at Brooke Danza, who ran the Esprit

Travel agency and was responsible for planning all of the PAT IV and other staff travels, and said, "book him on the rest of trip." Then he turned to Phil Danza, head of NOW productions and said, "give him a walkie talkie and radio." He looked back at me with a wink and said, "You're on my personal staff." I had no idea what that entailed, but I didn't care. I just wanted to be next to J-R.

To add even more icing to the cake, on the train to Leningrad, I was initiated into the Sound Current of God. It was an amazing and very sacred experience. I would say that all my aura balances, ordinations and initiations have been on trains or exotic, adventurous locations and places I've never thought of going to. I definitely will never forget any of my travels, especially this one. Then, in Germany, on the way to Russia, everything came grinding to a halt.

Looking back, I was experiencing the process of dying to this world. The eating of the manna and what John-Roger was letting me see in the inner realms opened my third eye, yet I was still attached to this world. J-R would say it's not the attachment to things but the detachment that causes pain. Part of that was because I really missed my wife. I was really torn once I realized this was not just some side trip on the journey of life; it was becoming the main road for me. I was struggling to decide—really decide—if this was the life I wanted.

As I began agonizing over it, something became clear to me: I had crossed the point of no return. It was almost a stunning realization. I missed my wife, but, deep down, I knew this was the life I wanted. And I finally got clear enough about it to admit it to myself.

This spiritual movement that was happening inside of me was so strong and powerful. It was a tidal wave that could not be stopped, not by a relationship, not by a marriage, not by a career, not by anything. As that realization settled in, I called my wife. I was unquestionably attached to her, but I was also unquestionably dedicated to my "True Self." I remember her answering the phone and my telling her I would get on a plane and fly right back if she wanted to get back together.

There was a long silence on the line.

When I told J-R what had happened, he advised me to go back to her after the trip and get a divorce so we would both be free. He said he'd see me at his house in Mandeville Canyon in October—which was a couple months away. Recognizing the wisdom in his advice, I set out to do what he suggested. It came down just like he said it would. It wasn't easy—for her or for me—but we both knew this was what was best for us. And in November, everything was complete and I moved into John-Roger's house.

Despite the excitement and adventure of my new life, and even knowing that I could not sustain my marriage properly, it took me years to get over my ex-wife. It was hard. When it was bothering me a lot, J-R would tell me to cut the tail off right at the dog rather than slowly cutting it off a bit at a time. These little steps were so much more painful than one fast cut—boom—and never having to deal with it again. But the best I could do was cut it off inch by inch, and the hurt stretched out for a long, long time.

I never saw my ex-wife again after our divorce and parting in New York. God Bless her. Following the trip to Russia, J-R and John went to Korea and I finished making the Merchant Ivory movie, going back to do reshoots.

Then, my new life really began.

"John-Roger had passed the keys of the Mystical Traveler Consciousness to John Morton on June 19, 1988; the transfer would be completed and it would be confirmed December 18, 1988 to make sure John could hold the energy. Because John was moving into a new position, I felt a really desperate need to learn everything."

– JESUS GARCIA, D.S.S.

CHAPTER 12

Working for J-R

By October 1st 1988, I had moved into the house in Mandeville Canyon where J-R's staff lived and found myself clean of drugs, free of alcohol and without any legally binding relationships. It was like a rebirth. Then my training with John-Roger, the spiritual warrior, began.

Let me give you a heads up on something: I had always wanted to be a priest or some kind of monk. And Mandeville, when I moved up there, was basically a monastery. The rule was no sex unless you were married. Phil and Brooke Danza were the only married couple living there and had pretty much been grandfathered into the place because, later, if anyone on J-R's immediate staff wanted to get married, they had to move out of the house. Besides no sex, there was no alcohol, no smoking, no garlic, onion or pork. It was a pure spiritual home.

Mandeville was also a spiritual workplace. NOW Productions had their offices and studios and a ton of audio and video equipment stuffed into a half-ton of space in the basement. Upstairs were J-R and the guys who worked closely and traveled with him, including me. Aside from John-Roger's room there were two rooms on either side of the hallway where we lived and used for packing and preparation for trips. Those of us on J-R's staff did our work, did SEs, and would pack for trips out of those two rooms. We would be working away waiting for J-R to call over the intercom with our marching orders. When the call came, we had to respond quickly. For example, if J-R said we were going for a ride, we had only a couple minutes to get dressed for wherever we were going and rush out to the car park area. Take too long, and you'd be left standing there.

My first job with J-R was being his bodyguard for a meeting he had in a public restaurant. I loved it, it was like I was in a movie or something. I came on staff at the tail end of threats against J-R's life. J-R wasn't afraid but I didn't want to lose him if I could help it. He told me to sit over there and just watch. I did and nothing happened, thank God. J-R and this person talked and it was finished. It would be the beginning of many meetings and places I went with him where he would say, "sit there and watch." I didn't fully get it but now it's clear what he was teaching me then.

As far as finances were concerned, eventually, like J-R, I would take a vow of poverty, which meant I owned nothing; the church handled all my needs. That ran from 2007 to 2016. Before that, from 1988 to 2006, I was a volunteer.

The house at Mandeville was pure energy and magical. It was and still is phenomenal. It was really a club of spirituality and we were all very tight. We were doing the Lord's work and it was like the Beatles in a lot of ways. Of course, if one of the guys got married or started dating someone, there was a period of adjusting to the new person (girlfriend/wife) being part of the band. But we got there.

The favorite place at Mandeville was the living room with J-R watching back-to-back movies or in the kitchen going through the mail; every staff member had his own mailbox in the kitchen.

Jason Laskay, who lived at the house and who was a master fine carpenter did wonderful work that made the house look great. Mandeville is basically a ranch-style home built in the 1930s or 40s and upgraded a lot over time. The backyard had dogs ranging from

Weimaraners and Rottweilers to Boxers, and even a few Dalmatians. If you've heard many seminars you've heard J-R talk about the dogs.

One of the best times at Mandeville was Christmas, when there would be presents stacked waist high. It was quite an adventure opening all of them and sharing what the church members had sent. One day, though, around maybe 2011, J-R stopped opening presents so the rest of us decided to stop opening presents, too. It was weird; there would be wrapped presents sitting for years in a corner of the room. Finally, during a Christmas dinner in 2016, we open them all as a way of honoring John-Roger. It was kind of a rite of passage, too, I think.

One of the rules at Mandeville was if you broke something, get it fixed. We never got blamed for breaking anything but we definitely ate it for withholding that it broke instead of getting it fixed.

Another rule I learned was, "What happens at Mandeville stays at Mandeville." People would share very sacred things and it was not our place to talk about it. Also, J-R's work was sacred and he would let people know what he wanted them to know. So if we saw something going on at the house, we never wanted to get in the way of what the Spirit was bringing forward. So, we kept our mouths shut.

These were pretty much the ground rules. If you were anywhere close to J-R or planning to move to Mandeville, you would be told of these things.

As I settled in and the shock of such a major shift began to wear off, I noticed that the staff had changed. When I started working for and taking care of J-R on the extended PAT trip, there were a number of guys on his personal staff. But by November, some of them had gotten married or moved on, so when I got there it was just John Morton, J-R and me. John-Roger had passed the spiritual keys of the Mystical Traveler Consciousness to John Morton on June 19, 1988, and by December 18 of that year, the transfer would be completed once it was confirmed that John could hold the energy. Because John was moving into a new position, I felt a really desperate need to learn everything to help J-R personally in order to be effective on his staff.

I looked to John Morton as the guy who knew the ropes. His devotion and dedication were really shining examples for me. He'd be sitting in the kitchen by our mail boxes watching TV, with our cat Cheerio slung over his shoulder purring while he handled all the correspondence and mail for J-R. Back then, there were no emails or internet or computers other than an Apple Lisa and Mac II. John became a real model for me of what J-R needed around him.

Then John got married. I felt sad at first when he left the house. But then I felt great because that left just J-R and me.

In living with J-R, I learned a lot really quickly. One of the first things he started on was self-discipline. I had actually started learning discipline when I was in ROTC during high school. I liked being in a uniform and I liked the order that the class was offering. Though I failed in most things in the ROTC class, at one point the Army Sergeant asked me if I could shoot a gun. I said I could and he took me to the school shooting range. I was great. He put me on the school shooting team and we made it to second place in the Sharp Shooting State Championship.

Our ROTC class field trip was a weekend at Fort Ord in 1980 while I was at Fairfax High School. We stayed at their barracks and took turns guarding through the night while others rested. This was "acting as if" we were in wartime. Being on the lookout and serving to protect and defend was something that would begin to form in my DNA and prepare me to serve J-R.

It was actually my training for what we called the Night Watch at Mandeville. That was a job that was rotated among the staff where we had to stay up throughout the night, keeping the energy clean and holding for J-R and others as they slept. I loved this and eventually was very good at it. I'm still doing the Night Watch when Spirit calls on me.

Years later I would drive J-R by Fort Ord en route to Asilomar Conference Grounds for the Living in Grace retreats. The energy and light columns were always there for me to step into.

I want to acknowledge that when I first started on staff, John Morton was a big help. Working with and being around J-R is a unique experience, to say the least, and John really helped me ease into it—at least ease into something that's like being thrown into the deep end of the swimming pool.

One of the first things John Morton taught me when I showed up at Mandeville was to make it a point to "say what you mean and mean what you say." That may sound trite, but with J-R you really had to do that or there would almost certainly be trouble. (I learned about that big time.) I also did a lot of meditation to keep myself balanced.

Often, I watched over J-R while he meditated in his room. I would be in the S.E. chair trying to read or do computer stuff (unless the computer was making noises). After a while I would get impatient, tip-toe to the door handle and start to turn it. A voice from the dark would ask, "What are you doing?" J-R's awareness was omnipresent in its totality. "Nothing," I whispered. "Where are you going?" "I want to go out for some air." "Okay, come back and don't make noise when you return." He knew everything. It was impossible to hear him in a deep sleep and he could sense the entire house.

J-R had several types of sleeps. If he was snoring, it was a shallow sleep, so we'd have to watch him more carefully. When you couldn't hear his snoring, it meant he would have a great sleep. For many years I observed the rest state for J-R. I also discovered that how I was driving could make his sleep deeper or shallow.

One of the things I wish I had saved was a collection of all the notes J-R and I wrote to each other over the years. My room was down the back hallway of Mandeville. The staff would often get up early to go run errands. On many occasions, before I left, I would write a note and slip it under J-R's door closed bedroom door. Sometimes he'd ask, "Zeus? Is that you?" "Yes," I'd say. Sometimes he would want to come along; other times I would cancel my errands and we'd hit the road and get a bite to eat.

Something I learned early on after joining staff was that you can only be clear of spiritual "cobwebs" when J-R specifically asked you to go through his files. I recall a staff member who had gone through J-R's desk drawers, innocently looking through stuff without checking with J-R first, and he was hit hard. He felt his face and eyes reacting like a spider's web had trapped them.

They asked J-R about it that night when he arrived at Mandeville to help them. J-R said straight to their faces, "Keep your nose out of my stuff." He explained to me that all his items are protected by this spiritual web. We understood clearly that J-R's house in Mandeville Canyon was protected by beings. If you have bad intentions, you get karma. The staff that has lived here get this and we co-exist with these beings. They are guardians of the universe.

Once, during a Living in Grace retreat in the 1990s, I brought J-R's mail to him. The Initiates mail generally stayed in the retreat room, but this instance I thought I'd save him time by bringing it to him in the hotel room. I walked in, handed him the mail and he said, "Did I ask you to bring me the mail?" "No," I replied, feeling horrible. "I thought I'd get this for you and help you." He said, sternly, "Hell is paved with good intentions" and then told me, "I'm going to let you experience the karma that's in those letters." He looked at me and then the universal pain and darkness of all those people who wrote to J-R hit me. "You need to experience what I go through when you do things that aren't your concern unless I ask you," he said. I think he left me with this karma for an hour. I was crying and deeply crushed. He walked up to me, smiled and touched me on my shoulder. Suddenly, relief—I was Atlas for a moment and he removed the world that was crushing me. J-R said, "Take these letters back." "Yes sir!" I ran back to the training room. He loved me enough to show me what he goes through, what he does every day for his initiates.

The interesting thing is, just because I lived with a master, a spiritual warrior, doesn't mean that he was constantly on, always teaching me. Not at all. My relationship with John-Roger started, and was built first upon a strong friendship. He was definitely with me as a friend during my pain after the divorce. That's part of being a spiritual warrior: you cut out anything that's not the truth with the sword of truth. And your heart is your shield of endurance. If you get knocked down, you get back up again. While divorcing my former wife was one of the most challenging things I had ever endured in my life, I think I got through it because I had a good, solid friend at my side. There's never been a better friend for anyone than John-Roger was to me.

"A few days later an earthquake would hit that area. It got so common that when J-R said we had to go, I'd just expect an earthquake would follow. J-R used to say he was moving earthquakes, making them easier on the earth."

– JESUS GARCIA, D.S.S.

CHAPTER 13

Moving Earthquakes

I WORKED WITH AND TOOK care of John-Roger for 26 years. You have to understand, that was a 24-hours-a-day job, seven days a week. I mean that literally. Other than the times I was acting or shooting films, along with J-R's movies, I was with J-R night and day. And J-R was a 24-hours-a-day kind of guy.

It would not be unusual for him to come over to me at midnight or later and tell me to grab the car keys, we were going somewhere. Very often he'd say to drive east. So we'd get on the Interstate 10 Freeway and head out through Rosemead where he once lived and taught high school in his "Mr. Hinkins" incarnation. We'd go maybe as far east as Idyllwild.

We'd be out there in the boonies at 3:00 am for a while, then J-R would tell me to turn around and head back. A few days later an earthquake would hit that area. It got so common that when J-R said we had to go, I'd just expect an earthquake would follow. J-R used to say he was moving earthquakes, making them easier on the earth.

I mentioned that because I wanted to touch on the idea of some of the work J-R did. He did a lot of inner work that he would not tell us about. Maybe every now and again he would talk about something like that, but not often.

One thing he did tell us about was on the Europe trip in 1988 when we went to the Berlin Wall. At the time, Communism appeared to be at its strongest. J-R did an exercise with us where we put a "Light worm" into the Wall and he said the Wall would fall within two years.

Many of us who knew J-R took it at face value. But others just couldn't believe it. And they didn't believe it right up until the Wall fell in 1989.

I believe J-R was doing things of that scope and nature all the time. But he didn't talk about it. And we didn't know to ask. Even if we had known, I doubt J-R would have discussed it.

In a sense, if we were members of the Catholic Church, I have no doubt that we could prove he did three miracles and it would be Saint John-Roger.

An interesting side note happened a couple of years ago, when I headed out to Idyllwild with Nicole. We were going there to celebrate the birthday of another guy who had been on J-R's staff with me.

It was great driving Nicole that day; it felt like J-R was with us and I fell into telling stories of the times J-R and I would come out this way. And sure enough, Idyllwild had three earthquakes around the time we were there. Nicole felt the first one at 6:00 in the morning that day.

"Our doubts are traitors, and make us lose the good we oft might win, by fearing to attempt."

– WILLIAM SHAKESPEARE (*MEASURE FOR MEASURE*)

"When I came on board and we were traveling and going places, I'd get excited. Of course, if we were at a beach, I'd want to go hang with the girls. But I was with J-R. I'd ask him when we were going to hang with the girls. It didn't take too long before I realized that for us, there were no girls to hang out with. We had work to do. We meditated a lot, got out of the body, which is soul travelling. "

– JESUS GARCIA, D.S.S.

CHAPTER 14

Stories of Working with J-R & Things Learned

NOT TOO LONG AFTER I started working with J-R, we were on a plane coming back from some trip or another. J-R had a bunch of correspondence from Prana, the church's administrative headquarters that's now called Peace Awareness Labyrinth and Gardens (PALG).

(As a side note, people who first got involved with J-R's work before 2000 still tend to call it Prana, which stood for Purple Rose Ashram of the New Age. Hey, the Movement started in the late 60s/ early 70s, when New Age Spiritual seeking was big, especially with the hippies, etc. I remember J-R saying the hippies brought forward a loving, open and brave consciousness.)

J-R started going through the stacks and stacks of papers, which were mostly letters from Initiates and Ministers who would write to J-R. He separated out a pile and pushed it toward me saying, "You. The Spanish stuff." This was common as his personal staff.

I looked at him kind of blankly so he asked if I could read Spanish. I said I could. I said that because I would say anything to be able to hang with J-R. I basically thought of it as lying, but J-R said I was just doing whatever it took to stay around.

The fact is, I was struggling to read Spanish; I could kind of read a little bit. J-R looked at me like he was seeing through me, then flipped a piece of paper to me and asked what the woman was saying. I looked and tried to figure it out. But finally I just said I had no idea.

J-R shook his head and found someone else to translate the Spanish correspondence.

Once on staff, I quickly learned that J-R was very punctual. When I moved into Mandeville Canyon to work I was pretty punctual, because I had learned to be on time from my high school experiences in ROTC, then later in acting when I had to be on time for a shoot. Film companies call you in at 5:00 or 6:00 in the morning, and you have to show up. Time really is money in the film business. I quickly found out that if J-R said we'd be leaving at a certain time, if someone wasn't ready, the car would pull away without them. I've heard more than one story of a staff guy chasing on foot after J-R's car.

I learned about this myself because, in the first nine years when it was just J-R and me, it was very common for J-R to intercom me in my room to get ready to roll. That meant I had only a few minutes to pull myself together, get dressed and get out to the car before he'd be pulling away to have breakfast or meet with John Morton. Don't keep him waiting or he'd say, "Dollar bill waiting on a peso." That was especially true in Santa Barbara where I'd be driving J-R and John Morton to meetings over breakfast, lunch and dinner.

I have to say, as an aside, the best times I had with J-R were at breakfast. It was just fellowshipping around food.

J-R also traveled a lot. It was the nature of his work. We went to cities all over the country and the world so J-R could work with his Initiates wherever they were. There was nowhere J-R wouldn't go to save and do battle for their souls.

Neither being punctual nor being a gypsy were a problem for me. My stepfather took me everywhere, and we lived in hotels and sometimes slept in the cabin of the truck, so I was used to that kind of life when I hooked up with J-R. Later, I realized that not only was I able to tolerate that kind of lifestyle, I really enjoyed travelling with J-R.

Sometimes, especially at first, I would feel as if I were being torn from what had become a comfortable environment, a home. Then eventually I would just decide I liked Holiday Inns, Radissons and La Quintas. As our MSIA family matured and started becoming more successful in the world, we'd stay in better hotels because people would take care of J-R. But no matter where we stayed, Denny's was the restaurant of choice. I guess our systems got used to Denny's recipes. I think that was also another reflection of J-R's Depression-era upbringing. As I got used to the routine, I basically cooperated with just about everything (as if not cooperating would do anything but keep me upset).

When I came on board and we were traveling and going places, I'd get excited. If we were at a beach, I'd want to go hang with the girls. But J-R was the boss, so I'd ask him when we were going to hang with the girls. It didn't take too long before I realized that for us, there were no girls to hang out with. We had work to do.

Traveling with J-R always had lessons—much like life in general does if you're paying attention. But traveling had its own unique experiences.

Once I was with J-R, in Amsterdam on a layover, and we were at a big international airport checking in. I had the luggage cart and I was watching J-R's little travel bag where he kept cash that he used for tips, transportation, or to pay for the events of the day. On this occasion we were getting ready to go to the Russia trip and to Germany. J-R was checking us in at the counter only a few feet from where I was with the bag. He had told me to watch his luggage, and this became a defining moment that brought me a very profound learning.

I was being pretty vigilant, but I took my eye off the ball. I left the luggage trolley that had J-R's bag on it and walked over to J-R, who was only about four or five feet away. J-R looked up at me and asked if I was watching the bag. I said, "Sure," and then glanced back at the luggage trolley. My heart sank. J-R's bag was gone.

J-R didn't even blink. He looked at me, smiled, and said, "I guess that guy needed the money more than we needed it. God bless him." And that was it. We made a police report and we put the Light on it. I think the most amazing thing I experienced, though, was that J-R never once brought it up, never blamed me.

I'm mentioning this because it took that experience, just one time, for me to really be on guard with luggage around J-R at airports, and to be a lot more vigilant. I became very focused when I started having more responsibility on the PAT trips; I was very watchful because I was accountable for the luggage, which is a very responsible task. You better believe that after that one experience, not one bag was stolen on my watch.

The main thing I took from this was the love I experienced that was filled with Grace. J-R always taught with love.

On another trip, I was in Paris with J-R. I was feeling sort of depressed and couldn't figure out why. I started telling J-R about a past experience I had had being in a particular apartment in Paris we called the models' apartment. It was where all the models and actors would stay when they were traveling to and from jobs and we all shared the cost.

I was telling J-R about having been in the apartment during a shoot that took me from Paris to Italy, and I said I had been feeling very depressed when I had been there. As I told the story, J-R said to take him to the apartment. So I did. We stood outside the place and I pointed toward the window, saying that was the apartment. J-R just stood there for a moment like he was meditating, and then he asked how I felt. I said I felt great now, that everything was OK. He said I wouldn't ever think about this again. He told me later that he was completing whatever I left there and erasing any ectoplasmic energy that had kind of pulled on me.

From that day, I no longer had any pull toward the apartment or my experiences of having been there in Paris when I had been an actor.

What I learned was that you always want to erase negative past experiences of a person, place or thing. If you had a bad experience with a place, for example, you can update it by going back to that location and having a good time there. It's a way of updating the memory and releasing the feelings that can drag you down.

J-R was able to change my past footprints. He did that in other locations, too. When I joined staff I went with J-R to San Francisco, and he asked me to take him to the same place where I had been emotionally challenged in my relationship with my ex-wife. I did and he magically erased the energy I had tied to that place. I updated San Francisco with wonderful experiences with John-Roger, many of them book signings, J-R marathons and movie screenings.

As you can imagine, traveling with J-R was magical.

"That adage I learned from John Morton, "Say what you mean, mean what you say," applied in spades to J-R. Whatever J-R said, he meant, and if he said something like he was going to straighten me out, I knew I had better run. I learned that he was quick, he was a quick draw. Before I could blink he would have (figuratively) smacked me around and had a donut."

– JESUS GARCIA, D.S.S.

CHAPTER 15

Being with J-R Was Being in School

I'M NOT GOING TO SAY I was an angel. And since I was kind of at the peak of my acting career at the beginning of my work with J-R, my self-esteem was, um, let's say, high. So, I was not the easiest person in the world to have along on a working trip. But J-R must have seen something in me—or maybe it was purely the awareness of the lifetimes and lifetimes we had previously spent together—that helped him put up with me.

I'm not excusing my antics, but I do know that some of the time I was really pushy around J-R. I don't judge that now because at the time I didn't know any better. That's one of the key things J-R used to say: "Everyone is doing the best they can with what they know. When they know better, they'll do better." The way that I functioned, I hadn't quite learned to be sensitive enough.

Sensitivity ended up being the talent that J-R really brought out in me. A person like me can always come in hard and push to get what I want in the world. But to be with J-R, I didn't have to do that. In fact, if I did that, he would just go away.

While it may also sound like a contradiction, another thing I learned from J-R was perseverance. I discovered there's a difference between holding for something and pushing for it.

As soon as I started working with J-R, I began learning. Over the years, J-R basically trained me.

That adage I learned from John Morton; "Say what you mean, mean what you say," applied in spades to J-R. Whatever J-R said, he meant, and if he said something like he was going to straighten me out, I knew I had better run. I learned that he was a quick draw. Before I could blink, he would have smacked me around and had a donut. (When I say smacked me around, I mean that figuratively. But he did probably have a donut. J-R loved donuts.)

A really good example of this was in Egypt. We were on a PAT IV trip, getting ready for the sound and light show in front of the Sphinx. These shows are very dramatic and begin just as the sun sets. They're performed by British actors accompanied by thundering dramatic music. It really gives you a feel for the ancient times. So the sun was setting and J-R and I were sitting across from each other eating. I was talking, asking questions and frankly being annoying to him. Finally, J-R said, "Don't talk." I kept talking so he grabbed his glass of water and said, "I'll throw it in your face if you don't stop." I said, "I dare you." Before I knew it...*splash!* I was soaked. People were laughing and I was busting up. I really got it. J-R doesn't talk to threaten; if he says he's going to do something, he takes action.

I learned there that J-R was real. What I ended up realizing is that J-R would be accessing many things on multidimensional levels. I was young and not yet experienced in the art of sitting still and watching John-Roger work. But it was still fun.

J-R would use anything to teach, and, specifically, to teach me. When I first moved into J-R's house in Mandeville Canyon, I was not a television watcher. I was all about reading scripts and books because I was coming from the acting world. I loved the encyclopedia and I owned my own encyclopedia and book collection. This was before Google; I owned books because I was always curious about things.

That behavior continued with surprises when I moved to Mandeville. J-R loved to lay back and watch TV, but he flipped through the channels really fast. He never really stayed on one channel long enough to get engaged. It was really irritating for me to watch that way. I used to ask him what the heck he was doing. He'd say he was watching television. I'd tell him he was definitely not watching television because he was not on any one channel long enough to watch anything. He did this for months with me, maybe years.

I eventually discovered that he who had the remote was king. So I took J-R's remote control once and asked if I could use it. He said "sure," so I started surfing channels. Before long, I got caught up in a show. As soon as I started to get really involved, J-R told me to change the channel. Then we did this routine that was like a comedy act with him telling me to change the channel and my trying to stay with the show I had on. This happened more than once. Way more than once.

Of course, J-R was teaching me something, but I didn't get it. Did he want the remote back? Was I attacking him? Were the shows hurting him? When I asked him why he wanted me to change the channel, he didn't answer my question. Instead he told me that we destroy universes when we ask "Why." Of course I would say, "why?" He would reply, "You just destroyed another universe." It's a slippery slope, feeling like you are out on the limb. So I kept wondering what he was teaching me and he kept flipping through channels.

Another technique that J-R used to teach me this particular lesson went like this:

Zeus: J-R, I want to ask you a question about my initiation.
J-R: You hungry?
Zeus: No. Anyway I had a dream and was wondering…
J-R: I'm hungry.
Zeus: What would you like?
J-R: Tuna fish sandwich, make sure it's…
Zeus: Quartered. Sure coming up!

So I'd go off to the kitchen to make J-R a sandwich while he sat in his recliner watching TV. When I finished the sandwich, I'd take it out to him and try to get back to my question. But before I could get out a word or two J-R would jump in again.

J-R: Pepperoncini?
Zeus: Got it. Mayo?
J-R: Yes, please, easy. Toasted bread.
Zeus: Here it is.

J-R would inspect the quartered sandwich and I would be feeling great that the sandwich passed his inspection. So I'd try my question again.

Zeus: When I dreamt of an accident does that mean it might have happened in real life?
J-R: Can you get me some water?
At this point I'm getting frustrated.
Zeus: Come on J-R, you keep deflecting.

J-R would just chuckle and continue having fun.

What I eventually realized is that J-R would break my patterns by not giving in to my thinking. At the time I didn't know it, but the mind just keeps on going and to no real purpose. J-R was in the Soul and above and the way in to him is through Love, not questions.

At some point, I'd just laugh. I didn't care about my question or what was on TV any more.

I eventually realized it wasn't about TV or tuna sandwiches: he was starting to break patterns that weren't serving me. It was only after I finally gave up wanting to know why he was doing the change channel routine that he told me it was because he wanted to keep the mind distracted but not get overly pulled in by a TV show. J-R was showing me how to watch TV (or life) without getting caught up in the drama.

Sometimes J-R would be a lot more direct with me in breaking up patterns or habits...or addictions. Yes, I had addictions, and one of the ones I picked up was pretty insidious. It started when John and his then-wife Laura took J-R and Laura's adult son up to the Goodwill Games in Seattle.

One day, Laura's son took us to get a cup of coffee at some up-start coffee place. It was called Starbucks®. And Laura's son was all about coffee beans. So I tried a Starbucks coffee and their famous coffee beans, a roasted espresso bean wrapped in chocolate...and I couldn't stop. So that was it; I became a Starbucks coffee and bean addict. Over time, through all the PATs and myriad trips and events I attended, I was (I admit it) pumped up on coffee.

Of course, pretty soon after I got hooked, Starbucks stores opened up everywhere. There was nowhere you couldn't see a Starbucks. That green logo just seared itself into my brain.

So, from then on, every day when I drove J-R somewhere, I'd be like, "Oh, I want to stop somewhere and have a Starbucks." I think I got up to seven espressos a day. It was pretty tough. And that's the energy I was using rather than the inner, spiritual energy. So, J-R started working on me.

Soon the dialog became...

Jsu: Can I pull over and get a Starbucks?
J-R: No.

Then I started to work it with J-R.

Jsu: What does that mean?
J-R: It means no.

Finally, it started to sink in that Starbucks had gotten ahold of me.

What I ended up doing was switching up different brands so the pattern would be interrupted and it didn't feel like I was addicted. I started to go to all sorts of non-mainstream coffee places.

In the end, doing that broke my habit of coffee, because I still drink coffee, but I don't drink eight espressos a day. And I certainly don't go to Starbucks as much.

Another addiction J-R broke me of was...wait for it...popcorn. We went to the movies a lot. I mean a lot. I'd always get popcorn because I loved it, while J-R would get Red Vines®.

One day, J-R looked at me with my popcorn and said, "You know, you're having a bit too much of that, so how about six months?"

"Six months?"

"Right. I don't want to see you eating popcorn. Take a break for six months."

Oh, man, six months. But I agreed and after a while it didn't bother me. Do I eat popcorn now? Sure. But I enjoy it instead of eating it out of habit or addiction.

J-R was a master at helping me (and all of his students, really) break patterns and clear addictions. He was all about Soul Transcendence, and the nature of the soul is liberation. If we're going to reach into soul consciousness, we can't do it if we're chained to a habit or an addiction.

In my observation, J-R was able to live multi-dimensionally. He would let the eyes and mind focus on something that wasn't really terribly engrossing. He kept it just interesting enough to distract the mind, and he would leave his body. Here's a great J-R quote about this:

> *"Now is the time to go into your own quiet place. Nobody in the house even needs to know you're doing your spiritual exercises. You can have the television on with your eyes watching it and be Soul traveling. You can lie in bed quietly and chant the HU or your initiatory tone, and the one lying beside you need never know you are doing that."*

> – JOHN-ROGER, D.S.S.

That was one of the techniques that I learned from him. These days I find myself having the TV playing a lot, and I do let myself engage sometimes. But it's always like the television is used for white noise, and in the white noise, like J-R, I go to other places. The thing is, he never told me where he would go when he was watching TV, so I can't testify to the effectiveness of my Soul travel while watching TV. However, I can say that eventually I became really good at using the remote. I was talented and trained by the Master. I kept him happy. I knew how to stay on a channel long enough so that J-R would leave his body. When that happened we guys on J-R's personal staff would say, "J-R's down," which was our code for him Soul traveling.

J-R also loved to watch infomercials. During the nine-year period when it was just him and me, one of my jobs was to write down all of the orders we'd placed calling 1-800-SendUsYourMoney. This was before the Internet existed.

He always liked new technology and he wanted me to order things even though they seemed kind of weird. I used to have arguments with him about something being a con, and they would go like this:

J-R: Order it.
Zeus: Come on J-R. They're selling abs in 5 minutes and you know those dudes in the ads are on steroids and we are not.
J-R: Order it.
Zeus: But…
J-R: Order it.
Zeus: Okay.
J-R: Get the special accessories with it.
Zeus: I can tell by looking at this, J-R, it's all fake.
J-R: I don't know that.
Zeus: I do. We will not look like that in 5 minutes.
J-R: You don't know until you try it.
Zeus: So get one?
J-R: Yes. And the extra stuff.

This was a major lesson for me. J-R was a "seeing is believing and testing it out" kind of guy. Experiencing it and knowing was key. Letting the mind think assumptions and assuming all sorts of things stops the experience. We would order all sorts of gadgets and things that interested J-R—and he was interested in all kinds of things.

The key is that I now find myself checking these things out myself. (But I still need to find out how to get 5-minute abs.)

Apple® Computer exploded when Steve Jobs returned to the company and we were always at the gadget stores (before Apple Stores were created) looking at new things. J-R loved what Steve Jobs created at Apple because it was so innovative.

That definitely influences me today. I am an infomercial internet troll. I like to look at new gadgets. I love anything that's new, and I'm curious about new things. I think that's the way J-R was: his nature was Love and curiosity.

Another thing J-R loved to watch on TV was televangelists and motivational speakers. Gene Scott was one of J-R's favorites. J-R would comment to me that he was the best scholar out there. He knew the Bible and the different languages better than anybody.

When Tony Robbins was in commercials, J-R would send him light. He loved Jim and Tammy Faye Bakker, too—he never judged them. We also would watch Kenneth Copeland and Paul Crouch and his wife. J-R had big respect for Billy Graham. One time, J-R, John Morton and I went to see Benny Hinn at a giant arena, and we also visited Robert Schuller's Crystal Cathedral one Christmas for their pageant. Terry Cole-Whittaker was another of J-R's picks. We would flip channels for hours looking for televangelists; some days it would be church time all day on Sunday at Mandeville.

J-R didn't claim to know it all and watching him watch the televangelists was always interesting. Often when the preacher on the TV would say, "Raise your hands and receive the blessing of the Lord," I'd look over and J-R would have his eyes wide open and his hands in the air ready to get the energy of the Christ. He'd look over at me and say, "Let's go." I would raise my hands and join him. It was always church when I was with J-R.

However, being with J-R was not only being in church, it was like being in college—on steroids. In a way, life is like a school where there's constant learning. Being around J-R was like always being in a mystery school because I was always with the teacher. Where, in my previous life, when lessons presented, I could deal with them or ignore them, when I was with J-R, if lessons presented, I could deal with them or I could leave. For good. So I chose to deal with them, though not always happily.

One opportunity I remember came up when I was in the car with J-R. I was doing what I call "acting up." That meant I was pushing to get my way even though my Master/Teacher/Traveler knew what was better for me. I was in the middle of insisting I get what I wanted and J-R just turned to me and told me to stop the car and get out. What? We were a couple hundred miles away from home.

That got my attention and I asked him what he meant. He said he meant for me to get out of the car. So I got out of the car and he drove away. There was no turning the corner or slowing down. He just left me there, stewing in my own juices. I had the opportunity to get a good hard look at what I was doing for about five or ten minutes, during which I nearly crapped my pants.

About the time I realized what a jerk I'd been, J-R would show up in the car and ask if I was okay now. He wasn't judgmental, he asked in complete loving. J-R never held back any kind of bad thoughts or held a grudge. He was smiling and loving when he showed back up. I'd get in the car and I'd forget my misery and laugh the whole thing off. And I got the lesson. Unfortunately, I got to get that kind of lesson many times. I think J-R had infinite patience.

Sometimes my "stuff" went deeper and didn't clear after only a few minutes of being on the hot spot. There was one period when I wasn't having a good time, and I wasn't processing things very well. One night during that time, we got home from being out somewhere and J-R told me he needed me to move out.

Now, the fact is, he would ask all the staff to move out when we were out of balance, and it really used to get to me. For many years, even up to his transition, I would frequently ask him if I was interfering and would he like me to move out. I never wanted to get in the way of his work. Sometimes he would say "Yes" as a test and I'd say,

"NO, I'm not going." He'd look over with his smile and wink and laugh. J-R was a strength builder.

Fortunately (for me), most of the times he would say, "No, stay," so I didn't have to leave (and I would be sweating bullets every time I asked). Sometimes he'd say if you have to ask then you have to leave. But this one time he said I did—and it was real. It shook me.

The thought of moving out literally made me sick. Up until then, if he said to leave, I'd straighten out a little and he'd let it go. This time, that didn't cut it. With a gesture of his hand, he gave me back my karma, and he told me I needed to leave.

I was crushed. I tried to weasel my way out of what I had gotten myself into. I tried everything I could think of, including crying, and nothing worked. In fact, begging and being pathetic most definitely did not work with J-R. For hours, I was basically on my knees with my hands on his feet, kissing them. I was brought to complete humbleness. It had never gotten this bad.

Finally, he said he was going to bed and I could stay the night. I asked if the karma was over and he said it was not. Then I asked him if he could take it from me so I didn't have to go through this. No response. So, devastated, I went to bed.

In the morning I got up and started doing the things I generally did around the house. When it was time to go somewhere, J-R let me drive. That's when I knew I might have a chance to learn more about myself, and to course correct. I asked J-R if the karma was clear. He looked at me, and this time he said, "Ah, we'll see."

Little by little, as I would change my behavior, the karma would lift and I would find myself back in J-R's good graces. I think it was hard on him, but J-R was relentless in working with me, no matter the cost to him. I think that was true with everyone he worked with: J-R would not take the easy way out or leave something half done.

I know that with me, J-R would strip from me everything that I mistakenly would think I was or that I had. Sometimes, it was brutal. It was like I wanted to die a million times. And it was also an amazing process.

Over time I saw that J-R just knew exactly how to break my patterns. As soon as I would start getting stuck in my way of thinking, he'd break it. He was bold like that. His disruptions were very calculated and very daring. I was going to basically abide by him. Though he was my teacher, he was not working for me, I was working for him.

Sometimes to get J-R to pay attention to me (and mind you I'm an actor—I wanted attention), I would call J-R, "Roger." When I called him Roger, he would smile and sometimes he'd get teary-eyed. This tapped into Roger Hinkins; that part of him could still surface from time to time.

"Give every man thy ear, but few thy voice."

– WILLIAM SHAKESPEARE (*HAMLET*)

"Often when I was driving with J-R, I would get a kind of signal—things like purple lights and flashes—when something was up. They could relate to almost anything, but they always meant 'pay attention.'"

– JESUS GARCIA, D.S.S.

CHAPTER 16

Driving John-Roger

BESIDES TEACHING ME WITH THE TV, J-R worked with me a lot through driving. For example, I might be lost in my thoughts and miss my exit off the freeway. Then I'd start wondering what I was thinking about that could make me lose my focus. J-R really did not like that. He actually would move his consciousness and be inside my head so he knew where my attention really was while I was driving past my exit. Then he'd ask, "What have you been doing?" I knew I was busted, and had to own up that I had been wandering around in my mind. I couldn't lie or make up excuses or hide my thoughts because he was in there and he *knew* what I had been thinking.

At first, I didn't understand it, but it was hard for me to lie to J-R because I didn't have many barriers. He could really see through me. To him, I was pretty much an open book. So I would tell him anything and everything about what I was doing or thinking. There was nothing that J-R didn't know about me.

So when he would catch me woolgathering while I was driving, the conversation would go something like this:

J-R: What are you thinking about?
Zeus: That girl back there at the movie.

J-R: What about her?

Zeus: I thought she was fine.

J-R: She was, wasn't she?

(At this point J-R is getting me to talk more)

Zeus: Oh yeah…

J-R: You want her?

Zeus: No! No I was just looking.

J-R: I can help you get her. Easy.

Zeus: I know you can. No, I'm fine, I just want to serve and be here, but sometimes I get hooked.

J-R: Be careful what you create. I can help clear some of it but if you over-fantasize and over-create in your mind, you'll have to fulfill it and then I cannot help you.

By that point I would be begging J-R to clear it as I've seen him help people get what they want. I did not want that. I wanted to be with J-R, working.

So I had to learn to be careful where I put my mind because the heart will follow it and the physicality will follow that. I guess that's one of the reasons it's so important to be in the present moment.

J-R would show me how to range ahead and send the Light ahead to prepare a safe arrival. Also, purple dots and flashes would start appearing. On long driving trips—like on superhighways in Utah or Nevada—especially if we were driving a new car, J-R would say to go ahead and open this up which meant for me to step on it and see how fast the car could go. The white pinpoints or flashes were good; this meant that J-R was inside looking out through my eyes and checking my consciousness. The purple flashes were often warnings. From my experiences, I learned that these lights were indicators that J-R was looking in. They could relate to almost anything, but they always meant "pay attention."

I observed that his consciousness was everywhere but he would never inflict. You have to allow him in. It's not a possession or entity or anything like that: it was consciousness.

When J-R would show up in my awareness, I did not experience being "taken over" like some trance medium. On the contrary, J-R really wanted me to be conscious when I was driving and not space out, so these were reminders of that; they were warnings to be aware.

Being aware is always a good idea, but there was one time, in particular, I got a big payoff for doing that. I was driving J-R to a doctor's appointment in Beverly Hills sometime in the 1990s. I was super-aware that day and I noticed four people walking very slowly along the sidewalk. It really caught my attention and as I looked closer I realized it was former President Ronald Reagan and three Secret Service Agents around him. By that time Reagan's illness had debilitated him and he was pretty hunched over.

Ever since I can remember, I've had a connection with Reagan; when I was 16 years old, I dreamt he would be shot. Three days later, that's exactly what happened. So I told J-R I wanted to say hi to him and to send the Light. J-R said it was okay, so I pulled over very abruptly and got out of the car. I walked towards President Reagan and, of course, the agents warned me to get back in my car. Then the president saw me and recognized I was not about to cause any trouble. We locked eyes and he smiled. I waved and his slow hands motioned to me as to acknowledge us for stopping by.

The agents kept telling me to get in my car and I said to them to relax, that he's not in office, we're just saying hello. Then the Light moved between all of us and J-R was there energetically, connecting us all. It was a magical experience to see their tension drain. I got back in the car with J-R and we kept talking about the former president and praying for him. It was really one of those special moments, and it happened because I was paying attention. (Well, that, and I had the nerve to stop and not be intimidated by three Secret Servicemen.)

A lot of times J-R and I would just talk while I was driving him. We were just two guys discussing our lives. One time when we were driving from the Living in Grace retreat in Asilomar down the coast road in Northern California, I mentioned an experience I had had some years earlier driving through Big Sur. I told him about how when I started driving through a particular area, I got this really creepy feeling. It wouldn't leave and, in fact, it started to intensify. Before long, I found myself scared to death. I told him it was like when I had been young living in New Jersey with the feeling that there were witches nearby. As I was driving through Big Sur, I told him, I sensed something huge and powerful; the energy was thick and I could feel it above my car.

I described how it had been starting to get dark and most of the places I passed were closed. I came to a town, but I had no money to spend the night in a motel, so I sped through while it got darker and darker as redwood trees formed a canopy over the car.

J-R just listened to my story, then he "went somewhere" in his consciousness as he often did when he checked things out. He looked at me and said that I had been on the pathway meridian of the dragon that lives there.

Dragon?! Actually, I believed it because I felt it. Only a dragon could describe the enormity of this experience that was so real for me.

A little later J-R mentioned the Aloha Airlines Flight 243 in 1988 that had sustained extensive damage after an inexplicable explosive decompression occurred in flight. He said he had tracked inwardly that the plane had run into meridian pathways or ley lines that ethereal dragons used for traveling. That blew my mind because it actually made sense after my Big Sur experience.

The mind is limited to what it knows, and what J-R would talk to me about was beyond the mind and into the "known unknowable" if you have the eyes to see and if you have the ears to hear.

Driving with J-R was very awakening and these are unforgettable stories. I relate them to you, not to convince you of them, but to remind me of them.

*"Accept what is going on in the physical without judgment
and you will be able to handle things much more
successfully than ever before. Similarly, in Spirit, accept
what occurs and what doesn't, with no judgment, and that
acceptance will contribute to your spiritual progress."*

– JOHN-ROGER, D.S.S.
(FROM HIS BOOK, *PASSAGE INTO SPIRIT*)

CHAPTER 17

More Than Meets the Eye

As I HAVE INDICATED IN the last chapter, not everything J-R taught me was about self-awareness. He gave me a glimpse of some of what I call the fantastical stuff, too. For example, J-R showed me how to see etheric temples in the Swiss Alps.

J-R, John and Laura, their children Claire and Zane, and I had gone to Switzerland on some business and after John and his family went home to get the kids back in school, J-R and I continued traveling there. We went to places like Zermatt and other Matterhorn-type mountains. As we were driving, J-R would say things like, "Take a look at the Etheric temples." So I would look and, of course, I wouldn't see anything but mountains. So J-R would start giving me clues to open and to start looking for other dimensions rather than this physical dimension.

He would tell me to not look straight at them but to look off to the side and see them in my peripheral vision. It wasn't easy, but eventually I started getting glimpses of these non-physical places. To me, it looked like they kind of followed the upper layer of the Alps.

J-R also talked to me about the Spirit Rain and how to see it. He said that it's a form of spirit that rains down in green areas sometimes. It looks like drizzle, like light rain. Sometimes it's the Devic kingdom flexing its powers.

During a group tour of England around the late 1990s, the mysterious phenomenon of crop circles was all over the news that summer. The trip was organized by Brooke Danza, J-R and John Morton as the extension of an adventure in Ireland. We traveled in one or two buses to different parts of England visiting many crop circles that had been turning up in the United Kingdom.

You can't really see a crop circle when you are in it; you need altitude. Seeing them firsthand, it was almost impossible to imagine a human creating them at all, much less literally overnight. It seemed like a whole lot of work to produce those designs, perhaps the size of half a football field, on acres of hay. Each circle consisted of intricate, perfectly-laid, flattened patterns made from thick, elephant-grass hay that was bent over or smashed in a way that didn't kill the grass. The stalks would point precisely in one direction or another, in swirls or spirals, and sometimes they would even be woven like a basket. Clearly, no earthly instrument could do that so consistently, despite the skeptics insisting on their hoax theories. Just to create perfect, simple circles, you would need to cut a great deal of plywood symmetrically, then really lay down the pressure with a lot of manpower; and even then, some stalks would get broken or point in random directions. The tour guide told us that they were created using some kind of radiant heat and a lot of weight to lay down the different hay patterns, whether circular, clockwise, or counterclockwise. The unique designs were always unpredictable from one crop circle to the next and the method of producing them had never been believably explained. However, a common belief among more open-minded people is that they were created by Unidentified Flying Objects (UFOs).

One evening, when a lot of people went for a walk with the tour guide to try to see UFOs, J-R, Nat, myself and a few others stayed behind on the bus. J-R sat there pointing out the UFOs up in the sky. I remember it was out in the English countryside, up on a hill overlooking a small town, so there was no light pollution to dim the stars or constellations. We could actually see the movements of what appeared to be a large number of UFOs, which were clearly differentiated from the blinking lights of a plane or other human-engineered aircraft.

I mention this because J-R was always teaching us and demonstrating the subtle energies present in the inner and outer worlds, beyond this dense manifestation called Earth. He showed us that even within the physical body, there exist many levels—and J-R was in touch with all of them. I had also heard somewhere that J-R said some aliens are looking for a Traveler to connect with, although they might be from another dimension. But there is still manifestation below the soul realm, so if the Traveler is working all the levels, then it is a good bet the aliens want to connect in a friendly way and become partners. This is not a *Star Wars* or *Independence Day* phenomenon, although I've heard J-R say those kind of things do occur on the inner levels. We are talking about something very multidimensional. I laugh when the scientists say, "We've discovered more planets in other galaxies." No. What they discovered is a better telescope to be able to see what was already there.

When J-R was alive, there would sometimes be unusual phenomena around the Mandeville house. I definitely think some of what we would see or hear was related to aliens seeking spiritual Masters. A few weeks after J-R passed, we had some non-physical visitors at Mandeville as we had had over the years. But this time was crazy. I was in Nicole's room by the kitchen and I got a strong sense someone was going through the house looking for their Traveler. It was pretty phenomenal and pretty profound, and at times, a little scary with the noises and vibrations that would shake stuff on shelves.

I mention these things to maybe give you a sense that J-R lived in many realities and was able to see into many dimensions, and part of what he was doing with us, his students, was introducing us to some of the things that proved there is more to us than meets the eye.

"One of those signs is that Travelers don't really promise anything in this world. J-R never promised me anything, but he always said to me privately that he'd always take care of me and that I shouldn't worry about anything. Even today, long after his passing, I really feel like he is taking care of me. And I'm sure he's taking care of thousands of others."

– JESUS GARCIA, D.S.S.

CHAPTER 18

J-R and My Acting Career

IN THE EARLY DAYS ON staff, while I was very much with J-R, I was also trying to keep my acting career going. Since that seemed like having two conflicting full-time jobs, I asked J-R how that would work. To my surprise, he said I didn't have to give up my career. He said he'd work with me on it. I figured, "Yeah, right."

I had been studying acting for a pretty long time (I'm still studying it to some extent) and it was a real focus for me from 1981 to about 2001. I was looking for my true Self in acting. Unlike a lot of acting that can be hiding in a character, I wanted to use the true parts of me and use them in the character I was portraying.

A lot of the same exercises and movements studied in acting classes are similar to those used in Insight and USM. My whole quest has been in search of my true Self. Uta Hagen talks about revealing, not canceling, one's self. I studied with John Abbott, a Shakespearean character actor, for 10 years. I felt very moved finding myself through his words. J-R would tell me that Shakespeare was a Traveler. The wildest thing is having J-R read Shakespeare to me. A Traveler reading a Traveler's words.

Not long after my conversation with J-R, we were at a cafeteria-type place, and I recognized Angela Lansbury across the room. She was starring in a top television show at the time called *Murder, She Wrote*, and I wanted to work on it. I mentioned that to J-R and he told me to go over and tell her I wanted a job.

Now, I'm pretty outrageous, but I thought that was really ballsy. Still, he encouraged me so I went over to her and told her it was nice to meet her and I'd like a job.

She said it was nice to meet me, was I talented.

I said I was, and she gave me an address where I could send my sample tape.

I sent her the tape right away and, sure enough, ended up working on two episodes of *Murder, She Wrote*. Ms. Lansbury liked me, and I liked her, and it was kind of cool. And I started to think maybe J-R *was* going to be working with me on my career.

This was a beginning for me. Every time J-R pushed me beyond what I thought was my limit, I learned something new. In this case I was learning to ask for what I wanted. He would often quote the Bible: "You receive not because you ask not." Over time, I learned to ask.

Speaking of asking, J-R was big on moving past concerns and asking questions to get information. It could be in any area. J-R didn't assume, he'd suck it up and appear foolish if he had to in order to get the information he wanted. That's one of the things he taught me, too.

Here are a couple examples of how that would go.

Example one:
J-R: Did you check and see if Jack bought the horse?
Zeus: No, he didn't say when I was talking to him.
J-R: You mean you didn't ask.
Zeus: Yes.
J-R: How much was the horse?
Zeus: I don't know.

J-R: You mean you didn't ask. If you think asking a question is bad or is going to look like you're not that smart, go ahead and look stupid and ask that question.

Zeus: (At that point I went silent, because I knew that the best thing to do was not to argue. Arguing for your limitation with J-R gets you demoted.)

J-R: Get him back on the phone and ask him all the dumb questions.

Zeus: Thanks, J-R.

Example 2 (after an audition):

J-R: How'd it go today?

Zeus: Great, they like me.

J-R: Did you get the role?

Zeus: Not yet. But they smiled and said I was great.

J-R: How do you feel you did?

Zeus: Okay.

J-R: You think you got it?

Zeus: I think so.

J-R: Follow the money

Zeus: What?

J-R: Don't think about fame, just follow the money.

Zeus: Got it.

J-R: It ain't over 'til the fat lady sings and the check's in the bank.

Zeus: It has to cash right?

J-R: Right.

Then I'd start asking about what I should do.

Zeus: Should I call that casting director for the big film I told you about yesterday?

J-R: I don't know.

Zeus: You know the cowboy one. Should I practice at Windermere?

J-R: I don't know.

If J-R didn't have enough information, he would not speculate or make stuff up.

Zeus: So I need to lean into it?

J-R: Yes.

Zeus: You can't answer it cause there's not enough information? Do you need more information?

J-R: Yes. If not, the answer is still "I don't know."

Zeus: Wow okay, got it.

That's not just what J-R taught, it's how he handled his life. He had a term, "don't push water uphill because you'll get mud in your face." I experienced this when I would think I aced an audition, but didn't get the role; yet, when I felt unsure and lost, I would get the role. There were a lot of times when I was sure one way or the other, but I was wrong!

Also, when J-R would tell Nat or me that something was "10%," we wouldn't move on it. Ten percent for us meant, "I won't support you with my energy and you're on your own." So, most of the time we never took action on anything if J-R didn't give his support. His saying "Fine or 10%" was not good. Ten percent refers to the small portion of human consciousness that exists on the physical level; J-R emphasized that 90 percent of our consciousness actually resides on the nonphysical (spiritual) levels, which we are generally not aware about. MSIA teaches how to become more aware of that other, far more important 90 percent of our existence.

There eventually came a point when Nat and I became a consensus team. We would be prompted from within and when we brought things to J-R, he would give an approval and it would all match what we had been thinking. That was the best proof that we were learning and growing.

While I was learning all of this, what I would call miracles were also starting to become more obvious to me. Many of my miracles actually manifested here in the physical world. It wasn't guaranteed, but I often saw them in advance. Many of them pulled me out of tight spots, but I couldn't just assume that J-R would help me physically.

One of the signs of a Traveler is that they work in the spiritual levels and don't really promise anything in this world. (See Appendix B, "12 Signs of a Traveler.") Accordingly, J-R never promised me anything material, but he said privately that he'd always take care of me and that I shouldn't worry about anything. What I have come to realize is: he meant that he is truly always with me, as close as my breath. And in that, I am unquestionably being taken care of. And I'm sure he's taking care of thousands, tens of thousands, maybe millions of others. But he never did that in a way that would weaken me or make me dependent on him. He's never let me down.

My miracles became very movie-like. I don't want to dwell on my Hollywood life, but that's where my karma was and, at that time, that's where my mind was. So naturally the Traveler, the Master, would work on me wherever I was.

In the year 2000, I hadn't had much of a breakthrough in my career, but it was the beginning of my comeback, and I was totally connected to spirit and J-R. It was amazing to use the teachings in my acting in every way. Using J-R's spiritual techniques like seeding and asking God for what I wanted—for the Highest Good—asking for the Traveler to be with me in the auditions and during filming, and just plain common sense allowed me to succeed with back-to-back films. This became true acting with my better self, my better angels. J-R would repeat Jesus' quote, "You receive not because you ask not." I would audition and that night, I would dream that it wasn't for me and I would hear the next day that I didn't get it. Rejection after rejection would make me stronger and stronger and believe me, I cried many times on J-R's shoulders.

This was before I had experienced the successes of *The Lost City* and *Along Came Polly*. Up to that point I had been doing B roles and TV shows, but I hadn't been able to make my way back into the movie industry. It's fickle. It's up and down. But you can get a big break anytime and become a big movie star, so in one way I really didn't have a problem with where I was in my career. At the same time, I was taking what happened to me—or didn't happen to me—very personally. But it's not personal. J-R taught me that this in-the-world stuff is not really personal.

They say that we choose our path and decide up there above the soul about our learning for each lifetime. Over time I discovered that the whole purpose of my life is for me to be courageous and strong. One year I had 80 auditions and didn't get anything. I came in second place for most of them. It seemed in my mindset then that I was a failure at acting. But I love Winston Churchill's quote: *"Success consists of going from failure to failure without loss of enthusiasm."*

It's all perception. J-R used to say it's your attitude. J-R wasn't helping me to become famous but he was helping me to endure and overcome and build strength within. He was helping me deal with expectations, feeling entitled, highs and lows and let-downs. There were plenty of let-downs; like working hard to get the role, then filming it, then finding out at the premiere that they'd cut me out. But, hey, that's showbiz.

To give an example of how Spirit seemed to work for me when I was working for Spirit, I had an audition for an Arnold Schwarzenegger movie called *Collateral Damage*. I had just changed my stage name from Nick Corri to Jsu Garcia, which is closer to my real name Jesus Garcia. In the eighties, a great agent gave me the name Nick Corri. He did that because, at the time, the only Latin actor of any stature was Ricardo Montalban. This agent said I'd never work in this town as a Latin. Later, people like Andy Garcia, Steven Bauer and all these other great Latin actors would turn that around, but at the time he was right.

At any rate, I went in and auditioned and they liked me a lot. It was really fun having changed my name because I felt reinvented. J-R helped me with the numerology to land on "Jsu Garcia." The casting directors who knew me didn't remember who I was from the B roles, but they thought I looked familiar. They loved the audition and asked if I could come back a little later to audition for the director—who happened to be Andrew Davis, the great director of *The Fugitive*. But I couldn't come back because I had agreed to do something with J-R, and I wasn't going to break my commitment to him. So, despite this great opportunity, I didn't hesitate to say no. From one angle it was career suicide, but I followed my gut—and my heart.

When I told J-R about the audition, he came up with a suggestion. He told me and my friend, Rick Ojeda, to get a camera and put the audition on tape. I really resisted that because I had tried something like that before, and generally, it looked pretty cheap and cheesy. This was just before the internet was really kicking it, and the whole notion of putting yourself on tape or digital file was unheard of. Nowadays, it's common practice put yourself on an iPhone video and submit it to your casting director. But in those days, in the eighties and nineties, we didn't have the technology and you had to show up.

Despite my reluctance, I heard what J-R said and I got a hit: Let's make a movie out of my audition. So Rick and I made a movie that was a super short version of *Collateral Damage*. It was a fireman whose wife and kids are killed by Latin terrorists. After the government fails him, he goes to South America and takes everything into his own hands.

We edited the tape with ten tracks of video and sounds and effects and music. We were totally jazzed and I sent it to the producers. Then I left the country on a trip to China with J-R.

In the middle of the China trip I got a call from my agent. He told me I had gotten a part in *Collateral Damage*. Miracle!

I remember flying into Mexico to do the movie, and when the producer picked me up he told me they had loved the tape. He said they thought I was insane and they had to have me in the movie. I was really jazzed about that, but it probably would have been better if I had never heard it. Because from then on I thought every producer would love my tapes. Which, of course, they didn't.

In any case, that became the beginning of the second surge in my career. Later I had roles in *Along Came Polly*, *We Were Soldiers* and *Atlas Shrugged*. And whenever I couldn't make an audition in person, I sent a tape. At that point, I was unstoppable.

But more than once I was faced with a choice like the one with *Collateral Damage*. Whenever I was going to do J-R's work and I would have a callback, and things would be rolling my way, I would have to decide, either/or. Would I sell out? Should I give up the spiritual work? In some ways it was a tough call for me. I had such a hard time, and I spent a fair amount of energy beating myself up.

I finally came to realize it happened this way to build my character, to strengthen my integrity. I know now that I could have just relaxed and let Spirit handle it. And that's what I ultimately it did once I really "got it." Of course, "getting it" was a bear.

This period would turn out to be the height of my career. I was really on top of the world. At the same time, I was connecting more spiritually and having a lot of realizations.

Also, in the midst of all of it, I was feeling like I was losing something. It's good to be connected spiritually and realize that you are out of balance. There's a difference between being out of balance when you're not connected and aware and being out of balance and realizing it. Without what I would call spiritual awareness when you're out of balance, it's easier to make choices that don't serve your higher good, your higher purpose. As a result, you're more likely to place yourself in a non-worthy area.

The miracle was that I was getting ideas that were inspired by J-R, and I began to open my awareness in such a way that I would get divine intervention and divine genius ideas. This is where I tell you that, although I'll say that *I* did it, this was really J-R giving me ideas; it was God within. And it was because I am open to receive these things, especially from J-R, and especially when I am in what I call the stream-of-consciousness.

To this day, I know that my ideas come from the higher source: Spirit, God, J-R. I can't live without these things that come to my mind. I have heard that Brian Wilson, from the Beach Boys, would be listening to what he called angels speaking melodies to him. I think it was hard for him because he either stopped listening or it stopped coming to him. I think that can be very, very devastating to an artist or to anyone. It's like what I heard J-R say, "once you eat of the manna, you can never turn away."

The way I learned about the business side of acting was pretty much through experience. Ultimately I started to see the ugly part of it, the wheeling, dealing and backstabbing; the things I didn't want to be involved in. I realized that although the money's good, sometimes it's not worth the pain, so I turned my full focus on J-R and my work with him.

In 1998, one of my films was accepted to the Havana International Film Festival in Cuba. J-R and I had co-directed *My Little Havana*, a 38-minute short that I was obsessed about expanding into a full-length feature. First, I want to express my gratitude to Marla Ludwig, who worked tirelessly into the late nights for months getting all the music cleared for the festival. J-R was with me the whole time during the shooting and after it ended; then came the period of submitting the film to hundreds of film festivals. Only very few accepted it, and I was very surprised to hear from Cuba, since it was a long shot. Once we were invited by the Havana Film Festival, we received permission to travel to Cuba to attend.

We scheduled 12 days in Havana (which ended up being cut short by my unfortunate bout of laryngitis), and traveled through Cancun, Mexico. It was wonderful, because I had heard that J-R and John had gone to Cuba several decades before and I had the privilege of private travel time only with J-R. This involves a lot of time with J-R traveling out of the body and doing spiritual work on the other realms. Doing spiritual exercises with J-R for many hours was a luxury that I became addicted to.

I was kind of arrogant in my approach: "I am an American, you guys are Cuban," but I remembered I was not feeling so good and they were perfect. It was obvious from the film festival that Cuba did not have a lot of money, but the experience was still a lot of fun. My parents are Cuban, so they told me all these places to visit—and it was literally like time had frozen since the 1950s, so I got to experience what Havana looked like when they lived there. I was even able to call my mom and dad from Havana. I would say,

"Hey, I'm at the Capri Hotel, is this is where you went?" They'd respond, "Yeah, yeah." Then I went to the famous Copacabana club with J-R, and it was exactly the same as my mom had described it. I was able to share that with my mom and my dad and J-R and we went to the Cabana with the famous lighthouse. I went everywhere with J-R.

It was quite hilarious when they screened our movie, because both times, instead of a theater, they put us in a room with only a dozen people and a tiny 24-inch TV. We definitely felt like we were sent to the corner; I guess they did not really want to expose the American footage or filmmakers. Some of the film dialog included comments about Cuba not being cool, but I figured since they accepted the film, they were OK with all aspects of it. Once we finished screening, we went to a couple of parties. I was getting feisty and talking to some of the locals about America being better, etc. I had something in my throat and instantaneously lost my voice for the rest of the trip. J-R and I left halfway through, on the sixth day. We just started to realize that they did not really want to do anything with the film.

J-R helped me with my laryngitis and took me to the tourist clinic. The funny thing is, we had to pay to go to a doctor because it is not necessarily free medicine over there. The tourists have to pay a premium in order to get the best medicine, but the people get what they get. Their doctors are humble and have great bedside manners.

It was wonderful to travel with J-R. Generally, after he visits certain countries, things tend to come into a more spiritual balance and a clearing of karma. Sometimes you can watch the news and notice all kinds of changes in those places. In my experience (and I've checked this out with J-R), almost always the karma clears up and the reasons for traveling to a country are mostly finished before we return home. Sometimes I would ask J-R, "Is the work complete?" He would reply, "Yes" or "Almost." Sometimes he would say, "Call Brooke and change our return."

Working with J-R for me was like working as an actor with a director you trusted with your life. The umbrella of J-R was amazing. All I wanted to do was get things done for him.

"With mirth and laughter let old wrinkles come."

– WILLIAM SHAKESPEARE (*THE MERCHANT OF VENICE*)

"I knew that I had known J-R before, and working with him was like second nature. We were like best of buddies. I remember one time when I got a little bossy he looked at me and said, 'in other lifetimes I paid attention, I followed you. In this one, you're going to follow me, you're going to pay attention.'"

— JESUS GARCIA, D.S.S.

CHAPTER 19

The Story of Scott

IN MSIA, WE ACKNOWLEDGE REINCARNATION. Not that we teach reincarnation, it's just that reincarnation occurs and we recognize that. You either have awareness of it or you don't, but that doesn't change the fact of it. I had evidence of it with J-R. I knew that I had known J-R before, and working with him was like second nature. We were like best of buddies. I remember one time when I got a little bossy he looked at me and said that in other lifetimes he paid attention to me and followed me. In this one, he said, I was going to follow him and pay attention to him.

This was not just a reference to some philosophical idea. This was simply a statement of fact—and I knew it because I had memories of that. I had had experiences of being with him in both genders and in all sorts of forms. But in this time we were just men, and my job was to be his student and his was to be the master, the Wayshower.

One incident testifying to this was at the Karnak Temple in Egypt, watching the sound and light show. It's basically an audio spectacle with the ruins as a backdrop. While the sun sets, the carefully crafted light show begins with a British voice-over actor leading the way.

It was balmy weather and, for no apparent reason, I was feeling like I had wronged J-R. All sorts of troubling negative thoughts appeared, so I asked him what was up. He told me that I had been his wife in the lifetime when he was the Egyptian pharaoh Akhenaten, and I cheated on him with one of his generals. That hit me like a wrecking ball and I felt awful. He didn't try to sell me on the story; I knew it was true the minute he said it. The impact of it hit me and I cried for hours releasing the pain and guilt. That was not fun, but as it cleared I began to feel lighter and "cleaner."

I came to realize that often I would identify a past life recognition through déjà vu. This was especially true with experiences where I remembered being J-R's son. J-R explained to me that déjà vu was either a warning, a sign I was on track with something, or a knowing that something had happened. I have come to see déjà vu most often as a signal that I'm on target with my life.

Through experiences like the one where I had been Akhenaten's wife, I started to see how people could get confused as awareness of past life experiences bled through to this life.

For example, you might become associated with somebody you knew in another life. In that lifetime, they were your baby and you were the parent and could tell them what to do. But in this lifetime, the situation is reversed; now they're your employer and they're telling *you* what to do. So you have this memory—consciously or unconsciously—of bossing this person around, and you can't figure out why it seems so wrong for them to be in a superior position with you. Even so, you have to live this lifetime despite your memories of once having been in charge of the person.

What's really important is to let go of old patterns. The way to do that is to be very clear about who you and the people you interact with are in *this* life, versus who you and they might have been in another lifetime.

Having said that, there were times when I would stand over J-R and watch him sleep. One night he came awake and when he saw me there, he asked what I was doing. I told him I was watching him sleep. He asked who taught me to do that, and I said that nobody taught me that—I had been doing it since I was little. I used to watch my mom sleep.

After a pause he told me that his young son, Scott, the one who had died, used to do that. A son? This was news to me at that time. And the fact is, no one, even his family, can verify that J-R had a son. Even so, much as I *knew* I had known J-R in many past lives, I *knew* this was true. One day I walked into J-R's room and said, "I'm Scott, right?" J-R just looked at me for a second, and then he said, "That's right." We even put a scene of me as his son in *The Wayshower* movie. J-R was co-writing that script with me and he didn't have me take it out, so I'm thinking there must have been some substance to it. Interestingly, since J-R never talked about it, people didn't know about it. As far as I know, it was a factual story.

Knowing about his son is why I chose the name Scott J-R Productions for the production company in association with MSIA, to make the films *Spiritual Warriors*, *The Wayshower*, and *Mystical Traveler*.

Even before hearing that J-R once had a child, I'd had an on-and-off experience that I was J-R's son. I can't explain it. I can tell you about an incident, though, that is pretty parallel with J-R's experience with his son.

Ever since I was little, I have had a feeling that I'd died in a car or a car accident. It started when I was young with my mother and stepfather. We often drove through New York, New Jersey, even down to Florida. On these trips, I used to curl up underneath the back seat floor mats because it made me feel safe and the road sounds were very soothing.

One time, my stepfather actually fell asleep at the wheel, and I remember poking my head out from under the mats when the car started bouncing around. I discovered the car had driven right off the road. We never talked about that incident and only my mother and I knew about it.

I don't know if that's where this feeling of dying in a car accident came from or if that feeling came from an experience in some past life.

"Pleasure and action make the hours seem short."

– WILLIAM SHAKESPEARE (*OTHELLO*)

"It was always exciting to be at his side learning to hook into that higher energy. The guys and I were always excited to see if our answers matched J-R's. We were always striving to access our intuition or that spirit that is of the Traveler."

– JESUS GARCIA, D.S.S.

CHAPTER 20

Nightmares

PROBABLY MOST OF US ARE familiar with recurring nightmares. I'm not referring to the terrifying, "the monster's going to get me," kind of dream; I'm talking about the "I was at an important business meeting and I forgot my pants" variety. J-R had a body and a mind and emotions like the rest of us (well, sort of like the rest of us), and he also had nightmares. J-R's was about being late to class.

My nightmares were about being late on the movie set. That actually happened when I was working with Ben Stiller and John Hamburg in *Along Came Polly*. I slept through my alarm and they had to wait for me for an hour or so. They were not happy—and with good reason: When an actor's late, everything on the set stops. But the producers still have to pay the dozens and dozens of people who are sitting there waiting.

I hadn't done it on purpose, but I ate the results of it. So I started having anxiety attacks all through the night, and it was awful. The anxiety came as I was trying to do acting. It was similar to J-R, who had been a teacher, having anxiety about running late to his class. However, I found that when I started to become my own man, directing and transferring all that creative energy towards spiritual films, and learning to tap in with J-R while working on his projects, it started to subside. In fact, it hardly ever happens now.

Of course, the physical reality also changed. With the J-R films, there was less of a crazy schedule. In the movie business, you're awake at 5:00 in the morning after being up late learning your lines. With J-R, it was really taking care of J-R, hanging out with J-R, then learning lines, and then going to work the next day; there really was no sleep—so there was no alarm to sleep through.

"Some are born great, some achieve greatness, and some have greatness thrust upon them."

– WILLIAM SHAKESPEARE *(TWELFTH NIGHT)*

"*There is a great privilege in this ministry and it comes through your own honoring, your own willingness to step forward, so begin in this moment and lift your head, for you are now in high ground from this day forward.*"

– From the Ordination Blessing
of Jesus Garcia, D.S.S.

CHAPTER 21

My Ordination

In 1988, I was approved to receive my ordination as a minister in MSIA. MSIA ministers are ordained through the order of the Melchizedek priesthood to do service in the world—whatever their heart dictates—and at the time of ordination there is a blessing from Spirit and a connection to a spiritual energy that needs to be used in service so it keeps flowing. It's really neat to be connected up to the Traveler energy in this special way, so I was very excited about it.

I had just completed the PAT IV training, traveling to Egypt and Israel. After that, we went to Germany, London, Russia, and Finland. J-R was supposed to do my ordination during a workshop in London, but around the time it was scheduled, he collapsed.

While this sounds dramatic—and it was—I would come to learn that it was not unusual for J-R to have pretty severe things going on with his health. It's not that he was unhealthy, it was more that, being so sensitive, and due to the nature of the spiritual work he agreed to do, he would often take on physical things or energetic things for other people, when Spirit permitted.

J-R told me later that day that he had collapsed because he was very tied in with Sathya Sai Baba and was taking stuff off him that Baba couldn't handle well himself. I didn't really know who Sai Baba was. I knew that he was known as the Christ of India and was considered an avatar, but I only knew that from what J-R said and what I found when I researched him.

In any case, while J-R was in the room and not far away, John Morton, the newly anointed Traveler, ordained me and came through with a pretty good ordination blessing.

This Blessing is a delicious presence, something that you can feel in all of your being, through all of your body, through all of your cells, through every part of who you are.

And begin this blessing each moment as you breathe in that you renew your life, that you are purifying your consciousness to stand into the heritage that is this line of the Traveler, to step forward and honor the true self, beginning to open your consciousness now as you allow yourself to step forward.

And as you honor the integrity of your being, words of wisdom can come forth, and you speak the words of truth. Let your words be ones that are the loving nature, that are the essence of this being that is of the Traveler. Bring your discipline from the heart. Let it be a loving waltz with God that you dance and sing the heritage of your being. No man is a fool who lets himself sing and praise the Lord.

There is a great privilege in this ministry and it comes through your own honoring, your own willingness to step forward. So begin in this moment and lift your head, for you are now in high ground from this day forward.

We stand by you, we love you, we support you and we bless you. Baruch Bashan

(*Baruch Bashan* means "the blessings already are" in Hebrew.)

Later, I showed the ordination to J-R and he liked it. I knew he meant it because, in almost every case, when I would ask J-R for his approval of something—or his approval of me for something I had done—he would simply reply, "That's fine." Now, when J-R would say "that's fine" it could mean a lot of things, not always endorsement. In this instance, however, he expressed a real and thoughtful approval.

In MSIA, ministers are ordained through the Order of the Melchizedek Priesthood and the office of the Christ. It is a very powerful lineage and I have found a lot of strength and support from my ministerial blessing.

It's time for you to look at yourself to see if you're doing what is required of you to open your Spirit, to receive of the greater Spirit, to shed more of your light and love.

This is all of us. And it's not just on occasions of bombing of objects of the material world, because eventually they are all going to go away anyway and our bodies are going to go away also. And you people, thank you for just showing up. There's a big something that happens in the Spirit world when we bring our material body and our spiritual body together and we focus it towards that object that is the unification of the world into the Spirit and the Spirit into the world, knowing full well they can never be the same.

The only thing that's the same in both of them is who we are as a spiritual being, and it is through that that we pray. Not through our ego or through our body, but through that that is the telephone between both worlds— who we are as a being.

Lord God, Father of Lights, you've seen it, you know it— attempt to give us the wisdom and understanding that we may withdraw from the pain of suffering and enter into the wisdom of your glory and why we are here and why all this took place. Illuminate our ignorance, so we may not judge erroneously from that ego that knows little.

Lord, help us not to discriminate against the living, because of those who are the dead. For the dead were told to bury themselves, and for the living to live and follow the anointing of the oneness of the Spirit.

We ask this through each one individually as they step forward, as they choose to bring forward greater love and Light into this world. Father, help us step aside any revenge. Let the revenge be the Lord's, as He said. Let us be the share-takers, and share-givers and the lovers of life and the lovers of those who died and those who took life, for they didn't know what they did or they wouldn't have done it.

And, Father, help us not judge them in their ignorance, nor us in our ego, but let us come into harmony with the living and those who are no longer materially alive. Let them come into the fullness of their own creation and, Father, let us stand in the face of our fear. Let us stand in the face of those who would do good and even the face of those who would do bad equally to us, and let us just love them.

Let us bring forward the sound of your love and the Light of your light and the glory of your being. Bless those who are here at this time, because once again, they chose themselves to put their body on the line and bring their holy holy which is the Soul, forward, and to present it to us.

Lord, we know we'll be hit at by negativity because of what we say and do here. Lord, that's fine with us. We will still live to present ourselves before God as those who have learned and those who have shared, and those who have loved and those who have cared, and those who will continue to place themselves forward in Light.

We will not end this prayer, Father. We will not say "Amen." We will do nothing except to continue on, but in this, I—and I ask others just in their heart of hearts—say, "Thanks."

And we continue on with this service in memorial— not to the dead—they are memorized already in the hearts; they are memorialized in the materiality that has gone before them—but for those of us who are left to suffer, to see, to hear the pains, to know that our suffering is our missing of that that is a beloved.

So seek more to place your belovedness inside of us— to let us share and cross the barrier of the physical and spiritual into the heavens, where we may all, once again, be united—where we may know the promise has been fulfilled. Thank you, God. Thank you, Father.

– John-Roger, D.S.S. (Post-9/11 Prayer, September 14, 2001)

"When in doubt, don't."

– BENJAMIN FRANKLIN

"Spiritual Warriors are people who confidently make choices about where to focus their internal attention, even when the external realities of their everyday lives are chaotic, troublesome or just plain annoying."

– JOHN-ROGER, D.S.S.

$\mathcal{J}$-$\mathcal{R}$'s $\mathcal{I}$nvisible $\mathcal{W}$ork

FROM WHAT I OBSERVED, J-R's ministry was whatever he put his energy on.

It's not about the places where J-R went, whether he'd go to a casino in Las Vegas or walk through a red light district in Amsterdam. The Spirit was the minister. The ministerial directive of the Movement of Spiritual Inner Awareness is to minister to all regardless of race, creed, color, situation, circumstance or environment. J-R demonstrated that in spades. He would go anywhere he needed to go to "save a soul." That's what I saw J–R do. That's what we're told Jesus Christ did. And I didn't think there was any difference.

When the Twin Towers in New York fell on September 11, 2001, it really shook up a lot of people. America essentially stood still. J-R, and all of us working closely with J-R felt like we were walking around in a fog. You could see that J-R was very involved doing the inner work. Later, he would confirm that the people in the towers had agreed spiritually to sacrifice their lives for the greater good. It was something on the order of Spirit allowing the Twin Towers to fall as a lesser event so that something like a dirty nuclear explosion would not happen. It was some kind of karmic clearing.

J-R went to New York twice after the World Trade Center fell and we would do his version of a vigil: sending Light and anchoring it into the area. Sometimes the souls of people who die in sudden, unexpected, or calamitous events don't realize their body has died and they hang around the earth plane sort of baffled. J-R was really good at releasing souls that got stuck like that, so they could move on in their progression.

When we were in New York after the 9/11 event, the energy was really palpable, very strong, very thick. A friend of J-R's was able to get us really close to the site, and the energy there was pretty brutal. But J-R always went where he was directed and did what he was guided to do, no matter how challenging it was.

Not only did J-R's work involve traveling physically, he also did a lot of his work traveling out of his body on other realms. Sometimes, J-R would be gone for weeks. He wasn't physically away because his body would be lying in the bed. He'd get up, eat, use the bathroom, and then lay back down. That could happen anytime, and would happen frequently when we were in Hawaii. A lot seemed to be going on spiritually in that area of the Pacific.

He would take off and go to meeting places, especially in Hawaii and Bora Bora. There were meetings of different spiritual boards, spiritual lords, and different gods and spirits of different realms. This could also happen in geographically high places, like in the Swiss Alps.

On occasion, J-R would take short-term trips on other levels, where he would need someone from the other side to take care of his body while he was gone. Apparently being fully in the body would hold him here so he needed someone to run the body while the soul traveled beyond and out there, to work in different areas. He actually had to detach from the physical body so he could go to some of these places spiritually.

There were several high spiritual beings who would take on the task of maintaining J-R's body while he was traveling very far away.

They agreed to switch with J-R while he was off doing stuff so that they could experience "now" on earth. When that was happening, somebody needed to feed and move J-R; that was staff's job. I know this may sound crazy to you, so imagine my reaction the first time I saw it happen.

It was in Nof Ginosar in Israel. I was just getting used to being on staff and working with J-R. We had been hanging out quite a bit and just having a lot of fun together. One day I was in the kosher cafeteria and noticed the other staff guys had walked in surrounding J-R. He seemed to be moving very slowly as they made their way toward the cafeteria line.

As they passed my table, I saw that J-R did not appear to recognize me so I reached out in a playful way to grab J-R's hand. One of the guys immediately blocked my hand and told me to not touch J-R, especially when he was out of his body. Then J-R looked at me and, in a sort of strange voice and with an unfamiliar cadence, asked who I was. What? I'm the guy you've been hanging out with for the last few weeks.

Seeing my confusion, the guys explained that J-R was away and this was a being they called The Ancient Man or the Old Man from the Bible. Apparently he was not terribly familiar with this level of existence, though he had some interesting abilities. For example, he was able to see through me and see through things, microscopically.

I learned that when he glanced at a glass of water I had on my tray. It looked perfectly fine to me, but he said, in a sort of biblical way of speaking, that the water was terribly dirty. I looked again and it just looked like clean, crystal-clear water. But when I got to my table, I held up the glass to the sunlight and saw what looked like particles floating around in the glass. There was no way he could have seen that from where we had been standing.

When I moved into the Mandeville house and began working with John-Roger, over the years, I saw this Ancient Man from time to time. Everything was new for him in the 21st-century, so he was always curious, as many of the seekers were. He is a friend, just a funny old guy. He's almost like a baby and he doesn't know these levels. But he's really fun to be with, and he can read you like a deck of cards. I never had anything to hide from him, so it was a blessing to get to know him. God bless him, wherever he is.

I have also experienced J-R's caretaker as a Native American; Nat and I talked to this caretaker, and he spoke like an American Indian. I thought we were with Sitting Bull.

When J-R would wake up out of a long meditation, we would sometimes ask who was there. And if the visitor was willing to tell us, we would know whether it was the Biblical character, a Native American, or even a Japanese emperor. The emperor only came once, and when I later asked J-R if he was a traveler, J-R said he was.

In addition to these beings who maintained J-R's body when he was out traveling, there were other spiritual beings that worked with J-R. One was a being J-R named Jodi. Jodi was a truth seeker and Master. He was also very intimidating, at least to me.

I was tested many times by these spiritual guys, and frequently I failed those tests. However, J-R did tell me that despite how I had done, Jodi liked me. The first time he said that I asked him who in the world Jodi was. J-R explained he was a guide, a very high spirit that protected him.

I was really happy that Jodi liked me because Jodi was able to filter the people around J-R that were full of BS. I believe that I was always clear and honest with J-R, and loved to talk with him. I always wanted his guides and spiritual friends to like me. I could feel the spirit especially strongly with J-R when Jodi was around.

Sometimes when J-R's consciousness wasn't present, his basic self would be in charge of the body. J-R's basic self was named Daniel and he had the aspects of the guy in the Bible who had been tossed into the lion's den. It wasn't that it was literally that person, it was the energy that he represented. Daniel was not always happy with me because he knew I was going to get in the way of some of the things (like pralines and cream) that he wanted. He was very precise and pretty strict. He was a pretty tough guy. I had a lot of run-ins with Daniel, especially when he wanted his goodies, which were always at the top of his "I want" list.

Daniel also very much wanted to be told what was going on and wanted things to be explained. I was forced to be totally honest and true with Daniel, and I'd definitely be taken to the mat with Daniel if I kind of pushed too much on J-R. When Daniel was the one primarily running the body, it would be pretty tough for me to goof off. No screwing around when Daniel was in the building.

There were times when J-R talked about the Light, that it came so powerful with him that sentient beings just wanted to hang out and learn with J-R. There was nothing really negative because he used to say anything that was negative would eventually burn up.

Some beings would end up going to J-R and attacking him because it was like a moth to a flame. They wanted to go home so they'd enter J-R like he was a doorway to another dimension. So it was not necessarily a negative thing if they attacked him. He was a vehicle through which they saw a way out. If those beings that were trapped and bound to the earth could see somebody like J-R who was multidimensional and able to access all realms, they would go to him and he could get them home. I saw that happen from time to time.

Not everything J-R did on the non-physical realms had to do with his spiritual work. On one occasion I heard J-R running around in the back of the house and it sounded like he was chasing someone. I made my way back to where he was and I saw J-R chasing air and moving around as if he was playing with an invisible person. J-R was laughing and just carrying on. Later, when I asked J-R what he was doing, he said he was playing with a child. About 6 months after that, J-R told me that he was playing with Zane, John Morton and Laura Donnelley's adopted son, before he was born. These were the kinds of amazing things I witnessed.

I know I've described things in this chapter that not many people have seen. You can believe them or not, though I can tell you, It's beyond the thinking and feeling, it's experienced from a place of "Knowing."

"There is no darkness but ignorance."

– WILLIAM SHAKESPEARE (*TWELFTH NIGHT*)

"I've learned that dreams can be a lot of things ranging from wish fulfillment to working out subconscious issues to just having had something too greasy before going to bed. However, dreams also can be very real experiences or past-life memories. I've noticed these 'significant experience' dreams have a different feeling than garden-variety dreams. My initiation dream was definitely one of the former kind."

– JESUS GARCIA, D.S.S.

CHAPTER 23

More Traveling with the Traveler

I DON'T KNOW HOW MANY miles I traveled with J-R over the years I worked with him, but I can tell you it was a lot. Traveling with J-R was really a unique experience because he would go wherever Spirit directed, often despite what was on the pre-planned schedule.

Whenever John-Roger traveled, you could bet unusual things would be stirred up—such as weather, earthquakes and other strange phenomena. One incident illustrating that took place in 1994 when J-R, John Morton and I went scouting locations to visit for a new trip they were getting information on. J-R and John were talking outside a café in Cairo and instantly a sandstorm blew in. We couldn't even see each other. I can't say this was typical, but I can't say it was that unusual either; but these kinds of things could always be expected when traveling with J-R. In any case, this particular trip held some other unique experiences for me.

The possible 1995 PAT V trip that John-Roger and John were scouting for was intended to be another pilgrimage to the Middle East—but, rather than a repeat of the PAT IV trip, we wanted it to be an expansion of that. In planning it, we visited Jordan, Syria, Lebanon and Egypt to investigate.

I love history, and in preparation for the trip I had done a lot of reading about the Palmyrene Empire. A couple of the things that stuck out for me were Queen Zenobia and a beautiful Roman city called Palmyra, in what is now Syria. Palmyra is still there today, a well-preserved and beautiful ruin, though ISIS has, in recent years, destroyed some of the city's artifacts.

Here's what Glenn Barnett, a friend and historian, has to say about Palmyra and Zenobia:

ZENOBIA, EMPRESS OF THE EAST

Zenobia was born to be a queen. She was a descendent of the famous Cleopatra of the Nile and went so far as to procure some of the tableware used by her ancestor. Zenobia became a queen when she married Odenathus, a client king of Rome and ruler of the wealthy caravan city of Palmyra, which was strategically located on the famed Silk Road.

In 260 AD, the Roman emperor Valerian was defeated and captured by the Persian king Shapur I. Odenathus earned the thanks of Valerian's son and successor Gallienus by executing a Syrian claimant to the throne and by defending the eastern empire from Persia.

Odenathus was assassinated in 267. His army proclaimed their loyalty to his widow Zenobia. She found herself the ruler of Syria, eastern Anatolia, Palestine and Arabia. In the pre-Christian era, educated rulers favored philosophers at their courts. Gallienus in Rome welcomed the neo-Platonist Plotinus while Shapur welcomed the mystic Mani. For her part, Zenobia summoned the Director of the Platonic School in Athens, a man named Longinus.

When the Goths overran Greece, the Roman garrison in Egypt was dispatched to deal with them. This caused secular violence in Alexandria. Zenobia dispatched an army which restored the peace. She now found herself the ruler of the second and third largest cities in the empire (Antioch and Alexandria), as well as Egypt, the breadbasket of Rome.

A new emperor of Rome, Aurelian, was not willing to allow her control of the eastern empire. He marched against her, captured her and restored the empire to his authority. Zenobia was marched in his Triumph through the streets of Rome, shackled in chains of gold. At the end of her humiliation, she was allowed a comfortable retirement outside of Rome.

Knowing this background, I was fascinated to be part of scouting the region to see if we could bring a tour of 150 people there. On that trip, I was J-R's personal valet and the camera man—and since he was out of his body a lot, meditating and soul traveling, I was also learning to guard his body. I was observing and learning and watching John-Roger and John scout and seeing how preparation for a trip works. On the physical is one thing and on another level there's the energy. I would watch J-R meditate, leave the body and bring back amazing information.

Before the trip I had begun having strange and vivid dreams. After one particular dream, I checked with J-R and he said I had been there before; in fact, I had had a lifetime with Zenobia. Then came the icing on the cake—J-R said I was clear to have my Soul Initiation. He initiated me in Syria, a country that has been very dear to me.

When we were at Palmyra, I had a re-awakening to the experience of that initiation. It was very powerful and it became one of the experiences we ended up portraying in the movie *Spiritual Warriors* film shoot in 2004.

We ended up not returning to Syria on the PAT V, but I went back ten years later in 2004, with a crew of ten people, to shoot our *Spiritual Warriors* film. I remembered all the places John-Roger had taken me on that scouting trip and Palmyra was indelibly stamped into my consciousness. We shot some really great scenes there that portrayed some of the things I had seen in my dreams.

I've learned that dreams can be a lot of things ranging from wish fulfillment to working out subconscious issues to a reaction to having eaten something too greasy before going to bed. However, dreams also can be very real experiences or memories of past lives. I've noticed these "significant experience" dreams have a different feeling than garden-variety dreams. My initiation dream was definitely one of the former kind.

After J-R, John and I returned from that scouting trip in the Middle East, we started to gear up for the big 1995 PAT V trip. It would be sort of a reunion. For us, it would be two 3-week trips to the Middle East with a Greek cruise in between to give everyone a break.

When the time came in summer of 1995, we got through the first trip and headed for the cruise segment. The cruise started out to be fun. But that didn't last long. Apparently some of the food was tainted and a number of the people in our party got sick...*really* sick with Salmonella poisoning. I was officially the worst of them. In fact, I nearly died.

It got so severe that I ended up being sent to the hospital, and J-R went with me. He wasn't really bad off at all and had come to be with me while I went through my misery. I was hallucinating and seeing a lot of what J-R and I would later write in *Spiritual Warriors*: battles and scenes that seemed like they came from *Lord of the Rings*. I remember J-R telling me to just go with it. By that time, I would go with anything.

In addition to being deathly sick, I was very sad because I thought that this was the way I was going die. I had always thought I was going to die a hero or something. Dying from diarrhea is not a very heroic way to go. I could see my tombstone: *Here lies Jsu Garcia. He pooped himself to death.*

I would have to say that I saw God in that hospital because I thought for sure I was going to die there and it took God to save my life. He was next to me. It was J-R sitting next to me watching over me and I was comforted with that inner knowing.

Meanwhile, John Morton continued on back to Egypt to finish the second part of the PAT V while J-R nursed me and also took care of others on our trip who were sick.

Eventually, I recovered and everything was great. I learned a lot, got stronger and I was definitely humbled. Once again, Spirit had a way of kind of knocking me off my pedestal and disillusioning me, so I could get down to being real and seeing what reality is all about.

Everyone is a spiritual warrior, and everyone handles situations in their life differently. Getting through that illness really opened my eyes to a lot of things. When I wrote my doctoral treatise about living with a spiritual warrior many years later, I reflected back on this as a key experience in my life. I was able to see life is really about living with myself, living with John-Roger, living with many people who represent the spiritual warrior and carry that mantle.

When I recovered, we joined up with the second PAT V trip. Afterwards, J-R and I took a trip to Italy, in order for both of us to more fully recover after the Salmonella attack. I was having a hard time and he took me to a town near Milan, not far from Switzerland. We spent 10 days in that town and there was a hole-in-the-wall restaurant where we ate pizza almost every night. This was a time for clearing and J-R supported me through one of my darkest periods. This private Italian trip was a time of reflection for me; I wanted to continue working with J-R and I was trying to figure out about acting.

Italy was a place for me to get well. I knew I could leave the planet because J-R had said that I had a window to go. What this meant, he explained, was that when certain situations in life all lined up, like a slot machine, you could die. You didn't have to die, necessarily, but the opportunity was there.

Then there's the idea of "dying to this world." Very much like in the movie *The Matrix*. The red pill and its opposite, the blue pill, are popular culture symbols representing the choice between embracing the sometimes painful truth of reality (red pill) or remaining in the blissful ignorance of illusion (blue pill). As Morpheus says to Neo in the film:

> *"You take the blue pill, the story ends. You wake up in your bed and believe whatever you want to believe. You take the red pill, you stay in Wonderland, and I show you how deep the rabbit hole goes."*

I experience J-R the Traveler like this. The rabbit hole is the Sound Current. This pretty much describes my life since I tasted of the manna.

I was having a similar experience then in Italy, and I sometimes experience it even now. Every time I glimpse through awareness that's not the mind but out of the mind's domain, when I glimpse the *maya*—see the illusion for what it is—then I die to this world. It's profound. The rededication and the eating of the manna. This is a knowing, not an intellectual thinking.

That trip taught me what love is and J-R consistently demonstrated real caring and love for me. I remember great comforting words he used. He would hug me and whisper in my ear, "Stay close."

On another trip, I experienced some different lessons. We had gone on an Adriatic cruise on the *Windstar*, a modern, cutting-edge, amazing sailing ship. J-R and I had gone on a side trip on a small boat while the larger ship was waiting for the tide so it could enter a grotto in Capri, which was the ancient entrance to the Villas of Tiberius. I was looking out over the edge of the boat into the water and I fell back into the boat with severe back pain. J-R held me up and cleared me of the water spirits, undines, sylphs and salamanders. He explained that there are elementals that live in the water and in the ocean in particular. His helping me and explaining like this was a way of raising the awareness on all levels.

We took another private trip off the cruise to visit Medjugorje, Yugoslavia, before the wars there. J-R was interested in checking out the kids that were seeing visions of the Virgin Mary and praying for peace. We did meet those children and pray with them. I would never have thought in a million years while cruising in the Adriatic Sea on the *Windstar* ship with J-R, John Morton and a group of MSIAers, that war would break out and over 100,000 would be killed. We recognized it as a balancing action or a clearing karma event.

J-R was very hands-on with me, teaching and showing me things that were invisible. I tried to be a good student and sometimes I got it and sometimes I didn't. This was one that I got: the importance of not having any againstness. On some occasions he would lean over while driving him, and ask "How am I inside you?" "What?" I would respond. He would touch my chest and repeat, "How am I inside you?" I would say, "Great! J-R, I love you." He would smile, "Good."

This was what he did often to check how we all got along. I use it still to this day. He would explain that you can love everyone but you don't have to like everybody. He pointed outside the car and said, "You can love them over there."

"If there is someone you feel againstness for, always try to hold them in loving and Light inside yourself. Keep your temple clean. Try to remember them when you first met or when they were young or when you used to get along. When you have them in that nice place, tap your chest and anchor that experience. You can always tap back into that energy of openness by tapping the chest." Having againstness from within doesn't work, so this is one of many techniques we used around J-R. He needed the energy to be clean around him. You had to drop issues pretty fast if you wanted to hang with the boss. I've heard J-R call it the "circle of truth."

I think that because J-R had become such an integral part of my life, I became afraid that he would die before me. I used to worry and tell him I didn't know what I would do if he died before me. He would always tell me with a mischievous smile, "Don't worry, you'll die before me." Those remarks would stop me in my tracks. Then I would get sad. Those thoughts went through my mind for years. Then the days came when J-R was getting sicker and preparing for transition. The craziest thing is, one day I took a break from tending to him at the hospital and walked to the market. I became aware how much I needed to watch around me crossing the street or while driving. J-R was not gone and, if I wasn't careful (care-full) I actually could die before him. I thought about it and realized that I was changing, that parts of me were dying.

As J-R got closer to his transition, the more I felt that both Nathaniel and I were dying. Aspects of ourselves did die as J-R passed.

It has been almost two years since his passing, and I can say that I'm not the same person. This "death" was a very subtle thing, which explains my falling to the Astral realms, looking for J-R's body. I realized he's bigger and he's not there; only grief and despair lay waiting for me when I want the comfort of his physical presence. It was all in the thinking and feeling and that became my temporary imprisonment. I've since been released and I'm becoming more aware of the dimensions and the traps they hold.

Insight II Saturday Stretch, 1986; facilitated by Terry Tillman and Lawrence Caminite. My affirmation: "I am a beautiful, powerful, sensitive man loving myself and you."

The Karnak Temple Complex at Luxor, Egypt, planting
Light and Love with J-R and PAT IV participants, 1988.

John Morton baptizes me while J-R watches
at the River Jordan, Israel, 1988.

PAT IV Group on the southern steps of the Temple where
Jesus walked and taught his followers; Jerusalem, Israel, 1988.

With J-R on Mount of Olives during PAT
IV; Jerusalem, Israel, 1988.

Walking with J-R, Joe Ann Cain and Connie Stomper on the Germany and USSR tour following PAT IV, in 1988.

Planting light columns in Moscow's Red Square with
John-Roger, Howard and Maxine White, Cleora
Daily, Angel Harper, Merle Dulien and many other
awesome souls; extended PAT IV trip, 1988.

Playing in Red Square with J-R, 1988.

Flowers for peace in Red Square, 1988.

Taking a moment with J-R in Finland to plan
my future; extended PAT IV trip, 1988.

Honoring the Beloved John-Roger and the completion of
the Passing of the Keys to John Morton; December, 1988.
Here, I'm impersonating Yoda trying to make J-R laugh.

J-R checking on his 60-plus Arabian horses
at Windermere Ranch, 1990.

J-R riding Sonlight, his favorite Quarter horse; Windermere 1990s.

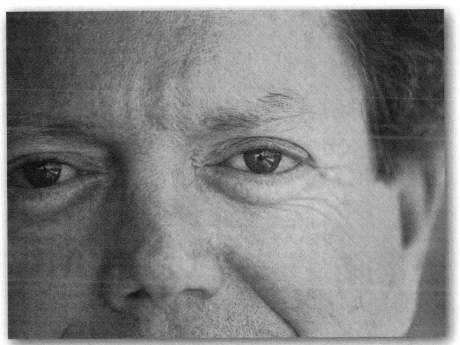

When the Master looks at you: Twaji, the gaze of God; 1990s.

On the stage with John-Roger, laughing and
breaking crystallizations, 1990s.

Playing with J-R, the Traveler and Preceptor, 1990s.

J-R's and my handprints for a ceremony debuting
Mandeville's basketball court, 1997.

Traveling to the Serengeti, Africa, in the early days; waiting
for Phil Danza to set up sound and video for a seminar.

J-R giving orders on the walkie-talkie, Maasai Mara, Kenya, Africa.

J-R schooling me on the Li River, China, 2000.

J-R's personal staff: Zeus, Nat Sharratt and Erik Raleigh, on
the watch while J-R soul travels; Li River, China, 2000.

J-R sitting in as the real Director of *Spiritual Warriors*, filming at Prana, 2004.

On top of the Great Pyramid in Cairo, Egypt, with
Director David Raynr, Producers Rick Ojeda and Michael
Hubbard, camera operators Robert Cain and Joshua
Benson, and Director of Photography Evan Nesbitt,
while filming *Spiritual Warriors* on location, 2004.

John-Roger and me, having fun at a Barnes
and Noble booksigning event, 2009.

Collage and Ideal scene.

Collage and Ideal scene.

Collage and Ideal scene.

Collage and Ideal scene.

Collage and Ideal scene.

Collage and Ideal scene.

Collage and Ideal scene.

Collage and Ideal scene.

Mystical Traveler premiere in Tel Aviv, Israel, celebrating J-R's 80th birthday on September 24, 2014: Integrity Day. There were 141 participants for J-R's final tour.

Elda and Delile Hinkins, J-R's brother and sister-in-law, at the *Mystical Traveler* premiere in Price, Utah, a few months after J-R passed into spirit; 2015.

Nicole and I celebrating John-Roger's 81st Birthday
in Jerusalem, Israel, one year after his passage into
spirit; September 24, 2015: Integrity Day.

Nat and me with J-R one month before he passed into Spirit
in Jerusalem, Israel; September 24, 2014: Integrity Day.

Arriving to celebrate J-R's 81st Birthday with Nicole,
me and Benji Shavit in Tel Aviv, Israel; Setting
up for September 24, 2015: Integrity Day.

Graduating from the final 2-year Master's of Spiritual
Psychology degree program with Ron and Mary
Hulnick, University of Santa Monica Class of 2016.

Celebrating J-R's 80th birthday with 141 family and friends in Jerusalem, Israel, one month before he passed into Spirit, September 24, 2014: Integrity Day.

Twaji with the Master during an Insight Seminars
event with Russell Bishop and John Morton.

"*Nicole and I traveled to Israel in 2015 to celebrate J-R's 81st birthday. September 24th was approaching, almost one year since John-Roger's passing into Spirit and I must say it had been a difficult year. While in Jerusalem, I knew I shouldn't try to repeat what I had done there with J-R in the past. J-R was showing me inside that I needed to try new things and go to different places to share J-R's teachings. So I did, and there he would be.*"

– JESUS GARCIA, D.S.S.

CHAPTER 24

Traveling Without J-R

By the time I completed my first year at the University of Santa Monica Master's program in Spiritual Psychology in 2015, I had had many experiences of J-R coming into my consciousness and letting me see some things since his passing. For one, I saw I needed to travel, and I got very strongly inside that I needed to go to Israel with Nicole. One of my dreams was that while John Morton was traveling in France that fall for the Peace Awareness Training, PAT VIII, Nicole and I would be in Jerusalem. I envisioned that we would be screening the *Mystical Traveler* film in Tel Aviv on September 24 (J-R's 81st birthday) and we would share a marathon nine hours of non-stop J-R seminars on September 26.

My intention was crystal clear. It was an impulse that was burning inside. J-R kept talking to me in pictures. When I cautiously shared this with some friends, I realized that J-R had been talking to folks in their dreams about helping me. I asked for, and I received, a lot of help.

Nicole and I traveled to Israel in 2015 to celebrate J-R's 81st birthday. September 24th was approaching, almost one year since John-Roger's passing into Spirit, and I must say it had been a difficult year. While in Jerusalem, I knew I shouldn't try to repeat what I had done there with J-R in the past. J-R was showing me inside that

I needed to try new things and go to different places to share J-R's teachings. So I did, and there he would be.

The previous year, 2014, in Jerusalem was a spectacular and unforgettable moment in time. J-R was still alive then, surrounded by 141 souls all loving each other. During the three-day fundraiser with John Morton, Michael Hayes, myself, Benji Shavit, our tour guide for all the PAT trips, and Paul Kaye, it became surrealistic and mighty; it was truly a moment in time and space. We were basking in the Love and Light of John-Roger, the Christ and God.

My attachment to J-R's physical body was immense. I could not just forget and move on. I moved through this with a hole in my heart.

By October 2014, one month later, J-R's health had declined and I was in the bubble of wanting him to live forever. We were all doing our best to care for him and make his life comfortable. I had fallen in love with Nicole Tenaglia on the birthday trip. I was always honest and transparent with J-R and I wanted to get clear with him. I would never do anything without J-R's blessing and support first. When we returned to California, I told J-R about my strong love for Nicole that had started at the end of the Israel trip. I looked at him and felt tears on my face; J-R paused and said, "I can see that." I asked, "Can you marry us spiritually?" I wasn't even thinking, I spoke from my heart and soul. I had this instinct, an intuition that I'd better hurry up and get it all out into the chalice of John Roger's consciousness. That is all I ever wanted and to me that is all I ever needed—it was that approval from the Christ/Preceptor/John-Roger's consciousness.

I said "marry us." He paused and went out of his body and came back. I thought it was going to be a "no" and then he nodded like it was done. J-R did a lot of that, he took off and checked with the BUS ("Boys Upstairs") or GAS (Gathering of Angels Society").

He touched my face and head. It was our daily thing for years. Sometimes he would gently slap my face. We always connected and touched. Towards the end of his last two years, although he might not have verbally said a lot, I knew how to talk with J-R and so did Nathaniel. We just knew "J-R code talk," because he was all there mentally, but his body was slowing down. It was quite easy to just ask the questions. In the early days, it was always the way that you asked the question. It really depended on the way you asked the question, because that was how you were going to get the answer. So the clearer you were, the clearer the question, and you could bet that J-R's answer would be right on.

After asking J-R to marry Nicole and me spiritually, I asked if we can share Discourses and the whole thing. I knew what to ask and he approved it all. I have never been rushed in my inner self and I've learned that when situations like this happen, it's a high self and spiritual part that knows more than the ego. It's a divine unknowing that takes the lead. It's beyond the mind and emotions…it's spiritual. I never thought that a few weeks later, he would pass away, but I do know that Nicole is a gift from J-R to help me stick around after he passed, because I certainly did not want to stay here. I knew I'd never meet someone like J-R again in this lifetime. When J-R was going through his transition, knowing that I was with Nicole assisted me to keep the energy up and hold the loving for J-R as he breathed his last earth breath.

Before he passed, one night I brought Nicole to J-R at Mandeville, and for a moment it was wonderful to love Nicole and J-R and be in oneness. I loved that J-R knew that I would be okay as he was ready to travel and transcend. I miss you, buddy.

On the trip in 2015, I noticed Nicole and I were looking for J-R in everyone and everything, much like "the Force" in the *Star Wars* movies. The trip turned out to be in the middle of Jewish and Muslim holidays: Celebrations of Yom Kippur, Sukkot and the Eid al-Adha Festival surrounded us in our activities. Finally, with fasting, no driving and restaurants closed, we surrendered and just observed. In the midst of having to walk to places, we found love and fellowship between families and friends. We planted Light columns in the Temple Mount on Yom Kippur and walked around the Dome of the Rock. The air was pregnant with the honoring of God. We let it infect us as we were honoring our Beloved John-Roger. My heart is filled with thanks to all who gave their light, love and donations that made this dream come true, to John Morton, and to the MSIA Presidency for their support.

This trip was the first of many to come where I was not thinking about getting back to the hotel to check on J-R and see how he was doing. It began to sink in that J-R was with me so I didn't have to go anywhere to make sure he was okay. Still, after 26 years, it was a hard habit to release. As I started getting used to the idea, I began to feel him inside in a different way. He was young and energetic, and he was showing me where to go. If I tried to recapture him in those old places he would not be there. Maybe it's the same with the Christ; it's a process of being here and now. He's in the here and now. I have so much deeper appreciation for the title Ram Dass chose for his book, as I kept hearing: Be Here Now.

It was graceful when we arrived in Israel, and for the most part it went smoothly. Everything came true for us. We did screen the *Mystical Traveler* film (all 3½ hours) on J-R's 81st birthday. That same night, we celebrated J-R, overlooking the Old City on the rooftop of Notre Dame Hotel. We Skyped with John Morton and the PAT group in France and the energy was awesome. It felt like we were transported to J-R's universes. It cemented the harmony, alignment and consensuses to the fellowship of the Christ inside us the way we experienced it in 2014 in Israel with John-Roger. Some divine connection took place. Then, on September 26, we held nine hours of non-stop John-Roger seminars at the yoga studio of Benji's wife, Zahava, called "Spirit of Tabor."

Decades earlier, with the first PAT IV trip, Benji had started as our tour guide; but over the course of the many years we did the PAT IVs and beyond, we all grew very close. Benji loved J-R and flew to L.A. to be with us at J-R's memorial service. That's more than friends, that's family.

Benji, his son Gilad, and Mia, Gilad's girlfriend, all helped to set the stage for this great event honoring J-R. Many people came to the Mystical Traveler screening, about 60 new folks, and 10 folks came to the J-R Marathon we held later in Tabor. J-R has said on several occasions that ascendant beings on other realms also come to MSIA seminars, so I imagine we had some of those, too. We also went to the newly discovered 1st century synagogue in Magdala near the shores of Galilee. (I encourage you to Google it.) The age of this synagogue indicates that Jesus and Mary Magdalene might have prayed or taught there.

Thank you, John-Roger, for guiding me on this trip, for Nicole and for taking care of us.

Another opportunity I had to look back on my earlier travels with J-R was when Nicole and I recently traveled to China together. I couldn't help the flashbacks from a group tour to China with J-R, John, Nat, Erik and a whole lot of MSIAers in 2000. Not only was it a great trip, but several things stood out to me from that time. J-R spoke of the stagnant waters in Suzhou, then placed a blessing and prayed that the waters would flow again. We all climbed the Great Wall in massive heat. My favorite place was Tiananmen Square where there's a photo of me filming and J-R doing a Moment of Peace. The uprising had been in 1989, and by 2000, Tiananmen Square had so much dense energy in the air, you could cut it with a knife. We had also visited the Forbidden City, which was quite raw. There was not very much tourism going on at that time. We took two boat cruises, one on the Yangtze River and the other on the Li River.

I felt such a connection with China and J-R. He predicted many things that were documented on video. Phil Danza, head of NOW Productions, and Nancy Carter put together at least six Moments of Peace clips during this trip, and in at least three of them, J-R spoke clearly of his predictions about the future of China. Here's my take on it: he spoke privately about this to staff, but I remember him saying the "yellow race" would be taking the lead and that China would be a global leader and a superpower. But first it would need to go through an internal change to become closer to a true democracy, post-Communism. The country would become part socialism and part capitalism, and together it would be a better demonstration of government.

Jump forward to May 2017. Nicole and I were invited to visit China by a good friend, Ribal, to participate in Iman, an international conference featuring dignitaries from many countries to promote greater freedom and democracy in the world. While the conference gave me many opportunities to share John-Roger's story with new friends, I was having many experiences of déjà vu and flashbacks to 2000. It seems that when I'm away from home, I have deeper experiences with J-R on the inner levels. So I was particularly aware of huge changes and developments in Beijing from 2000 to 2017, and how J-R really called it in regards to China's future. That experience was very similar to his prediction of the "Worm in the Wall" in Berlin back in 1988, an event that I was lucky to be a part of. I remember laying down at the base of the Wall with J-R and friends, meditating.

Beijing really blew me away because I didn't even recognize it. Although there was quite a bit of pollution, the Chinese have really invested in their infrastructure and I felt the energy of happiness in their consciousness, relating to this new venture of owning modern, cutting-edge material items. I believe in 2000 there were more bicycles, but in 2017, I saw many more cars, including American brands like Tesla. I even found a wider variety of food to eat than before! It is like a new world in my eyes—I felt like Christopher Columbus discovering a new civilization. While I did not travel to Suzhou on this trip, I met several people from that region who told me that city was nearly as developed as Beijing.

"The energy was powerful. Muhammad Ali wished us off to a great start. I've watched Ali my whole life, and there he was cheering us on. I ran a good 7 miles, walked and ran until I hit the 18th-mile marker. By then, my left knee was giving up and I began to develop a massive blister at the bottom of my right foot. Pain was my friend and it was visiting. By the time I hit the 22nd mile-marker, I was walking. The knee locked and I could not run. I was carrying my cell phone, and I called J-R for help. He delivered and I kept going."

– Jesus Garcia, D.S.S.

CHAPTER 25

ℒife's a ℳarathon

On March 7, 2004, with J-R's agreement and support, I ran in the Los Angeles Marathon. Actually I ran and walked the Marathon. It was my first marathon. It will probably be my last.

First, let me give you a little background on how running marathons came about. It's what contributed to my mindset as I decided to run. There are many points of view, of course, and this is the one I like best, written by my good friend and local historian, Glenn Barnett. Of course, you are welcome to find your own version.

PHEIDIPPIDES AND THE MARATHON

When the Olympic Games were revised in 1896, the logical place to hold them was in Greece. Olympic organizers wanted to include an event that would honor Greek history. They came up with an idea for a long- distance run that would commemorate the deeds of the ancient Greek runner Pheidippides, who, after the Battle of Marathon in 490 BC, was dispatched to Athens some 26 miles away to announce the victory.

Pheidippides was a professional runner. He was a messenger who was often dispatched to carry news and announcements far and wide. He had marched with the Athenian army to Marathon and fought in the battle, before being tasked with the assignment of rushing ahead to Athens to inform the city fathers that their army had won the battle. In the dry heat of late afternoon, Pheidippides ran the 26 miles over the rocky Greek terrain back to his city, mindful of his duty and his heart filled with pride. The heroic story ends with Pheidippides entering the city and announcing, "Rejoice, we are victorious," before he collapsed and died of exhaustion.

On the day of the first modern marathon in 1896, the runners began on the actual Plain of Marathon where the battle took place, and ran to Athens where they finished the race in an ancient Roman stadium. When the Greek audience in the stadium saw that the first runner to enter the stadium was their countryman, Spiridon Louis, they stood. When it became obvious that Louis would win the race, they began to joyfully chant "Rejoice, we are victorious."

Today, the marathon is the most popular race in the world because all are allowed to participate, not just professional athletes. As many as 50,000 people run in a single race, men and women, the disabled and the elderly. All are welcome in this most democratic of all sporting events. All in memory of the sacrifice of Pheidippides.

Let me begin by saying, I did not train or even prepare for running the marathon. That was mostly from my naiveté; I had no idea what a grueling experience it was going to be. All I did was eat a lot of carbs and I began to tell myself that I could do it. I was not planning to finish first, but I absolutely intended to finish. I wanted to show myself I could do it. I asked John-Roger to be with me the whole time, and he was.

The way I looked at it is that in my personal category I came in first place. I've been on five PAT IVs, I climbed the Pyramids, I've traveled around the world with J-R. I was near death in Greece and

I climbed Mount Sinai. I've been to Russia with J-R twice, and I had two horses at Windermere roll on top of me (and J-R once again healed me); and I co-starred in a film, *Along Came Polly*, which had grossed over 86 million dollars. So, running a marathon was not a big deal. (Okay, it really was.)

At the starting line looking down the road, it looked like an ocean of people for miles. The energy was powerful. Muhammad Ali wished us off to a great start. I've watched Ali my whole life, and there he was cheering us on. I ran a good 7 miles, walked and ran until I hit the 18th-mile marker. By then, my left knee was giving up and I began to develop a massive blister at the bottom of my right foot. Pain was my friend and it was visiting me. By the time I hit the 22nd mile-marker, I was walking. The knee locked and I could not run. I was carrying my cell phone, and I called J-R for help. He delivered and I kept going.

At the 25th mile-marker, I was seeing people collapsing and quitting. Also, it was 92 degrees out there. When I saw the finish line about 1/4 mile away I ran in and got my gold medal. Everyone who finishes gets a gold. I didn't run to win, but I ran for me. Downtown Los Angeles was Athens to me and I was *Pheidippides*, running to save Greece (myself). I loved it and I'd do it again—if I found a reason to do it. Which I don't expect to. The people were great to all the runners. I ran for the MSIA inside of me, and for the John-Roger inside of me. It was a beautiful thing to watch in myself, and the inner talk with J-R for over 6 hours was an amazing experience. I thank the Lord. I thank the Lord. I thank the Lord.

To bring this full circle, sometime after the marathon, I was at a *Sports Illustrated* awards show with J-R and a couple other staff guys. The great Muhammad Ali was there and I told J-R I wanted to meet him. J-R said if I wanted to meet him to go and talk to him. So I walked down to where Ali was sitting in the front row at The Shrine

Auditorium, not paying any mind to his bodyguards, and said that I'm with my friend J-R. We love you and it's great meeting you.

He looked up got close to my face and he raised his shaky hand and touched my greasy hair, saying, "Nice hair." We hugged and I left feeling cool that I met the champ. I felt like I was cheering him on in his marathon.

"I have a pre-birth memory of being somewhere in darkness; a black void. There were men, or elders, which I later surmised were members of a karmic board somewhere in Spirit. They were asking me if I wanted the tough father or the more sensitive father. I said I wanted the tough father, the protector. Then, boom, I'm in life somewhere, and that tough father was my stepfather. He was very tough; he looked a lot like Sylvester Stallone in Rocky."

– Jesus Garcia, D.S.S.

Jesus

"Jesus Christ is the spiritual head of the Church of the Movement of Spiritual Inner Awareness, and the Traveler's work through MSIA is based on Jesus' work. Jesus Christ made it possible for all people to enter the Soul realm, whereas before that time, this was available only to a few people. Soul Transcendence, the spiritual work that John Morton and I do, builds upon Jesus' work and makes it possible for people to be established in the Soul realm, traverse the twenty-seven levels above Soul, and to go into the heart of God."

– EXCERPT FROM JOHN-ROGER, D.S.S.,
"FULFILLING YOUR SPIRITUAL PROMISE"

CHAPTER 26

Heroes and Judgments

As I WROTE THIS BOOK, I came to realize that it's important to look at the heroes throughout my life and how I related to them. The first one was, of course, my stepfather, who stood in as my father. My biological father left my mother when I was pretty young. I have no idea why, though I knew they had never married. I met him later, when I was 16, as I mentioned before.

My stepfather, who stepped in and married my mother, had his own kids. But he raised me as if I was his own, and he was unbelievable. He was a tough guy. I used to hang off his muscles.

I have a pre-birth memory of being somewhere in darkness; a black void. There were men, or elders, which I later surmised were members of a karmic board somewhere in Spirit. They were asking me if I wanted the tough father or the more sensitive father. I said I wanted the tough father, the protector. Then, boom, I'm in life somewhere, and that tough father was my stepfather. He was very tough; he looked a lot like Sylvester Stallone in Rocky.

I really admired my stepfather. I worshiped him—even though he was not exactly flying straight. Actually, he was pretty crooked, and he cheated on my mother. He did a lot of what I would call bad things. But what's interesting is that, as a child, I didn't judge him. I really had problems with him for hitting my mother, fighting and cheating, but they were not what I would now identify as judgments.

Even as a youngster, I fought with him and told him that I didn't like that he was hurting my mom. But at the same time, I loved him and forgave him. I loved him and I loved my mother. It really seemed like they were good together much of the time.

He was great to me. He gave me presents. He took me to cool places. I remember waiting for him during my school summer vacations in Miami. Eventually I'd hear the blast of his 18-wheeler truck air-horn and he would pull up outside my grandmother's house. I'd run out the door and into his arms and he'd take me out go-karting or some other super place for a kid and dad. We had great times and strengthening times. I hated going to his Spartan training grounds that consisted of the terrifying Coney Island Cyclone roller coaster and being dropped into the water at the beach so I learned to swim on my own. These experiences were traumatic and not recommended for present-day child-rearing. I still loved him. I appreciate it all now, I know how to swim and I can ride any roller coaster in the world.

That, to me, was a very heroic time. He was my hero. To me, he was Superman. He looked like Superman. Nobody could mess with him.

In my forties, I created a short film with J-R called *Me and My Daddy*. It's about a boy who's always waiting in the car while his father did everything from having adulterous relationships to beating up people who didn't do what he wanted. Obviously, it was semi-autobiographical. But the great thing was that, as I was going through that childhood, I didn't have a judgment on it. In that particular time of my life, I had no moral compass saying that's right and that's wrong, so to me it was just what it was.

I love the innocence of being young when it seems like every-thing's okay and nothing really matters. My stepdad was not killing anybody, thank God, but I couldn't disassociate and say, "this is right and that is wrong." I was just a blissed-out, loving kid. I loved people, no matter what. I would say that's an expression of the innocence of God consciousness. Then later on, religion entered my life and all of a sudden I learned some things were "wrong."

Growing up in that non-judgmental way, when I would see pros-titutes, or, as J-R called them, "counselors of the streets," I didn't have a judgment about it one way or another. As children tend to do, since they haven't been brainwashed into the judgments that society tends to generate, I just saw through the eyes of innocence without the mind traps that get instilled in us over time. I would say to myself that they were beautiful people. I didn't stand there in my pulpit and talk about damnation. I didn't tell them they'd burn in Hell for their sins. I didn't have any of that in my heart—at least not until I got into the whole Catholic phenomenon.

The funny thing about my brush with religion is, rather than learning the Christ doctrine, which is forgiveness and love thy neigh-bor, I was brainwashed into worrying about sinning and going to Hell.

Here's a brief digression. J-R put the Christ doctrine into prac-tice and he taught it to us on his staff in practical and profound ways. J-R would leave the table if he didn't like the conversation. If he did leave, we would blame the staff person who had promoted that con-versation and ostracize them for making J-R leave because when he was around us it was magic. We began to hold the Light and keep things on the positive for fear of losing him.

We were a lot like brothers, and there were times when a couple of us would be having a problem with each other. J-R would al-ways let us go at it—arguing, not physical violence—and sometimes we'd get pretty intense with each other. However, at some point J-R would take us into his office and have the two of us who were fighting wash each other's feet. I can't begin to describe the power of that. Then he would have the other three wash each other's feet. J-R said that at Mandeville, while under his roof, we were our brother's keeper.

I know I sometimes fought the process, but I always eventually gave in. I can tell you, we staff guys became close friends because of it. J-R always said that he who apologizes first wins.

On the PAT IV trip in 1988, we had an overnight layover in Amsterdam before our flight to Cairo. J-R walked me around the Red Light District, and I could see he had a lot of compassion for all of it. Interestingly, we never, on any of the trips, went cruising through rich neighborhoods. And I started to learn that getting lost when we were on our way somewhere was not really a problem and likely presented a divine opportunity for planting Light columns— which is asking the Light to come through your body and anchor into the earth leaving a pure column of white light for the highest good. That's what we did if we ended up in an unfamiliar area— which somehow seemed to happen a lot.

As we grow more mature, we tear down our heroes, I guess. I know that at some point I started to realize my stepfather wasn't exactly a fine example of a hero, from the point of view of an adult. So I looked around for more heroes. As I became interested in acting, Scott Baio became someone I could admire. He was my first sort of professional hero because he showed me something that I could attain—a star-level of success on T.V. And I did attain it.

Then I wanted to go further. Marlon Brando became a hero, then it was Robert De Niro, and then James Dean. All of these men are what I call Spiritual Warriors. Outside of my immediate universe of Hollywood, I considered Robert Kennedy, John F. Kennedy, Martin Luther King, and Abraham Lincoln to all be superheroes, in a sense, spiritual warriors, because they attained something that was so beautiful. They embodied courage and honor. They embodied many things to me. And they each had their own problems that, I believe, served to keep them grounded here in the physical.

I believe spiritual warriors—heroes—have to have some sort of physical issue, condition or situation to anchor them here to this earth. I think they need to be, in a sense, crippled here, as they transcend and lift themselves and others.

When I met John-Roger, I realized he was my true hero. I knew on a very deep level that this was the guy I'd been looking for. I saw that in all areas he was definitely a great leader. In all the years I knew him, I've never seen him depressed, never seen him complain. I aspire to be such a man, such a warrior.

I definitely have failed and fallen many times. But I've gotten back up. I've come back, through the grace of God, and through prayer, and found myself back on my feet. As I learned from J-R, it's not how many times you fall that matters, it's how many times you get up.

When I was in the Doctoral of Spiritual Science program through Peace Theological Seminary and College of Philosophy, I had to write a 100-page paper called a practical treatise exploring some aspect of life of my choosing. I picked "Living with a Spiritual Warrior" as the theme for my doctoral treatise. In writing it, I had to explore what being a spiritual warrior meant to me, both inside myself and outside, living with John-Roger.

I came to recognize that everyone is a spiritual warrior, and everyone handles situations in their life differently. Being a spiritual warrior, to me, is just pretty much taking life and the situations it presents one step at a time. Not being stupid about it, but there are things in life that really come at you and challenge you. I saw that they can either finish you, or you can spin it and make it funny. You go through your sorrow, your tears, you write those things out, you express those things, and then you look on the bright side and stay in the present and move on and breathe.

I'm grateful that I am an actor, because, probably in the worst times of my life, I was able to express what was challenging me through my roles in movies, TV shows and plays. I also sing, so I was able to sing and to write and express what was inside of me that way. I realized that through those difficult times—there were actually very few—I was able to create gorgeous work, whether a song or a script or a scene or a play. I was able to use these as ways for getting it all out.

As I examine my life, I think the toughest time I ever had was when John-Roger was hurt. He had an accident and seriously injured his eye. In a nutshell, what that taught me, more than anything, was to stand up in myself, reach inside myself, tap into the knowing and take command. I found that in the act of doing, the Spirit matches the action. Perseverance was a key. I realized that a person who needs help doesn't need the person helping them to be in drama mode. They need them to be in leadership mode, to assist and help, without the energy and the scatteredness of freaking out. A leader in an emergency has to be direct and keep moving deliberately to carry out the mission, which is to assist and serve.

I also learned that on the set of the *Spiritual Warriors* movie. John-Roger and I wrote and produced it together. It was J-R who brought out my courage and gave me the reins to do the filming in the Middle East.

Ten of us went out there to get the film shot. It was amazing. It changed my life. Doing that movie put me in the hot seat and I had to stand on my integrity...or not. It was doing that movie that I first really began to learn how to stand on my integrity and not back down from what I knew was an inner connection and being clear inwardly.

One example of this was when we were in the middle of the desert in the Wadi Rum in Jordan. It was late in the day and the director and everyone on the crew were hungry and wanted to eat. Keep in mind that this wasn't a place where we could pull into a McDonalds and have a couple of burgers. This was the desert. There were no roadside fast food restaurants because there were no roads; there was sand.

We were in five Land Rovers and Fadel Gad, my co-producer and guide who knows that region, took us further and further into the Wadi Rum, which is pretty much like the Grand Canyon in the desert. It's awesome; Mother Nature at her best. I was fascinated. Wadi Rum was where David Lean had shot *Lawrence of Arabia*, and I was creating my own little fantasy that I was going to shoot my own *Lawrence of Arabia*. So I asked Fadel if he could find the sand dunes where that film was shot.

What was happening for me was that I was starting to get inner guidance from J-R, who was physically back in L.A. But I was not telling my director this.

Finally, Fadel shared with us that we'd have to quit looking after no more than another half hour, so I agreed. Unfortunately, we kept looking for more like an hour, and the director was pissed. He stalked over to me and read me the riot act, and I gave in. I collapsed inside myself and said we'd head out without the shot I wanted.

We got into the Land Rovers and proceeded to go back to the bus, which would then take us on a regular road back to town, an hour away. In other words, I had a crew of angry, hungry people and we were about two and a half hours away from anything to eat.

As we drove, I had a conversation in my head talking to the inner master, the spiritual warrior, A.K.A., John-Roger. I was talking to him as if he and I were in his living room in Mandeville after the trip. It went like this.

J-R: How was the shoot?

Me: It was great, great. It was fantastic. Thank you so much, J-R.

J-R: Did you get everything you wanted?

Me: Well, yeah, yeah, mostly, except for…

J-R: What?

Me: Well, we didn't get…there was this shot I wanted in the desert that represents dying in the desert and thirsting for spirit, but the director said I broke an agreement, so I didn't get it. And it would have been beautiful. It was just like *Lawrence of Arabia*.

J-R: So you didn't get the shot?

Me: No.

J-R: So you just collapsed and went ahead and did what the director wanted to do. You didn't get to do it?

Me: Yeah, that's it.

When I heard myself say that in my head, it was like a flash of lightning hit me. I was stunned at the learning I had just received from the Traveler. I looked out the window and found we were driving through an area that matched what I had in my mind pretty well. I was getting a second chance!

I pulled out the walkie-talkie that we used to communicate between the cars and hollered for everyone to stop. They did and the Director and Director of Photography stormed out of their cars. There was a potential mutiny in the middle of the Jordanian desert. But I had my inner marching orders and basically, all hell came out of my mouth. I told them we were going to shoot the scene right here and if they didn't get the camera out, I would fire all of them.

At this point, half the people were on my side, the other half were not. The D.P. gave up and said, "Peace, peace, peace. Let's shoot this."

I set up the dune shot as the sun was setting and reflecting off the sand. I was wearing my Jellabiya (the traditional Arab/Muslim shirt), crossing the desert, just like Lawrence of Arabia. It turned out to be the most beautiful shot in the movie.

Later, the director apologized for being so angry and admitted what a great shot it was. That's when I realized that part of learning to stand in my integrity was to include others in on the process. I needed to explain to him what had happened in my head, speaking to John-Roger, my inner master. Because, when I told him that, he was really taken aback. He said he wished I'd told him that because all he heard was, "Get the hell out of the car!"

Hearing this, I apologized and there began my lessons on staying true to the inner knowing and guidance while still speaking kind words, sharing and communicating.

Those were really key things that changed my life. This is the story of the love J-R gave to me, the love of a Master. It's measured by the time he spent with me while I worked to learn to be true inside myself and follow that. Not to collapse.

Now I try not to collapse or fall apart. I try to keep strong about my inner guidance, or guide, which I feel is very connected to the Christ and to the Holy Spirit. But it's always challenging because it's hard to know what's intuition and guidance and what's ego. That's why J-R always taught us to check things out. Living with J-R meant constantly checking and experiencing one's inner intent, then adjusting, correcting and aligning. It was important to not be the weakest link.

From time to time, someone gives everything they are
and graciously loves the world.
A vision is seen, a word is spoken,
a heart begins to open.
Defying the strains of an imperfect world,
Love is born anew.
A guiding light to so many,
holding the vision with infinite patience and strength,
a demonstration of our highest aspirations,
wayshower, beloved friend,
our dedication is reborn, in honor of you:

– JOHN-ROGER
MINISTER OF THE YEAR
MINISTERIAL SERVICES IN ACTION CONFERENCE
OF EXCELLENCE, JULY 1, 1984

⌀ntegrity

IN THE EARLY 1980S, JOHN-ROGER created a foundation to recognize and honor people who exemplified the qualities of integrity. As J-R defined it, integrity is "Having the courage to go with the truth as you know it, as a heartfelt response, with caring and consideration for others."

A number of distinguished people, ranging from Lech Walesa to Jonas Salk to Mother Teresa, received the Integrity Award between 1983 and 1987.

The awards were presented at lavish galas. These were festive black-tie dinners, complete with top-notch entertainment and celebrity presenters. They were held at the prestigious Beverly Hilton where many high-profile Hollywood events took place, including the Golden Globe Awards since 1961.

Here's what J-R said at one of those galas:

"With our modern-day methods of communications, we can more readily see what is happening around this world, thereby keeping track of those in this world who are doers. Because they choose to stand in their integrity, their actions in the face of adversity have shown all of us new strength of purpose and have even hinted at ways that we also can become more fully in our own lives. Thereby

giving each and every one of us an opportunity to grow in our own individual integrity and to find out for ourselves more of the meaning of this substance and action that we call life. And that is what the John-Roger Foundation is here to do. We are dedicated to creating opportunities and expressions to renew our lives. And above all we are here to remind each other that the greatest gift we have is the gift we make of our loving.

It is our integrity that makes us fragmented or whole. Integrity is basically an inner process, a life-giving process. The people that we are honoring this afternoon, I assure you there is no question of their integrity."

For me, and for countless others, John-Roger was a model for integrity and a living demonstration of our highest aspirations. In recognition of this, he was named Minister of the Year at the 1984 Conference of Excellence.

"Any fool can criticize, condemn and complain – and most fools do."

– BENJAMIN FRANKLIN

"In awakening the heartfelt energies, you can't help but discover your own self-worth, your own self-love, your own magnificence."

– JOHN-ROGER, D.S.S.

CHAPTER 28

Milestones: Changes Along the Way

OVER TIME, THERE WERE A couple of really key events that resulted in significant changes in J-R's life, which also meant changes in my life. While they weren't chronologically close together, they were milestone events.

The first was our move to Santa Barbara.

Let me take you back to December 18, 1988, when we celebrated J-R's 25 years as a Traveler. At the time, it was viewed as a retirement party because at the ministers meeting of MSIA's annual International Conference that summer, J-R announced he had handed the keys to the Mystical Traveler Consciousness over to John Morton. It was sort of like J-R transferring that spiritual authority to John. While this announcement was the start of the transfer process, the final blessing and anchoring celebration took place at the John-Roger 25th Anniversary event later that year. It was a huge, formal celebration with tuxes and gowns. I was new to staff and J-R let me get up on stage and honor him with song and comedy; I enjoyed making the whole congregation laugh, including J-R. There were hundreds of people there honoring J-R; I loved to entertain J-R and I knew he loved actors and artists. He was a dance teacher when he was younger. At the event I sang him a song and did an impersonation of Yoda.

During this Honoring the Beloved evening, J-R completed the transfer of the keys to John and hugged him. And I thought, "It's on."

When J-R started the church, he had taken a vow of poverty, which means he didn't own anything; he'd given everything to the church. The church housed him, fed him, and took care of him (as they did me since I also took a vow of poverty). We lived and worked, we traveled, but we didn't own anything, and we didn't take a salary.

At this big anniversary event, it was announced that a home had been purchased for J-R's retirement. It was in the mountains above Santa Barbara, near the church property called Windermere Ranch where J-R often liked to spend his down time. (Not that J-R actually had real down time, but he'd go up there when he didn't have appointments or other responsibilities that required him to be in Los Angeles.)

Here's a brief digression about the ranch. Under J-R's direction, the church had bought this 142-acre plot in the beautiful Santa Ynez mountains overlooking Santa Barbara, California, some years earlier from the woman who owned the property and was living on it. Although we took it over, J-R told the woman and her old ranch hand that they could stay on the property as long as they lived. They remained there for several years.

Not too long after we purchased the ranch, someone donated a herd of Arabian horses to MSIA, and they were sent to the ranch. J-R liked having the horses there a lot.

J-R told me that the Fremont Trail used to go through the property to San Francisco with horses and carriages. The Chumash Indians lived there, and just below what's now Highway 154 are the Painted Caves.

We had been going to the ranch quite often, even though at the time I was still heavily engaged in the movie industry. I'd just finished *Slaves of New York* at the time of this supposed "retirement," so I went with J-R when he moved up to Santa Barbara. All of a sudden I went from being a city boy in Mandeville Canyon to a cowboy in a rustic setting on the ranch in the mountains. There was a lot of wind and at times there was some rain. Occasionally it even snowed. Spending significant time on the ranch was pretty daunting to me. I found myself wondering how in the world that had happened.

J-R often told me that if I didn't like doing something, to pretend I had gotten a role in a movie doing that thing. So I decided to pretend I had gotten a role as a cowboy in a movie. In my imaginary script, J-R was my buddy and we were going to be training horses. As a result, I started to have fun instead of being intimidated by the situation. I learned how to ride and soon I was riding horses with J-R—who was a pretty good rider from his childhood in Utah.

One time it was just J-R and me riding on the ranch. We were headed down to a spring that ran through the property and J-R led me toward some huge slippery rocks that had a face of about a 45-degree angle to the trail. Our horses stopped and I looked up and J-R looked at me. With a glint in his eye he told me try riding up that incline. I looked at J-R and I looked at the incline and said, wow that's steep. When J-R didn't back down, I kicked my horse and attacked the angle.

As we moved up that steep rock face I began to hear metal from horseshoes hitting the rock. My horse, Blue, couldn't get a grip, but we were committed to speed and force. Then gravity kicked in. Halfway up, which was about 50 feet, my horse went down. I was glued to him and he rolled over me on a huge shrub. I thought he crushed me. It wasn't good.

After the slipping and sliding subsided, the horse got up and came over and smelled my feet to check and see if I was alive. I was and I jumped back on. From my perch on horseback I watched J-R negotiate the rock. He did his share of slipping but he kept his seat and he went all the way to the top. At the summit J-R looked at me and smiled. He waved and hollered for me to get moving—he said to talk to the horse. So I did. I talked to Blue as I kicked and held the reins and his mane hair. I thought I was going to get rolled over again, but J-R encouraged me saying not to be fearful because the horse will pick up on it. "Be clear and direct," he told me.

With that, I changed the fear inside me and rocketed up to the Traveler who was sitting on his horse at the top of the rock.

The times I would fall, J-R would make the pain disappear. But I had to get back on the horse. That's a metaphor I use today. This experience is in my DNA.

I did not have a lot of experience with horses and J-R was asking me to do things with them that really challenged me. But I'd been challenged before. So I became bold like kids are bold and fearless. J-R often told me to "fake it until you make it." While some might consider that as being dishonest—saying I could do something when I couldn't—I looked at it more as if I was in the process of learning things. Neuro Linguistic Programming (NLP) also uses that type of approach as a method for expanding and moving past blocks.

So if people would ask me if I knew something I didn't really know, like, if I knew how to ride a motorcycle, I'd say I did. Of course, since I did *not* know how to ride a motorcycle, I'd pretty quickly get into trouble and crash. Or people would ask if I knew how to play drums, and I'd say yes. But I didn't and I'd end up looking pretty foolish. But I would consider that part of the "getting there" process.

J-R was big on "mocking things up" as a technique for getting to the point of doing something you couldn't currently do. Mocking up involved creating an image of doing the thing in your imagination and laying a foundation that way so that when the situation or opportunity to do the thing showed up, you had some sense of what was coming and what you needed to be able to do.

Another thing J-R was a proponent of was creating an "ability suit." In the Insight I seminar, there's an exercise where each person creates their own inner "sanctuary" and in that process, we learned about creating an ability suit. That's a suit you could put on any time in your imagination that would enhance a gift you have, empower a talent you want, or give you the ability to talk with someone you are having difficulty with. You could also create an ability suit to give you self-confidence, inner peace, or some other internal quality. In the imagination, there are really no limits to your abilities!

That's not to say you could create an ability suit for, say, performing brain surgery, and then go out and cut into someone's head. However, if you were learning something—maybe like public speaking or riding a unicycle—you could create and put on an ability suit and that would enhance your ability to do that.

The thing is, as a result of J-R's many approaches, I can play drums now, and I can ride motorcycles now. So, maybe that younger me said he knew how to do something he didn't know how to do because he saw ahead to when I would know. Now I can say that my talents are matching up to my ambitions.

Anyways, there I was playing the role of a cowboy. One day, J-R took me to the bunkhouse at Windermere. The place had been there for decades, maybe close to a century; it was the original bunkhouse, very Spartan, weathered, rustic, small, and not appealing in any way. It had a couple of rooms with bunk beds and sort of a sitting room with an old battered table and a couple of chairs. It was dusty, drafty and, in a word, bleak.

As I looked around, J-R told me we were going to live there and asked if that was cool with me. I looked at the dust and the mess and it definitely was not cool. But I knew I had to keep sacrificing ideas and ideal fantasies, so I thought to myself that I'd find a way to make this work.

I turned to J-R to let him know I'd work it out and he had a mischievous grin. J-R would get the neatest twinkle in his eye when he was doing something that he knew was going to surprise people. He'd been kidding. I was definitely relieved because, with J-R, you just never knew.

J-R did temporarily move his residence from Mandeville Canyon to the retirement house in the Santa Ynez Mountains not far from the ranch. Because it was located on East Camino Cielo Road, we called the place Miracielo. It was beautiful, and a far cry from the bunkhouse at the ranch.

Part of the reason for the move had been to provide J-R with a cleaner environment to live in, with fewer people around. J-R was always picking up energetic "stuff" from people, and having him in a more remote place seemed to be a good idea to keep him healthy. Of course, trying to keep people away from J-R or J-R away from people sounded good in theory. In practice, not a chance.

Before long, J-R had moved a lot of the church events, like fundraiser pool parties and MSIA's biggest fundraiser, the annual Founder's Dinners, to the Miracielo house. To accommodate this, one of our MSIA guys, Jason Laskay, who was a fantastic carpenter, made huge round tables that looked like something out of King Arthur's era. Large groups of people would come up for the Founder's Dinner and Paul Kaye, Vincent Dupont, and Mark Lurie—the three guys who made up the MSIA Presidency—and

I, and others who worked on J-R's staff would wait on tables or otherwise help with the event.

I had also become the cameraman for Now Productions, documenting J-R. That was my training ground to ultimately become a director and filmmaker. I would always drive him up to Miracielo and pack, unpack, etc.

By this time, John Morton had married and he and his wife had two kids. It seemed to be one of those cycles where a bunch of folks in MSIA were having kids. Since MSIA is, in a sense, a big family, all those kids would play together at church get-togethers. J-R always loved kids, so, soon, there were kids all over the Miracielo house.

Because the place had a nice swimming pool, it was important that every kid learn how to swim so they would be safe there. So someone found a character named Tom, who was an amazing swimming teacher for little kids, and arranged for him to teach swimming classes at the Mortons' house in Mandeville Canyon or at the house of one of the other MSIA families that had a pool. Classes were given at 6:00 or 7:00 am because that's when Tom was available. He would spend an hour or two teaching kids from infants to 4-year-olds how to swim. He was phenomenal.

He used to start out his classes saying, "Tom is boss." So, when Tom was working, the parents had to back off. They weren't allowed to rescue their kids or get involved in any way. *Tom* was the boss.

Many of those kids now are college graduates, and they certainly know how to swim, thanks to John Morton and J-R deciding kids were always welcome at their homes.

Meanwhile, back at the ranch, more horses had been donated to Windermere by other organizations and friends. As they foaled, we started imprinting horses. A movie came out called *The Horse Whisperer*, which was based on the work of Monty Roberts, a man J-R and I subsequently met and took courses from. J-R saw the goodness of the methods that were presented in the movie, so he started creating clinics and workshops that showed people another way of "breaking" a horse. It taught a loving approach and creating a relationship with a horse. This approach created less damage to the horse—and to the rider. Another man with a similar approach, Buck Brannaman, would teach courses at Windermere for all ranch hands and staff. Windermere horses started doing the most phenomenal things with people that traditionally broken horses would never do. For example, I saw one of the horses lay down in the grass and put its head in someone's lap, which is normally unheard of.

Windermere horses had a confidence and often a gentleness that was a testament to this type of training.

Here's a funny story about something that happened at Miracielo. It wasn't funny then, at least not for me.

There was big fire in Santa Barbara that started from the ocean side of the highway. But it jumped the 101 and rushed up the mountain toward Miracielo.

J-R was monitoring the fire with walkies and watching the news, because in those days there were no internet or iPhones. As the situation began looking more dire and like the fire was going to get to us, J-R told me to pack the car, the brown Lincoln we were using in those days, and prepare to evacuate. So off I went and packed everything important in the trunk—including the car keys.

When I realized what I had done, I walked the long road back to J-R, collapsing inside because I had to tell him the bad news. I got back to the house and into the living room, which was packed with people, and sheepishly said I had locked the keys in the trunk. Dead silence.

Then J-R said, "Well, we'll wait." I can't even begin to describe the feeling in the room or what I was feeling inside for having messed up so badly. We waited 30 minutes and, miraculously (yeah, right) the fire reversed its course.

Later, J-R told me that the keys getting locked in the trunk was part of the plan for him to stay there and work the fire. I might have thought J-R only said that to make me feel better, but then I realized that through it all, no one had thought to go out and hit the trunk release, which was inside the glove box of the unlocked car. When Spirit keeps the obvious solution from everyone's mind, I have to go with "it was part of the plan."

The second life-changing event was when J-R fell and severely hurt himself. We had long since moved back to Mandeville because we couldn't keep J-R away from L.A. and the work he was doing there. Though J-R had been a high school English teacher when he was in his 30s and had a great command of the English language, I don't think he knew the meaning of the word "retirement."

On Halloween eve 2004, of all times, J-R fell down the back stairs at his home in Mandeville Canyon. It was an event that would change a lot for J-R, and everything for me.

That day I had shot the final scenes of our movie *Spiritual Warriors*. I had even persuaded J-R to come by the beach and do a little cameo in the afternoon. I had gotten in around midnight and I was really tired. I remember pulling into the parking area by the house and saying to myself, "Wow, I made it home with no accidents. Everything's good." And then my bumper hit the corner of one of the other cars parked there.

After making sure the damage wasn't too bad, I went into J-R's bedroom because I always told J-R how the day had gone. He took one look at me and told me to go to bed. But I wanted to stay in J-R's room and do the night watch, which meant watching over his body while he was soul traveling. The fact is, sometimes beings would come in and "caretake" or use his body while his consciousness was out traveling the realms he went to. So I wanted to be around to make sure no harm came to J-R's physical body if that happened.

But on this particular night, J-R was really firm about going to my own bedroom. I was surprised because up until then I had slept in his room every night. So I explained to him that I had hit the car and damaged the bumper and that I'd get it fixed. I gave him a hug and he told me to get some sleep, that he was fine. So I did what he said and went to bed. It seemed like a great night, nothing to worry about. Then...

I was sleeping and I heard a huge bang. It was the most god-awful sound. Immediately I thought something had happened to J-R. I ran to the doorway leading to the basement and, sure enough, J-R had fallen down the basement steps and injured his left eye.

While this was to have a very profound effect on J-R, it also was life-changing for me in a very fundamental way. In that moment, I knew I had to take command of the situation—the immediate situation and things to come. This is where all the training from my war movies and from J-R helping me stay strong and persevere and not collapse came into play. I guess this is when I stood up and became a man. Nat, Mark and Erik instinctively moved on the situation as well, and we all worked as a team to handle it and get J-R to the hospital.

Many times J-R would hug me and ask, "Where's the safest place on earth?" I would say, "here," pointing to his heart area. We would finish the hug. This ritual started years ago with his poodle named Pookie.

I always wanted just to be safe under the J-R umbrella and not have to think, not have to decide anything for fear of doing it wrong. It had been so much easier to just follow J-R's lead: to like what he liked and go along with whatever he was thinking or doing. But, to my surprise, when this happened, I was ready. It was time to hear the inner guidance, to connect with and trust my intuition, and follow what was true in me as J-R had always taught me.

So I carried J-R upstairs and put him in the car. He was conscious but disoriented. I started directing everyone to do what they had to do. I was calling the doctors I knew to contact. Things were moving pretty fast as we headed to the hospital.

One of the challenging moments that showed me how much I had grown was when one of the hospital doctors came up to us and said that J-R's eye had to go. I said that was not going to happen and I had someone remove that doctor from J-R's case. I immediately called my two great eye guys, Dr. Griffith and Dr. Kraus; and later, two other great men and doctors, Dr. Chang and Dr. Song. They became my heroes. We knew that J-R's eye was badly damaged, and these were the doctors who saved J-R's eye. I thank them and always will love them for healing my friend.

That was my biggest test. I went inward and followed J-R and Spirit inside of me and made the best decision for him. I know it was Spirit, and I was held to the impeccability of it all. Courage was the theme. Courage and love.

With this event, Nathaniel and I stepped into being J-R's chief advocates with the medical industry for his health decisions. If I had three wishes, one of them would be that everyone in the world could have as good advocates as we were for J-R. We knew that mistakes were not uncommon in hospitals and that an error with medical care could be fatal. We were absolutely committed to making sure that nothing bad was going to happen to J-R.

Despite the excellent care he received, because of the extent of the damage, his vision would never return to what it had been. The process of his healing was grueling on J-R and not much easier on me because I was 100% dedicated to him. I also had to finish the *Spiritual Warriors* movie, which was our project together. I have to acknowledge Nat Sharratt, Erik Raleigh, Rick Ojeda and Mark Harradine who stepped into the caring of J-R, giving me the space to complete our movie projects.

It was an intense couple of years and J-R kept pretty much low-key so he didn't have to deal with people's concerns for him.

By 2006, J-R was back. He was more of himself and very functional, though he had cut back on his work. For example, he was doing few seminars and lectures at the MSIA events. I think this was another way for him to let his successor, John Morton, know it was time to step up even more, because J-R was turning his attention to other things.

That was the beginning of J-R and me doing even more activities together without the many work responsibilities that he normally took on. We got him more involved in making movies, traveling without being under the pressures of having to make public appearances and doing book signings. We started J-R touring as a way to get him out and about.

Sometimes I know what happened to J-R was not my fault; it couldn't have happened if Spirit hadn't allowed it. It was a spiritual action. Later, J-R would tell me that through this fall he took on someone's karma for them.

However, my ego was not so accepting of the idea that anything could happen to J-R. I thought it was my responsibility to stop anything bad that might come his way. I really tried to and if I could, I would move mountains for J-R to keep him healthy—although I have to admit, we were weak in the "staying away from donuts and ice cream" department.

Now my consciousness is showing me more of the Spiritual action. When I truly experience this awareness, then I'm not feeling the weight of responsibility and I have no guilt. I do remember J-R always telling me, "Zeus, ultimately you're responsible for everything." So, over the years, I learned to take the response-ability for many things. I grew to love it. If I saw something that needed fixing, it was my responsibility to fix it. When I did that, it gave J-R more freedom and I was okay with that. J-R gave me the strength to have the ability to respond.

Now, there are a couple of things that were going on for me that I want to talk about. Maybe it's more accurate that I *need* to talk about them. One was that I was blaming God for what had happened to J-R; I was really angry. The other is that I was grateful for knowing what to do. I was really surprised that I could actually be on top of things because, as a child, I had an experience that pretty much convinced me I couldn't handle the important things in life. I had been running that against myself ever since.

It had occurred when I was very young. My family and I were moving to a different house and my stepfather had loaded pretty much everything we owned into his 18-wheeler truck. There was no room for my younger brother or me so my stepfather told us to follow him on our bikes.

We tried to follow him as best we could, but he was going a lot faster than we could. Before I knew it, he had outdistanced us and was gone. I couldn't see him anywhere down the road. As the realization sunk in, I cried out in a panic, "Oh, my god, I'm lost." My younger brother, Eddie, told me not to worry; he had my back. I was grateful that Eddie had said that, but it didn't change anything: We were lost and it was my fault. This would be the base of all my triggers today when I felt a loss. I would say, "What now?" I had my brother then, but I had to learn that I had myself all along. I had the resources to connect to the all-knowing one inside of me.

Of course, my stepfather came back once he realized he had lost us. However, I had failed and the damage was done. Since that experience, I believe that I'd been afraid to be responsible for anything really important. I had let my brother and my stepfather down. How could I handle something that really mattered?

And now J-R's well-being was going to be in my hands.

That event with my dad had a huge impact on me; it literally changed my life. To this day I find myself checking things and checking to have the courage to proceed when I have to take an action. I have to remember to acknowledge that when I think that I'm alone, I'm never alone. J-R is *always* there.

Recalling the traumatic experience of my parents forcing me to choose who to go with when I was young, I can only imagine the pain I felt and how scared my basic self was—and still becomes—when faced with making decisions. The basic self is a young part of our consciousness, along with the conscious and high selves, that has responsibility for bodily functions and maintaining habits. Much like a four- or five-year-old child, it tries to assert its desires and wishes—and fears—upon the conscious self.

I believe J-R helped me face myself for the last 31 years and he continues to do so. Chanting the names of God gives me the altitude to comfort my basic self, mind and emotions, and see the totality of everything.

When his fall happened and J-R's health became even more of a consideration than it had been, I discovered I *could* handle things in a crisis. Through that experience I became a man. But it didn't happen because I was born that way. It happened because J-R taught me to be that way.

Maybe I even became a great man in my own way. I don't mean I think I'm great in terms of stardom or by outer measures. I mean great inside. There's a bandwidth that's powerful in my connection with Spirit. When there are things to be done, I move on them. That is the greatness that I'm talking about. This greatness that he instilled in me happened because he fell, and I had to look around and see how I was going to respond.

How did I respond? I got things done. I handled the most important things that had been placed in front of me: I was getting J-R's health handled, and I was finishing the movie. How well I did was brought to my awareness in a very special way.

One of MSIA's biggest events takes place in the summer, usually around the 4th of July. It is our international Conference and people come from around the world to participate in workshops and other events. The Conference culminates with two very powerful meetings: the Ministers Meeting and the Initiates Meeting. As part of the Ministers Meeting, the church gives a Minister of the Year award to two or three people whose ministries have been exemplary and have inspired others in our church. In 2007, Nathaniel Sharratt and I each received that award. It was the congregation's way of acknowledging and thanking us for taking care of J-R.

To this day, I'm so appreciative and grateful that I worked with J-R to the end and getting the Minister of the Year award was really kind of bittersweet. Sometimes I think I don't know how to take it. I need to accept that people appreciated what we did for J-R. But I would rather that J-R had been healthy and not needed our support and I got an award because I made great movies.

I remember what I said when I accepted the award. As I often do, I joked. "Oh, well, just in case I never win an Oscar, I'll take this." But sometimes it's hard to appreciate the award because it has tragedy connected to it. It's almost like receiving a Purple Heart. To me, that's heart-wrenching because our servicemen and women who fight get a medal for having been injured. I appreciate the award, the injury not so much. But we were acknowledged. And I can truly say, "Hey, thank you. I get it."

But for me, the Minister of the Year award was a lot like a Purple Heart. I'm glad I can reframe it and call it my Oscar. I do thank the ministerial body and all who truly loved us that day and beyond. Here is what was written on my plaque:

We have seen your many expressions of freedom
and your many antics bringing joy and laughter.
Today we celebrate you
in your devotion to the Traveler
at any hour day or night
and as one who serves
our beloved wholeheartedly.
We are grateful that you walk with the Traveler,
hold with the Traveler
and bring a smile to his face.
Many know you as a Spiritual Warrior
We know you as our Minister of the Year

REV. JESUS GARCIA

Baruch Bashan
Ministerial Services in Action Conference of Spiritual Promise, July 1, 2007

The wind bloweth where it listeth, and thou hearest the sound thereof, but canst not tell whence it cometh, and whither it goeth: so is every one that is born of the Spirit.

– KING JAMES VERSION, JOHN 3:8

"We were 'E-Z-linking,' 'cause we'd just had the computer and just set up and we were traveling and Zeus was working with me and we'd go, we'd take a message and go online to send it to Betsy, go offline, get the other message, put in on, go online, send to Phil, go offline and that was really efficient in its way. But what a waste! Because through a mistake I sent a message to the entire staff on my computer list because I hit the wrong key."

– JOHN-ROGER (1990 STAFF MEETING ABOUT EMAILING FOR THE FIRST TIME)

CHAPTER 29

Small Miracles

Unusual things used to happen all the time. Because I was working closer and closer with J-R, I began to look on them as small miracles. For example, when we would go horseback riding at Windermere, we had walkie-talkies so we could communicate if we got separated. On one of these rides, I unknowingly dropped my handset and couldn't find it. When I mentioned I couldn't find my walkie, John-Roger said the last time he remembered me having it was when we went through one of the ponds that had been dug when we were improving the property; it was like a tiny man-made lake. When we rode through that, the horses would be about chest deep in the water.

I thought it was possible that I had dropped it into the lake, but if I had, how would I know where? So John-Roger told me to go to the lake and he would start talking on the walkie. I hesitantly agreed; I didn't think I'd be able to hear it since it was underwater.

When we got back to the pond, John-Roger clicked on his walkie and started saying, "Breaking for Zeus. Breaking for Zeus."

I looked at him, baffled, but then I caught a movement out of the corner of my eye. I looked closer and there were bubbles coming up from the bottom of the pond.

Shaking my head, I went into the lake almost up to my neck and reached down where the bubbles were coming up. And up I came with the walkie-talkie. Maybe it was just J-R being practical. Maybe not. But with everything going on in the world and in my life, recognizing the consistent miracles and grace definitely helps me tap back into the higher power, the inner guidance.

Here's another example of the kind of things that would happen when I was around J-R:

J-R had been teaching about the basic self, which I mentioned in the previous chapter—this is like the inner child part of each of us. It's also the part of our makeup that really knows everything about our automatic daily rituals. You get up, brush your teeth, put your clothes on, get the keys to the car in the kitchen, grab your wallet, and go for a drive. The basic self tends to know how to do all those routine kind of things. When we do actions without really thinking or being aware of them, that's usually the basic self handling them.

On this particular day, I couldn't find my credit card. When it's not in my wallet, I keep it in a specific place, but it wasn't there. So that was strange. I'm also a good "finder" when people's stuff goes missing. But in this case, I couldn't find my credit card. It was bizarre. But I had a *feeling* it might have been in the trash because when I checked inwardly if it was in the house, the answer came back that it wasn't.

Then I asked J-R if he thought it was in the house. He's really good at knowing where things are but he said he didn't see it. He suggested I use a technique for finding things called "ranging." It involves telling yourself to "reach," asking the consciousness to extend itself for the information. Since my inner hit was that it was in the trash, I went out and picked through a few pieces of trash in the can. It was dark, the trashcan was dirty, and I wasn't into it at all. So I told myself I wanted it to be in the house so I didn't have to get into the trash. (That reminds me of the joke about the guy looking for his car keys at night under a street lamp. Another guy comes along and asks what he's doing. He says he's looking for his keys that he dropped in the alley. The second guy asks if he dropped the keys in the alley, why is he looking on the sidewalk, and the first guy says, "Because the light's better over here.")

A little later, still not having found my credit card around the house, I headed to bed. But first, I wrote a bit in my journal. I had been encouraged to start a diary or journal where I could write down things I wanted, or make note of things that had happened, and things that I wanted to let go of. I was told there's something that happens when you consciously write down something; it becomes like a contract with yourself. The ritual of going over the day in my mind, seeing how things went, and writing out my thoughts has become pretty much my life before I go to bed. At the end I write, "Oh, God, please help," or "Thank you very much," or "I'm so grateful." In this case, I wrote, "Please help me find the credit card." I could have called and canceled the card, but that's a hassle. So, instead, I asked God to please do something. To show me some powers!

That night I had a dream with a series of pictures. One of the pictures was seeing myself outside by the trash, grabbing a plastic garbage bag, opening it up, and piece by piece, emptying it out. When I woke up, I remembered the dream and wrote it down. All the time I was writing I was dreading having to go outside and take each piece of paper, one by one, going through seven garbage cans. But I committed to myself to do it, so I got dressed and got myself ready.

Out I went to the first can. I opened it up and opened the first bag. And I followed what I saw in the dream, taking out one piece of paper at a time. I pulled one, two, three pieces out. I went to reach in again and looked where I was putting my hand. And I saw my hand was reaching for...my credit card! I paused with my hand in mid-air and just praised the Lord. I couldn't believe it. But I realized the picture that I got in the dream told me all I had to do was look, as closely as I could.

This was a big realization. I saw that if I have a picture of something, and if I follow through on it, it can help me get what I'm after. I realized I didn't see the result of my finding the credit card in the dream. The dream just showed me a picture of doing the process. That was an interesting key.

The third incident that was significant for me came the night after I had lost a ring that was very special to me. It had the symbol of a "Hu" on it, an ancient name for God. The Sanskrit character looks something like the Om. It's our main logo in MSIA.

The next morning, in a dream, J-R told me, "Go check the car." So when I woke up, I went to the car, opened up the trunk and there it was.

Maybe you have experiences like these, and maybe they happen pretty often to you. I found them showing up a lot more frequently after I started working with J-R.

Now Elijah said to Ahab, "Go up, eat and drink; for there is the sound of the roar of a heavy shower."

– KING JAMES VERSION, 1 KINGS 18:41

"I thought, 'I won't know if this really works unless somebody else does it.' And so I got in back with Liz, and Zeus got in the front, and so he started driving. He started, like, watching how I do it, and he took over. And it's very easy—a very, very easy thing to do when somebody teaches you who knows what they're doing. Get a teacher who knows what they're doing. If somebody stands on the side and tells you how to drive 'em, just listen to them, but get on with somebody who's been driving them. There's a whole world of difference of standing and talking about it and getting up and doing it.

"Now those Clydesdales inside of me are in a very comfortable place. Very comfortable."

– John-Roger, D.S.S. (1990 Seminar at an Institute for Individual and World Peace event in Santa Monica)

CHAPTER 30

Life is Just a Dream

IF THERE WAS ANYTHING THAT produced a direct link from J-R to me, or from my intuition to my conscious awareness, it was dreams. I had some really amazing dreams throughout the years when I worked with J-R, and I got a lot of teaching in my dreams.

Sometimes I would have dreams that indicated something would be happening in the future. I discovered over time that often there was a six-month lag between a dream and its manifestation in the physical world, while other times, like with the dream about my credit card, it was almost at that moment.

An example of how dreams worked for me is that, at the beginning of my time with J-R, I had a manager who was handling my acting career. She wasn't really producing any results and I thought she didn't like me. I didn't know what was going on. But I decided I had to get to the point where I could be compassionate rather than blame her for not doing anything.

Then I had a dream where I went through her entire house, and she wasn't there. I saw her family photos on the mantel and I had a sense of extreme sadness in the household. It felt like an eerie, gloomy kind of feeling; a depression. A couple of days later, I was talking to her on the phone in real life, and I told her my experience and it freaked her out. Later I found out that she was an alcoholic, and she drank in order to bury her emotions. I realized this was J-R teaching me through a sort of remote viewing dream to have understanding and compassion for people.

When I learned that, I hoped my bringing it up it in that conversation might have given her a chance to address those feelings and then let them go. But that wasn't where she went with it. It wasn't long after that call that we ended up going our separate ways.

Getting messages in dreams is something that definitely does not go away. I will say, though, that I was completely weirded out by J-R's death, and for a while I had no inner communication with him. It is just now, about a year after his death, that it's starting to come back.

These realizations are all keys for me. I call them my lighthouses. The purpose of lighthouses is to provide warnings; they let ships know where the rocks and the shore are. I think these dreams and these experiences are my lighthouses to keep me aware that the Lord is very close to me.

In my early years working with J-R, while I was still focused on my acting career, I had a goal of working with Tom Cruise. I knew Tom from the early 1980s, before either of us had had a great deal of success. After moving into Mandeville, I had a dream in which Tom and I were going to get together. It was like we were friends and were just shooting the breeze.

About six months later, J-R and I went to the movies, and just after we got there he told me to get some popcorn. I went downstairs and there were Tom and Nicole Kidman. They just sneaked into the theater to get some popcorn and stuff. At the time, he was filming *Interview with the Vampire*, based on the best-selling Anne Rice book, playing the lead role of Vampire Lestat. I loved that series of books and, as I mentioned in an earlier chapter, had read all three of them when I started traveling with J-R. So, when I saw Tom, I told him about that, and we got into a really cool talk about them.

Then I reminded him that we had done paintball wars together in the eighties. He thought for a second and then exclaimed "Oh, my God, that's right. Nicole, this is the guy I told you about." That was kind of cool: he had been talking about me, because we had gotten together with Emilio Estevez before he was a star, and we had fought in this paintball game on their huge battleground.

That was just one example of how my dreams sometimes came true. I thought it was interesting that J-R sent me for popcorn just when Tom and Nicole happened to show up.

I also wanted to work with Andy Garcia. As with Tom Cruise, I also had dreams about meeting up with Andy. When I was on J-R's staff in the 1990s, I had sneaked into the Paramount lot and ambushed Andy in his office. I asked him for a role then, and, while he was very nice to me (probably nicer than I deserved, having sneaked in), he didn't have anything for me then. But J-R had taught me about perseverance and to never give up. Andy didn't have a chance even though neither one of us knew it at the time.

But, in 2004, 16 years after I had started working with J-R, and 14 years after ambushing Andy in his office, I was in New York on a staff trip. I had let my hair and beard grow out; I didn't know what was going on with me at the time regarding acting. Out of the blue I got a call that Andy wanted me to audition for the role of Andy's brother in *The Lost City* which was the story of the fall of Cuba. I did not get that role.

Feeling down and depressed, I shared with J-R what had happened and asked him to put it in the Light. Two weeks later, I got a call that Andy wanted me to audition for the part of Che Guevara in the film, because I had gone to the first audition with the beard, looking pretty disheveled.

I got really excited because when I was a kid, I had a powerful inner experience with Che, a key figure in the Cuban revolution who was originally from Argentina. That was extra cool because my parents are Cuban and, despite being born in New York, I considered myself Cuban.

I'd had a pull toward Che much of my life, not in a worshipful way, but a déjà vu way. I later came to realize that had been a sort of spiritual premonition, which, in playing Che, would be a validation of my earlier déjà vu experience.

So I was very excited about the whole thing. But when the audition came around, I was really sick. I had stomach issues and I kept forgetting my lines. It wasn't my best audition. So I asked Andy if I could come back and audition again. Fortunately, he said yes. I redid the audition, and, huge surprise, they gave me the role.

One of the things I learned from that experience was recognizing that the way I was seeing things was not necessarily what God had in mind. But once I started thinking outside the box and allowed myself to receive God's way, not push for mine, things tended to work out. I felt J-R's presence closest to me while playing the Che role than I had ever felt in a role before.

When we were shooting in the Dominican Republic, I asked Andy which audition he liked best, the first one or the second one. The second one had been a lot more polished, and the first one was just me when I was devastated on a lot of levels. Andy said he liked the first audition and that's why he picked me. And that told me a lot; that no one really has control over a performance. You just speak your truth as best you can, and if the people want to hire you, they hire you.

In many ways, the Che Guevara role was the ultimate role for me. Playing a person like him allows you such freedom that you don't have when playing a straight character, a one-dimensional hero. In a lot of countries he's known as a hero, but it didn't matter to me because I'm non-political in that way. It was all about getting a really choice role.

The Che role was a benchmark for the change in my life and my new chapter. During the shooting, Andy came up to me on the set and said that he felt that this was a career performance. After this, I could retire. Little did he know how prophetic that statement was. Maybe it's even indicated by both of us sharing the same last name, but in any case, I consider Andy my brother.

There are probably a number of other dream experiences I could relate where J-R sent me advance information on things to come, but I think you get the picture and the point.

Aside from career dreams, there were also very profound dreams that had to do with spiritual growing. For example, I once told J-R that I had this dream where I saw his eyes looking at me and heard the screaming, shrieking sound of an eagle. He said there was a time when you reach a certain level above soul and the "terror of God" breaks away any attachment, anything from the negative realms that gets hooked to you so it's just you, pure in that higher realm.

He said it a different way in a talk he gave.

"People are going to have special missions here, be taken to high places, high rocks, high peaks, high pinnacles, to high places and be abandoned to the forces of negativity. **The forces of negativity come in like screeching birds with talons just ripping,** *but the person who's there can't be hurt, because there's nothing to hurt them. But what you do is you start to release all the fears, the impurities, and they just sort of drop away and you just come into the beingness of, 'Oh, ok, this is what's going on,' and it's very natural and very normal again."*

Dreams are an amazing resource and they're also puzzles that we need to figure out if we're going to get the full message. I think that's a never-ending challenge and a great spiritual exercise.

"And it's amazing, right after that, when we were riding horses, he rode the horses with grace. All of a sudden, he became a good horseback rider. I was going, you know, I taught him up to a point, but all of a sudden he gestalted a big leap. 'Cause he was centered. The horse picked up the centering. So he wasn't doing anything, like, "Hey, I'm going to center and be one with the horse." He was just handling his thing, and the horse picked it up."

– John-Roger, D.S.S. (1991 PAT Trainings at the Windermere Church House, talking about Zeus)

CHAPTER 31

ℰxperiencing ℊrace

IN 1991, THERE WAS A PAT II training at what we called the Church House, a house MSIA owned adjacent to the Windermere Ranch property in Santa Barbara. J-R had come to the training to share with the group, as he often did, and he used me as an example of how to get in touch with a place of peace and grace inside. He was referring back to a retreat we had had in Asilomar, California, called Living in Grace.

As a bonus, right in the middle of J-R's sharing, something happened that was really quite phenomenal.

John-Roger: "We know peace of the Spirit, because we have, through these physical incarnations, been in those levels. And there is no way you can understand this because that peace, as Lord Jesus says, surpasses understanding. But it does not surpass the ability to experience it. But after you experience it, it's like how do you understand an orange. You don't understand an orange, you eat an orange.

"So it's really difficult. It's like saying, 'What's your middle name, true or false?' And you go, those do not apply, that's not applicable, I cannot relate. But inside of you, you say, 'Well, my middle name could be True and False, just as easily as any other name could be.' So it's an experience.

"Now, what the depth of yours is would be quite different maybe from everybody else's. You may go deeper, or not as deep, or, I suppose it could be on the same vibration, but interpretations would be quite, quite, quite different.

"When we finally got around from the Christmas time, Zeus was saying, 'You know, I don't have the grace. I want to go back to Asilomar with all exactly the same people. And be there, and I want you to come in, I want you to do your magic.' And I said, 'Well, you know, why do I have to go to Asilomar to do it? I mean, can we just drive down the street, and go, "Here's Asilomar," and do it?'

"And it was like, 'No, you see, it was at Pacific Grove at Asilomar, in that room, with all of these people. Each one has to be accounted for to be precisely that person.' I don't know if it meant precisely the same chairs. But it was, 'Grace was me,' in that experience.

"So we were working with energetics with a person, and the person said, 'Did you experience grace there?' And Zeus said, 'Oh yeah, oh yeah, oh God, I really want that.' He said, 'Well, if you experienced it there, then it's in you.' He goes, 'Well, yeah.' He goes, 'Well, if it's in you, IT'S IN YOU; it just showed its head up there. So move back to that place inside of you where that's...' And he couldn't get it...and he said, 'Go to Asilomar, inside of you. Go to the grace inside of you.' "So he did. See, we're able to do it if you give us some kind of tricky directions."

Suddenly, J-R stopped and got one of his faraway looks.

"Just a second, I'm under Spiritual Guidance here now. (pause)

"So what we're required to do now is to just sit very quietly and beam Light to the Masters in the Inner Worlds. There's something going on over in the Persian

area that's really not really good. It's not necessarily in the physical world, it's in the Spirit World. And there's a call for more Light. So we're just going to call up our own Spiritual Light, and then it is sent to the Masters of Light, and they'll handle it. (pause)

"Okay, that will do it.

"You know, sometimes when you send Light, people say, 'Well, what do I do?' Hold that thought, and let me finish up with Zeus's. Because otherwise we'll get fragmented here, and a lot of stuff comes dropping down. It's like, 'Say the magic word, and duck, and there's words dropping down all over the place.'

"So he went in his mind—we were in Los Angeles—but in his consciousness, he went to Asilomar, found the grace. And I said, 'When you got that, let me know.' And he said, 'I got it.' And I said, 'It's in you right now. Claim it, acknowledge it, right now.' And he did. All of a sudden he was full of grace, in Los Angeles. And I said, 'Notice where that is inside of you, notice how that moves, watch, pay attention to it now.' And it was about 30-40 minutes of real intense looking. And there were three or four of us that were holding Light and energy. And he found it. And there was this profound peace entered the room. That his grace could not be held by him. And all it took was one person to find it, and the rest of us had it by contagion. And I thought, 'God.'

"And now he knows how to come back to his area here, the heart. He located it here. And so, we'll be going down the street, and do something, and he'll go like this. (J-R was tapping his chest, showing how to anchor the awareness of a moment of grace.) And he wants to stay in that heart. But you know, sometimes you stay there, you can't move, cause it's a thing where you say, 'I want to be salubrious in my own inebriation of this grace.' So you sit there and just slop out on yourself. And we become space cadets real easy.

"And then, when he got up, he realized that he had the grace in him. And it could be at Asilomar, or in a car, or in this place, or in a movie, or seeing a movie, or riding a horse.

"It's amazing; right after that, when we were riding horses, he rode the horses with grace. All of a sudden, he became a good horseback rider. I was going, you know, I taught him up to a point, but all of a sudden he gestalted a big leap. Because he was centered. The horse picked up the centering. So he wasn't doing anything, like, 'Hey, I'm going to center and be one with the horse.' He was just handling his thing, and the horse picked it up.

"So we know that whatever you get here doesn't have to stay here, in this house. If you get it here, all we're doing is like, it was awakened here and it's awake, it's yours, you claim it, you take authorship over it, you own it, you ingrain it, you, like, anchor it. We use anchor points to keep reminding you. Like, 'There it is, there it is, there it is, there it is.' When you walk down the street and somebody cuts you off, you go, 'There it is, there it is, you dirty son-of-a-bitch, there it is, there it is.' So, no matter how many times you go out of it, that's not even important.

"I don't even want to hear anybody tell me how many times they've gone out of grace and peace. I just want to hear the one time, how you got back. That's the one I want to hear."

Speaking of grace, J-R created a retreat that used to take place every year around Christmastime up at Asilomar, a beautiful rustic retreat center in Northern California.

Living in Grace retreats were life-changing and produced profound spiritual experiences in people. Significant elements of the Grace retreats were the processes participants did with each other and the sharings with J-R.

Taking the training and enjoying the God Rounds—the optional processes people could choose to do late at night at the end of the official retreat day—was amazing for me. And I always pushed J-R to share even when he didn't want to.

In the later years, J-R was pulling away more and more and allowing John Morton and Michael Hayes to share on stage without him. I remember one night at the 2012 Grace retreat when I was pushing and J-R wouldn't get dressed to go. I begged him and shared how much I missed seeing him on stage. I told him that folks would love to see him and he replied, "Why don't *you* go."

What? I was pissed. I got a hit at that moment that he wouldn't be sharing on stage anymore; that things were slowing down. My stomach sank like a punch to my stomach realizing he would not be on stage again. I begged him to go and share with John and Mike. The more I pushed, the more he kept telling me to go up on stage and share with Michael Hayes and John Morton. I said no. I wanted him to share like the old days. There was even a time I was shown to start muscle testing and doing what Michael Hayes does but instead I took D.S.S. courses and wrote my PT. I was afraid, I guess, to go up and do the work.

I did go on stage on the Saturday of the retreat when people were kind of letting loose and performing. I sang and shared with the other participants that I had tried to get J-R up on the stage and he said for me to get on stage and share. So here it was.

I remember saying to J-R that there was no way they would let me share. With hindsight being 20/20 vision, I realize that I should have gone up on stage with John and Michael and shared when people asked questions. But that was then and I didn't.

J-R was always encouraging me. Now I believe, after much thinking and waiting over the two years since his passing, that my consciousness is changing. It's wanting to grow and experience. I can't stop remembering how J-R would do things or how he would respond or react. J-R is in my DNA.

So now I'm taking that leap for sure. I will share.

I hope you found value in what J-R was saying about how grace—or whatever we might have experienced at any time—is always available because it's inside, not outside of us. And I hope this also gives you a small sense of the magnitude of the work J-R was doing all the time.

"More than the sounds of many waters, Than the mighty breakers of the sea, The LORD on high is mighty."

– New American Standard Bible, Psalm 93:4

"*I was with old Zeus the other night in Cardiff, Wales, and there's this place that said 'Billiards,' so I said, 'Do you want to go in for some billiards?' And he says, 'Sure,' so we walked in there, and then he walked up to the bar, and he said, 'Can I have a glass of billiards?'*"

– JOHN-ROGER, D.S.S., 1988
SEMINAR IN CARDIFF, WALES

ℳaking the ℱirst ℳovie

I THINK THE BIGGEST PHENOMENON in my life, living with the Spiritual Warriors who showed up for me—and that includes J-R, myself, and many people in the church—was making the feature-length film *Spiritual Warriors* with John-Roger. We wrote the script together. It was inspired by his number one *Los Angeles Times* bestselling book, *Spiritual Warrior: The Art of Spiritual Living*. I saw a lot of miracles while I was working on that film. J-R and I also wrote some other scripts, including the shorts *My Little Havana, Mandeville Canyon,* and *What's it like being Cuban?*

But I don't know if I would have ever made the *Spiritual Warriors* movie if it had not been for a very frustrating experience peripherally involving Steven Spielberg in 2004.

At that time, I was working on the TV show *Crossing Jordan* at Universal Studios. Across the road was Amblin Studios, where Steven Spielberg works, and where he created most of his movies. I had been there years before and had turned down a movie called *Batteries Not Included* because I had agreed to do another film.

Hoping to get on Spielberg's radar, I wanted to give him my audition tape for *Band of Brothers.* So when I happened to see him, I gave him the tape and a couple of J-R books for good measure.

He didn't want to take the books because he didn't want to get sued down the line if someone accused him of stealing ideas from them. But he did take the tape. Great!

When I hadn't heard anything from him by the next day (not that I'm impatient or anything), I decided to go over to Amblin and hand the tape to him again. I had no idea that he had been getting death threats because of working on the movie *Munich*, which is about the PLO killing Israeli athletes during the 1972 Munich Olympics. But he was getting them and had taken steps to make sure he was protected. So when I got to his office, there was a big to-do and Security actually detained me for a couple of hours. It was really an awful experience, which was not made any easier by the fact that they were waiting for me back on the set to film a scene from *Crossing Jordan*. It was more than frustrating, believe me.

I used the frustration of being detained to motivate me to talk to J-R about the *Spiritual Warriors* movie. I had been sort of avoiding dealing with the movie and, after this situation, I decided I wasn't going to let anything get in the way of my doing my own film.

J-R did give the go-ahead and I got David (Hubbard) Raynr—the same famous teen actor and director who had facilitated the Teen Insight event I had attended so many years ago and who had later become a good friend—to direct the movie. I ran everything past him and I learned a lot from him. But there was something about that experience at Amblin that was still bothering me. The healing of that came through in a really strange way.

It was like this: One night, the staff guys and I had taken J-R out to a sushi place for dinner. As it turned out, Steven Spielberg and his wife were also there. His wife kept looking at J-R and it was apparent that she was pulled by J-R's energy.

I surreptitiously arranged with the waiter to pay for Steven's bill, and at the end of the meal when he found out his meal had been covered, he wanted to know who had picked up his check. The waiter pointed at me. So I smiled and went over to him and told him what had happened that day when I was detained. He had no idea that that had taken place and I found a sense of forgiveness and release inside of me by having told him about it.

Then his wife asked who was that man sitting at our table; she said she just sensed so much love coming from him and the friends around J-R. I had no idea that Spielberg knew J-R, but I had heard stories from Leigh Taylor-Young that they had met before. So Steven walked over with his wife and introduced her to J-R. Steven and J-R locked eyes and in that moment I became aware that there was definitely some sort of connection there. You can see Steven's wife was attracted to J-R's light and really loved the energy. The energy was very powerful that day.

Sometime after that, we arranged to show the *Spiritual Warriors* movie in several theaters and we had made postcards promoting it. I ran into Steven and his wife in Brentwood and handed them a postcard. On another chance meeting, I gave him another postcard and he looked at me and said, "Kid, you got a lot of guts. One of these days I'm going to see that movie." That was pretty cool.

This business with Steven Spielberg was literally about a three-year process. I appreciate how much that really motivated me, and how much J-R guided me through the whole thing, and how much he really brought the healing in on top of that. I've heard a number of stories of John-Roger interacting with important people in the movie industry and maybe that experience helped him help me.

But back to the movie. After J-R green-lighted it, we got to work. We shot it in a number of locations, including the Middle East, as I described in an earlier chapter. I felt more alive than ever in the Middle East. I loved those trips; I love to lead, and it was my first experience of doing that as the head of the film production called

Scott J-R Productions. With all the training that J-R had given me as I worked on the three PAT IV (1988-90) and two PAT V trips (both in 1995), I felt like we were doing another one of those, but with new people, and this time we were filming it. After nineteen days of shooting, I felt like we'd accomplished quite a bit.

When we came back from the Middle East, J-R, John, the rest of J-R's personal staff, and I went to the Olympics in Athens, and then we prepped for about 25 or 30 days of shooting in L.A., Utah, and Santa Barbara.

Around that time, my mother called me from Florida to say she was going to have some medical tests. It was something about her chest. She wasn't very specific. So I wished her good luck and said I was in the middle of shooting so I'd see her when I got back. She went to the doctor, got the tests, and was immediately scheduled for bypass surgery. Apparently the arteries to her heart were blocked. Who knew?!

So, while I was fully immersed in writing, filming, directing and acting in the *Spiritual Warriors* movie, my sister was calling me every day from Florida telling me how things were going with my mom and her open-heart surgery. Through it all, I was constantly on the phone with J-R who was not only working with me as my spiritual teacher, but as my friend.

Actually, when I first learned about my mom's surgery, I had called J-R and I asked him for help. When I was little, I wanted my mother and my granny to be saved. I would pray and cry begging God to take my Granny and Mom and have a place in Heaven for them. I loved them so much and there I was years later with J-R, the Lord, and I asked him to help my mom and Granny. He did. I actually asked him if he was working with them, and he said, "Through you I am." My mother is now an initiate and minister in

MSIA. In fact, I had the honor of doing her ordination. I'm very proud. Thanks J-R.

After the shooting it took about 40 weeks to edit the film. To say it was really hard would be an understatement. There's a saying in the film business that your film will never be better than your dailies and will never be worse than the first cut. I found out just how true that is. I loved every one of the 91 hours that we shot on this film. Because of that, the first cut was about three hours and 45 minutes— about twice as long as a contemporary feature film. However, the editing process solidified the whole spiritual warrior story for me. It ended up being a challenge, and it was a lesson within a lesson: a lesson in life, and a lesson in filmmaking.

It turned out that we were making a movie about a lesson, to entertain and teach, and we were learning that lesson even as we were filming. I guess that makes sense. How can you teach something without learning it?

"I went out on my back porch at Miracielo, and I just opened the door and looked, and it (the snow) was like stacking up, so I reached down like this and grabbed a handful and went in and said, 'Zeus, have you ever been snowballed before or played snowman?' He said, 'Yeah, I think once.' I said, 'Here's another one—peeow.' So he jumped up and grabbed and tried to scrape it together to snowball me back. We've got a lot still—(there was) a little bit there as I left."

– John-Roger, D.S.S. (1991 PAT
Trainings at Windermere talking
about snow at Miracielo nearby)

CHAPTER 33

More About Making the Movies

WHEN I STARTED THINKING ABOUT making movies, I was hesitant, because I couldn't see myself spending much time apart from J-R. I knew J-R wouldn't be able to come along on all the shoots, but I could see that these movies could be important.

So I was really thankful for other staff members, who would be there to take care of J-R while I was away. J-R used to ask me what I thought about most things; he liked hearing my point of view. On one occasion, he asked if I was okay with new staff coming on board and living at Mandeville. I was okay with these guys and I always said I was. Anything for J-R. I was particularly glad I had agreed to their staying around. They have contributed tremendously in many ways and only J-R's staff truly understands what it means to be on staff. I related to it like being a Spartan—J-R's republican guard. We were all close and bound together as brothers.

J-R was always in support of me doing the movies and I've never had anybody be there for me like that. He let me not only do these movies but he also allowed me to go out in the world, publicizing and marketing and screening them. He once said to me that if one person got touched by the Spirit through the movie, then I'd done my job.

Also, I appreciated John Morton because of the work he had done and was doing. When I was looking at all the film footage, I realized that what J-R and John, Michael Feder, other staff at the time and the MSIA Presidency had all done in the early days of the PAT IV trips had laid the foundation for what I was doing with the movies. The revelation for me, as I watched the old 8mm footage, was seeing that everything was laid down by John-Roger and Staff. J-R encouraged me to go back to those places. I did just that in the movie. We did it again in Israel and with the work that John was doing along with J-R.

A while back I did an interview with David Sand that was published in MSIA's magazine, the *New Day Herald,* in November 2013. I'm including sections of that interview here as it gives other insights into the making of the movie and other things that I think are important parts of my self-discovery and self-revelation.

Adventures in the Un-Comfort Zone:
The Making of "Mystical Traveler: The Life and Times of Dr. John-Roger"
An Interview with Jsu Garcia
by David Sand

Jsu Garcia recently completed a 3-1/2 hour film biography of J-R that was shown at the 2013 Conference and in London. We caught up with him in Los Angeles in October, just after the month-long John-Roger travels in England, which Jsu and Nicholas Brown organized and facilitated together.

DS: When did you start work on the movie?

JG: Right now it's all a blur. In the winter of 2010, after we completed the film *The Wayshower,* I was inspired to start interviewing the "elders" in MSIA to get their stories down on film, while we still had the chance. Laurie Lerner came along and offered to produce it and got us a camera. It was great to have our own camera, because to rent one every time we wanted to interview someone would have cost a huge amount of money.

I was able to travel with that camera all over the world to do interviews. I didn't know what I was doing. I just knew I was going to gather "data." Thor, the cameraman on *The Wayshower*, jumped on board as the Director of Photography (DP). So I started getting interview after interview, asking everyone the same five questions: How did you meet J-R? What was it like? What's your favorite food? What would you like to tell J-R? During times of controversy, how did you get the strength inside of you to keep going?

DS: At what point did you realize you were doing a documentary?

JG: As soon as I rolled the camera, I realized I had something more than just interviews, that this was something bigger. We interviewed a lot of people who were there from the beginning, including some who have now passed over like Norma Howe, Joe Ann Cain, and Steve Ferrick. The rolling of the camera was like the Traveler and the Light overshadowing the microphone when we share at Living in Grace. People were intense—laughing, crying. It was really affecting me. I was watching testimonials from people who had sweat, blood, and tears in the Movement. These were the people who created the Movement and were part of it. I was being completely humbled. Just because I live with J-R, it doesn't mean anything—these guys are the *real* guys. When I heard their stories, I thought, "Wow, I'm sorry I judged you." We went to the original sources, the people who were actually there in the beginning, like Pauli Sanderson and Candace Semigran, and we got their stories in their own words.

I wanted a lot of points of view, so that no one person would alter or compromise my search. I didn't care if they were people who had left the Movement, because at the time they were involved and the

Movement was blossoming—just like in the Shakespeare lines that J-R quotes in *Mystical Traveler*:

> *There is a tide in the affairs of men*
> *Which, taken at the flood, leads on to fortune;*
> *Omitted, all the voyage of their life*
> *Is bound in shallows and in miseries.*
> *On such a full sea are we now afloat,*
> *And we must take the current when it serves,*
> *Or lose our ventures.*
> *(Julius Caesar Act 4, scene 3, 218–224)*

The first couple of editors started piecing the interviews together and asking for other footage to fill in the blanks. Those early editors, especially Matt Rondell, who edited *The Wayshower*, would ask questions like, "When was J-R born?" So we'd find footage that dealt with that, and pretty soon we'd have footage about his whole life. We found seminars where he talked about early parts of his life, like the car accident before he got the keys to the Traveler consciousness.

So we would pull this footage together and we had sections of different eras of J-R's life. We created a board that listed all these different eras and what we had on film. So I was floating around with a ton of material, 8mm film that had been scanned in the 1990s. The scanning quality was OK, but today the scanning quality is off the hook, so we needed to re-scan it. (We ended up scanning it at 2k and HD.)

I didn't know where it was going, however, John-Roger approved me to have access to the MSIA archives. I asked Barbara Wieland, the MSIA librarian and archivist, to help. Through J-R, I was approved to have access John-Roger's archives and Data base to have full range of resources for the making of the Mystical Traveler film. Phil Danza and Barbara Wieland were able to get me all excerpts and media for the editors upon request. Whatever we asked for from the archives, Barbara and her many volunteers would find it, and then when we needed the media, Phil Danza, the Don of Now Productions, along with Nir Livni, would organize and copy and capture the footage. Chuck Moore of NOW Productions would make 24-hour-a-day trips to the vault where all J-R media is stored to get whatever I needed. In the process, we even had a chance to upgrade the archival system because sometimes there were discrepancies between the database and what was in the vaults.

As the project grew bigger, the original editors needed to go on to other projects because I couldn't afford to keep paying them. We were floundering and I was desperate to find editors. You can't really edit this stuff without "getting" J-R. And that can take years. It's taken me 27 years to "get" J-R—like so many of us. So if you find an editor who's really good, how do you get him to a place where he understands enough to really do the editing? It would take a month to two months in the editing room just for an editor to "get" J-R. Finally, I found two great editors, Aaron Thacker, who did the graphics, and Josh Muscatine.

I called Lisa Day, who edited *Great Balls of Fire*, the Jerry Lee Lewis biopic, and told her I was in trouble. She told me to relax and just build the skeleton first, and then later on add all the different layers. That gave me a direction, and we started to build the bones of the movie—all the different phases of J-R's life— and find the footage that related to those. Then we could fill in the missing parts with photos, interviews, seminars, etc. Someone would talk about a person in an interview and I could call up Barbara, and ask her to get photos of that person, and suddenly I'd have hundreds of photos.

Without J-R, Zoe Golightly Lumiere—my #1 soldier, Laurie Lerner, John Morton, the MSIA Presidency, NOW Productions, and all the MSIA tithers (people who tithe to the church) and seeders out there, none of this would have been possible. I got to see how the money is spent and the amazing job that's being done in organizing, storing, and making all the media available. Anybody now can punch in what they're looking for and access media from any point in the history of J-R's work. I was able to look for footage not just by date or seminar number, but even by city, so we could recreate the history of MSIA in any area we wanted to.

We went through **100 terabytes** (that's a huge amount) of data. We narrowed that down to 190 gigabytes for the final film. So you can imagine how much information we went through. We were driving ourselves hard for two years. I don't know if the machine will ever run as hard again as we ran. I would say, "Phil, I need this NOW," and Phil would say, "Yeah, I'm on it." And it would get done by either Greg Fritz, Nir or Chuck. Mark Lurie was my right-hand man to keep the legal area lined up. Mark always had the attitude of, "I'm here for you. Whatever needs to get done, we'll do." I work for free. I don't have enough room to name everyone, however, NOW Productions (you know who you are) did a wonderful job to make J-R's film *Mystical Traveler*. What I get is the enjoyment of being part of history.

It was almost as though there was nothing I couldn't do, nothing I couldn't create—mostly because I would go to J-R. I would say, "J-R, I need to interview Larry King, can you put it in the Light?" The next thing I know, I have an appointment with Larry King. I'd say, "I need Tony Robbins, how am I going to get to him?" I ran into his lawyer the next day. I didn't go looking for stars, I went looking for the people J-R touched during his life.

We went through an incredible number of rolls of film to find stills. There is even film that was never developed, and we had to scan it to make contact sheets just to see what was there. And luckily, some of the early staff people filmed J-R with the old 8mm film cameras. The bulk of the expense of the movie was restoring all that 8mm footage. We had something like 55 hours of this stuff that had never been seen before. We made a big investment in restoring that 8mm film, thanks to John-Roger, Mark Lurie and all the ministers and initiates who have tithed and seeded. Your money made this movie. Thank you. And it looks gorgeous. There is also an old Laren Bright interview with J-R that was shot with a camera that was tethered to a recording device. That technology doesn't exist anymore, so we had to find someone who could scan that to get it into a format we could use.

DS: What was it like to look at all that early footage?

JG: The 8mm film really reveals a bygone era. It's like a time capsule. You see J-R in that context and of course you're in love with him. Just imagine having film of the time of Jesus, and seeing all the people with him. Now you can be a witness to something amazing that happened in our own time. In 100 years, we'll all be gone. Will the film be what people look at to know how it was? I don't know, it's digital, and who knows how long that will last? It might just disappear with the ones and the zeros. But the journey was amazing and I was investigating J-R like a reporter.

I learned to be a reporter, and then I learned how to be a scholar. I'd see a person in the background of a piece of film from 1970-something and wonder who it was….and then the editor would come to me all excited and say, "I think I found out who this person was… look at this!" And then we'd see them in the 8mm footage. We'd be looking at a piece of film and have no idea where it was from, and then we could enhance it and pan down and see a San Francisco newspaper under the table, and we'd know the location. We'd piece together times and locations according to J-R's hairstyles, or a car he was driving, or some other detail.

I don't know if there have been many people with as much archival footage of their lives as J-R. (Maybe George Harrison—I highly recommend the documentary of his life, *Living in the Material World*.) I was pushing everybody hard to get all this material together, especially NOW Productions and Barbara Wieland. Even with all that material, there are still gaps where there is no film. There are places where we've had incredible experiences, like in Egypt on some of the PAT IVs, where we don't have everything filmed, so we had to go to photographs or interviews.

We finally assembled a two-hour version. We used code-words for the different assemblies of the movie that came from the different Space Shuttle models. That first two-hour version that we finished in 2012 was the Endeavor. The final one would be Atlantis.

When we screened that two-hour version, we got feedback that there wasn't enough of the teachings of J-R. We had purposely held that back because we didn't want to preach or proselytize. But it didn't present a full picture of J-R's work, so we added 50 minutes of the teachings, in depth. Watching the movie, you can feel how it drops you into the depth of the energy. Aaron Thacker added amazing 3-D graphics to create 3-D versions of still photos, and to show the realms of consciousness, using a level of software technology that's used in sci-fi movies. It brought the picture to a whole new level.

In April of this year, we sat down with the editors and made a big board outlining Atlantis, the final version. We had a 3 hour and 50-minute movie. We tried to cut it down, and we were able to cut out some little things, but we realized that at 3 1/2 hours, that was the movie. No more adding and no more taking away. At that point we just had to decide on how to order what we had.

We divided it with haiku-like titles and little sections of 8mm film that we called chapter breaks. Rather than say something literal like "Utah—The Early Years," we would use short J-R quotes from the film, and that would "gestalt" that part of the movie in a way that sparked people's interest.

DS: What was J-R's role in the film?

JG: The best part of the movie was that I got to work with J-R. He's always involved—and he's involved in my head. And those are the best times that I have in making movies. I ask myself, "What would J-R think? What would he do here?" And I had every answer. Sometimes I'd be with him and I'd be depressed and he'd ask me what was wrong, and I'd say, "I'm not getting such-and-such for the movie." And the next day I'd get a call about it. J-R was always my oracle that I would complain to, and he would magically change something. It was like there were no obstacles in making this movie. J-R was like Ganesh—the remover of obstacles. If J-R didn't give me the green light, it just wouldn't happen.

All along, we were showing J-R clips of the movie to get his OK. I can't claim credit for any of this. I wanted to become a conduit so that Spirit and J-R would talk to me. In all my decisions, I would defer inwardly to the Spirit. All along I kept hearing J-R's voice echoing in my head, "Do it right. Do it right." And when I became aware and caught myself cutting corners, I can hear J-R in my head, "do it right," "the little things turn into the big things."

I knew I needed to stand strong in the conviction of what I needed to say, of what I know as J-R. The overall purpose of the movie is to show that J-R served the Lord. I just wanted to put J-R out there as honestly as I could. Then the secondary part is to make it artistic and cool. There was one time when one of the editors didn't think I'd care, but he edited a J-R quote. When I asked him to replay the original, I could see that it was changed so it made sense in the storyline of the movie, but it also changed the meaning. It reminded me of the way the teachings of Jesus were changed in the Bible. We changed it back to the original. It was very important to stay as true as I could to J-R.

I didn't feel that I had to be defensive about anything. I wanted to reveal everything. And I'd like other spiritual organizations to do documentaries like this about themselves so we can know more about them. I've had so many people come up to me and say, "I didn't know that about J-R," and they were spouses of people in the Movement. They would say, "I totally see J-R now. Before I was seeing him through my spouse's eyes. Now I get it." It was worth it because of that. J-R puts an energy with the movie, and you just get it. He saw it on July 5, 2013, and said the energy is on it, the Christ is working with it.

I'd love to take credit for all this, but I can't. I'm just the bus driver. It was J-R who opened the door, and everybody just participated and participated hard-core. Zoe, the line producer, was a killer worker. And Laurie Lerner, the producer, always came through when I needed anything.

DS: Were there things that changed in your perception of J-R through making the movie?

JG: He's a (expletive), he's intense. I knew him for 27 years, but most of that was after he gave the keys to John. And it was still a hard school. But I can imagine what it must have been like when he was in his thirties. When I moved in with him, I really had to learn how to move, but back then I'll bet you had to move twice as fast, or you'd get left behind. In making the movie, I saw how he was clearly following an inner direction.

I'm friends with J-R the funny guy. Up here at Mandeville we're with the J-R that's just hanging out, and that's the person I grew up with. But when he's lecturing, that's the other J-R. And I love all the old staff members who have come and gone. They're like rock stars. And the women who were around in the 70s and 80s—I would think, thank God I didn't know her then, I would have fallen in love with her and married her. And I was shocked by who actually married who. Most of all, I'm shocked by how much J-R has done. By the way, on a good day at Arrowhead during PATs, you literally fall in love with everyone. A higher love. I think it's a song.

I love the early days, the hippie time when everybody was sleeping on the ground, and working hard; when there were fires and floods up at Mandeville, everybody pitched in to help J-R. I learned that people follow J-R because of the love. That's what it was about.

That's the great lesson for me—you always come back to the love. I came to the conclusion that either J-R is who he says he is, or everybody's crazy—because he affected all those people. Maybe he could have brainwashed a few people—but all those people had the same inner experiences. I've interviewed probably 100 people, and the ripples and effects that J-R has had on people—it's incredible. I don't get that when I'm just up here at Mandeville with J-R. But then when I interviewed all these people, I got touched by how J-R touched them. And I could see all the ways that he touched them privately—not just through seminars—but he held everyone's hand as they went through their lives. I was moved by their being moved. The average interview was about 20 to 40 minutes, and it was like a mini-seminar inside of me. I interviewed Steve Ferrick just before he died, and when the interview ended, he said, "Well, J-R, my bags are packed." That really trips you out, to interview someone who knows he's going, and who knows he's going with the Traveler.

DS: Were there ways that you changed in the process of doing the movie?

JG: I think I got more impeccable. I became ruthless in my pursuit of making the film as good as it could be and to stay connected to my inner vision. With that focus, I think I sometimes became insensitive. When you're with J-R you learn to take on more and more, and I could forget that others are sensitive and not as thick-skinned as me. So, I'm trying to learn to be more delicate with people. But I learned there is a giant core inside me, and that's my true self, the part that J-R helped to grow. And it grew by listening inwardly and staying true. Part of the test for people in the Movement, and for everyone else, is whether we get thrown off our path by other people, or whether we stand up and fight the fight of what we need to get done, without hurting someone. I would just make it known that, "Hey, we're going to finish this movie." People would tell me it was impossible. And I would tell them the possibilities, which was me seeing from the higher levels. Sometimes it felt like I was leading them on because I was trying to explain to them something I was seeing in the Spirit. But when my lower self (mental, causal, astral) would kick in, I would succumb to the doubts and fears that reside on those levels. But then I'd go back to SEs or I would go to sleep and travel. In the morning, I would confirm with J-R that I was still on track and he would nod yes. And that's all I needed. I would tell the gang what we were going to do, and then I'd leave the room and go, "Oh my God, what are we going to do?" But that was my job to do, not theirs. My job was to go cry to J-R and go, "Please, you've got to do something. I think I've bitten off more than I can chew." Then he would help me see it though by bypassing the mind straight into Spirit. I learned that it's the Spirit that gets it done and it's important to articulate the spirit in the minds for folks and at the same time hold in my integrity. As J-R says, "Having the courage to go with the truth as you know it, as a heartfelt response with care and consideration for others."

We had plenty of time, and plenty of time for disaster. And at the end we got to mix the movie at Warner Bros. with Danetracks and Dane Davis who did sound design for "The Matrix." These were people who aren't in the Movement who love J-R, who have met him and who like what he has to say. As we were mixing the movie you could see how J-R's seminars would make these people think. Some of them are believers, some are atheists…it doesn't matter. In the midst of making a movie we were having discussions about philosophy and spirituality. So, working with J-R, or doing a movie with J-R, is always fun, even though I was working so much. I found that it's not about what we all think about but that we get together and create, the fusion and synergy. It was a demonstration of "When two or more are gathered there he is."

It was hard but it was worth it when we saw the result at the screening on July 5. When I looked out in the audience and saw that full house, with J-R there, the pain was all gone. We flew, like the Wright Brothers. While you're making the movie, as soon as you think about it you get overwhelmed and it's over. So what I got out of making this movie was a high-speed line, with high bandwidth, in my connection to the strength and knowledge of what is clear and not clear inside of me. Sometimes it rubs people wrong because I'm not going to make a move until J-R says I can make a move.

So that brings us to right now. A lot of people want it on DVD, so we're working on the Blu-Ray. J-R said we're like Johnny Appleseed, just planting seeds to make the teachings available. If I could keep making movies about J-R I'd love it. We're showing the film at the film festival in Mar de Plata, Argentina.

(We're showing the 2-hour version.) I want to interview more people, and there will be more on the Blu-Ray. I don't want to change the movie, but I can add bonus features to the DVD.

You just don't know who's going to be digging J-R. So we're getting subtitles in a lot of languages so people can see it all over the world—Polish, Japanese, Chinese, Farsi, Hebrew, Russian, Spanish, French, Arabic, Bulgarian. Some people from Abu Dhabi came to the London screening. They didn't understand all the language but they got J-R. So now we're doing Arabic subtitles. I meet people from different cultures and send them the movie and ask them what they think. I met these Chinese women at the Four Seasons in London and asked them to look at the movie and could they check that the Chinese subtitles are good. They probably thought I was crazy, but they ended up loving it.

And I want to do more screenings. We do a J-R seminar marathon, and then do the movie, and we're thoroughly doused in J-R. I want to do screenings in San Francisco and South America.

DS: What's your hope for the movie?

JG: I've given up the idea of trying to make money on the movie. If that was the goal I'd be fired, and luckily J-R did not require it. J-R told me that sometimes the movie is for that one person at that one time. There was this one man in London who rode the bus all the way from Scotland to see the movie, and he got on the bus right after it was over to go back to Edinburgh. I said, "The movie is for that guy." He was so into the movie, and as he left he said it was totally worth the trip. Inside I was like "Yeeeeeahhhhh!!!" That's what you make the movie for—people like that. I'm hoping we can touch people like that. We can be jaded here in California because we have so much of this stuff. But you can show this to someone who's thirsting for it and they go, "Oh my God."

People here say, "I've taken Insight, thank you." Well how about taking it again? Sometimes you have to get out of your comfort zone. I showed the movie to one famous guy, a friend of Oprah, and he said, "J-R gave me the answer that I needed for the book I'm writing. Thank you." That's all I need to hear. I don't need him to join

MSIA. That's what J-R was always about—what key can he give that one person that would make that person go out and change himself, or change the world?

As I look back on it all, I'm sometimes amazed about how many layers and levels that movie works on, both in what it communicates to audiences and how working on it molded me.

Man: Do you like to fall asleep watching TV?

J-R: No, I really don't. No, because I tend to incorporate what I'm watching on TV in my dreams. They spook the shit out of me. And, uh, Zeus, you know, whatever happened that day, he's going to…I'm going to hear about it tomorrow. "I had this neat dream last night!" He's going to tell me, and I'm going to say, "Was there also this, this, this?" He goes, "Yeah." I say, "That was in the movie." "Yeah. But it's, you know, it's really neat."

– JOHN-ROGER, D.S.S. (1991 PAT
TRAININGS AT WINDERMERE RANCH)

CHAPTER 34

What Spirit Wants, Spirit Gets (or Things Can Get Really Tense)

LIVING WITH A SPIRITUAL WARRIOR is like God has shined a light on you, and you can't go wrong. It's also similar to being given the job of taking care of a child: You're in protective mode. It's really not hard work to be in that protective state of awareness, to be on heightened alert. Awareness, to me, is what it's about. You have to be careful about what you say, what you do. You're always watchful. You're more in a defensive state about others. You're just watching this child, which is probably what God does for us.

Creating the movie *Spiritual Warriors* was like that for me, too. The movie was like my child. I took care of it, which required a lot of responsibility.

During pre-production for the film *Spiritual Warriors*, J-R and I were invited to dinner at Katherine and Frank Price's home with Jan Shepherd, an annual event. As with most of J-R's private dinners, I was also present as the "fly on the wall." Frank was very much into DNA testing and his quest to fill in his ancestry's family tree. He offered to test my and J-R's DNA by swabbing our saliva into a vial, and sent it off to a lab in Oxford, UK. A few weeks later, Jan called to relay the message that J-R and I both originate back to the

Gilgamesh time period. I did my homework and learned that he was a warrior king depicted in statues and paintings holding lions by the tail. Then J-R told me Gilgamesh was a Traveler. Very cool! That is why I named our LLC after Gilgamesh.

Managing money was part of the responsibility. And sometimes it didn't happen the way I wanted it to. So I learned the hard way that sometimes when things weren't going my way it was because I wasn't seeing the perfect way that Spirit had put in front of my face.

This was brought home to me when we were shooting a scene in which I wanted to depict the soul. I had wondered how we could represent the soul visually, other than just a floating ghost, which would have no emotional quality to it.

The scene was very similar to one in the film *Contact*, where Jodie Foster is looking at her father and reconciling things between the two of them (which was really within her). In our scene, I had decided that one way to depict the soul was to use an infant. So I was reconciling things with this infant, which to me was like a Christ figure or myself. The intention was to do it in such a way that the love between me and the baby was emanating from the screen, and the audience would be hit with it and blissed out.

So, we found the infant we wanted for the scene and we were shooting. For a number of reasons, it cost a lot of money to do that one-day shoot, and that was on my mind as I was striving to get the feeling I wanted. I was able to relax a little because John-Roger was there and keeping an eye on the whole thing.

The baby seemed to be okay and, mechanically, we did everything we needed to do. But it didn't feel like the magic was there.

We finished and the parents took their baby home. Then, about a half-hour after they left, we found out that the camera had malfunctioned and the scene that we had spent two hours working on had not been recorded. We were in a pickle.

We immediately located another baby and had the mother bring the child to us. But that baby did not want to have anything to do with me. It was crying and fussing. I saw disaster looming in front of me.

At a loss for what to do next, I basically knelt down to my teacher, J-R, and asked for help. I told him this was just crazy and I didn't know how to get what I wanted to happen. With barely a pause, J-R told me that Spirit didn't want to do what I wanted to do, It wanted to do what It wanted to do. He advised me to find out what It wanted to do.

I asked what Spirit wanted to do and I told J-R that whatever it was, I'd do it.

Now, it just so happened that I had invited my friend Michael Hayes and his son Danny to the set that day. Danny was eight and it was his birthday. He's a very loving kid. They arrived about the time I was talking to J-R and Danny came running into my arms and hugged me. He was just flying high.

J-R watched all of this and, while Danny was hugging me, J-R asked why I didn't use Danny. In that moment I realized that Danny was doing just what I needed: he was displaying love. I got it!

The director saw it and asked if we could do that again, with the same authenticity and genuineness. I didn't know he could do it, so we offered to give him a birthday gift if he could do that again. He did every take perfectly. The gifts kept on coming.

I learned that lesson, to do what Spirit wants, not what I want. And that Spirit often will present what it wants in a very natural and spontaneous way. That doesn't mean give up my life or anything like that. It was just a demonstration of how cooperating with Spirit gave me way more than what I had hoped for.

In hindsight, I can remember countless times when something just showed up and J-R would go with it, regardless of whether it was what he had had in mind or not. What a great lesson.

Voice: *"Can we touch Jesus?"*

J-R: *"Yeah, you can touch Zeus, he likes it. (Laughter) And we're, we're one of the few organizations that has two Jesus's in 'em. You know the one that travels with me, and is my personal clown and one that's down at the Church headquarters who keeps track of all of the money. And I don't think we're in probably better hands, really."*

– John-Roger, D.S.S. (Q&A, 1991,
Unitarian Church, Santa Barbara)

CHAPTER 35

Techniques for Getting Through Life

IN WORKING WITH J-R, I was shown a bunch of techniques that really helped me get through the challenging times—or times that weren't even that challenging but added some juice to the day. I'm sharing some of them here with you. They're all part of the mystery school teachings, as far as I'm concerned.

JOURNALS

For me, journal writing and praying have become core activities in my life. I don't know how many journals I've filled but I can say that I had so many at one time that I had to burn some and throw some away. I believe some of it was too karma-ridden, and I needed to get rid of them. I don't think there's any special way to do journaling; just write what seems important in each day.

PRAYING

I recall countless instances where I really prayed to receive messages. Several times it actually worked and I actually got what I was hoping to learn. I started to track and found my requests were fulfilled in about six months to twelve months. For example, I would decide I wanted to be working in an acting job. Then I would pray, and I would have a dream that I was in that kind of situation. Then, six months to a year later, it would come to pass.

TRACKING

One of the really valuable things from the Doctor of Spiritual Science course that I took to a really deep place inside was the practice of tracking the things in my life that I wanted to pay attention to. Things like how many hours a night I slept, or how much water I was drinking, or important areas of life where I was spending my time. I found that what I thought I was doing did not match the reality of what I was actually doing when I tracked. Writing things down is a way for people to really prove to themselves what they have done because memory is silent, faint, and often does not match the reality of life.

When I try to pull into my consciousness those experiences that I had—which is really another way of God talking to me—I found that whether those things actually happened or not, they could become very vague if I didn't write them down and track them. Plus, tracking is a great way to compare what I thought I remembered and what I actually tracked at the time.

FREE-FORM WRITING

Living with a spiritual warrior, I have found that free-form writing has worked very well for me. I have found it especially helpful during times when I have had pain and anger or when I have been working through an issue that was boiling inside of me. That can be the best time to do free-form writing. And sometimes it's very good to do that before something builds up. It's good to just nip it in the bud.

Rather than describe the process here, I will refer you to J-R's book, *Spiritual Warrior; The Art of Spiritual Living* or in one of the books in the 3-volume set, *Fulfilling Your Spiritual Promise*. Both provide an in-depth explanation and instructions of the process. You can also get the information in audio format on one of the CDs (or MP3s) in a package offered by MSIA called the *Living in Grace* packet. *Spiritual Warrior* is also available to download as an audiobook on Audible.com.

SEEDING

Seeding is a process by which you can energize a vision of what you want by "planting a seed" for it with God, with your source. The seed is planted and fertilized with a donation to whatever you consider to be the source of your spiritual teachings. For me, obviously, that's J-R.

You can pick any amount you feel is right—could be a penny, could be $100 or more. And you ask the Lord to deliver this to you if it's for the highest good. You could seed for a car. If you wanted to seed for a $30,000 car, you could go inside and seed $30 or $300—or 50¢ for that matter. So, from time to time I would seed for a really big blockbuster movie, a great career, whatever. Seeding actually resulted in opportunities to work with Mel Gibson in one movie and with Arnold Schwarzenegger in another.

Seeding has worked to bring me a lot of things. But along the way, I learned that it works best when you seed for what's for your highest good. I wasted a lot of time seeding for things like being in a movie with Richard Gere and Julia Roberts. But with those, I wasn't really asking for God to give me the movie that It thought was good for me, I was asking for what I wanted, not for the highest good.

In fact, when I learned to give it up to God, I can truly say, I couldn't have designed my career any better than God did. God gave me good roles with great actors and stars. It was unbelievable, the amount of work I got to do when I really did let it go. God's design was better than the design of my imagination.

Seeing that was when I realized I had been limited in my thinking. That's when I also realized we're all limited. But when I tap into the source, to God, and I build something, and I act in something, or I create with the Divine watching me, I outdo my limited mind, my limited emotion, and I expand.

Where I love to live is outside the box. I think that's where geniuses are, and I think all the geniuses are connected with the Divine and the creative source whether they recognize it as that or not.

You can learn more about the specifics of seeding from MSIA on their website, www.msia.org/seeding-in-msia.

Working with Dreams

I've had many experiences in dreams. I love to dream. John-Roger very much encourages people to write down and track their dreams and their experiences with spiritual exercises (SEs). It gives us an external feedback mechanism and can make the experiences more tangible.

That idea was very much ingrained into me when I did the PTS Doctor of Spiritual Science (D.S.S.) program.

In the early 1980s, before I moved in with J-R, I would write things mostly related to my acting classes and my process with that in my journals. So, when I moved in with J-R, writing and tracking was second nature. It was easy to transfer the habit of writing for acting to recording my dreams and spiritual experiences, it made them more real and it strengthen my tracking abilities.

GETTING NEUTRAL

As an actor, I learned a kind of Taoist way of working that really applied to many things in the world. I found that what I chased would retreat from me and when I appeared disinterested and detached, things would come toward me.

An actor's job is to get the job, to really go after it. That's a game that I eventually had to stop playing. What worked was to pretend that I didn't want it. Maybe a better way of saying that was that I had to release my attachment to getting a particular role. I really, truly, had to be neutral, or it would kill me.

It was the same thing with dating; when I really wanted a girlfriend, I could not get a date. But when I was totally taking care of myself and was into whatever I was doing, along would come the opportunities for relationships with the ladies, and they were interested in me. But *trying* to be interesting and *trying* to get a girl or an acting job that way just didn't work. In acting class, I learned, "Be interested, don't try to be interesting." The Tao or in the "Zone" is where I focused on the moment. J-R taught me to use the Tao in many things. The ability to want it but not chase it.

For me, that is the case with pretty much anything I want in life. When I go for it, if it's meant for me to have, I'll have it. So, pushing for it doesn't do much. It's more a matter of asking myself why I want those things, getting clear that I really want them, and then relaxing and letting them come in.

It's not just about the American dream: I can say for sure those things in our culture that we idealize sometimes are not for the highest good. Here is a constant affirmation I tell myself: *I want to live my life and achieve those things that I've always wanted.*

Living my life and achieving the things I want are not exclusive of each other. However, there's only so much energy I have to put on things, otherwise I would be cheating myself. Creating a family and a career and all those things people want in life requires a great deal of energy and it's impossible to give 100% of your energy to each one of those things. So I've found you have to choose what you really want and put your energy and focus into those.

There are many other techniques I learned from J-R that you can find out more about through his writings and seminars on the MSIA website, www.msia.org.

"Self-love, my liege, is not so vile a sin, as self-neglecting."

– WILLIAM SHAKESPEARE *(HENRY V)*

John-Roger: *"When I was teaching Zeus how to ride a horse and he didn't do what I want, I took the reins and whipped him. Do you ride, Zeus?"*

Zeus: *"Yeah."*

J-R: *"Didn't I, Ginger? Virginia? Didn't I, Jack? Who else saw me? Connemara saw me. Is he a better rider now than he was then? Are you a better rider now than you were then?"*

Zeus: *"Yeah, a lot better.*

J-R: *"Did the whipping help you?"*

Zeus: *"Yeah. I think it whipped the ego thing out of there."*

J-R: *"Not him. He's a hell of a good rider. But he thought he was in some movie we weren't shooting."*

– John-Roger, D.S.S. (PAT Church house seminar)

CHAPTER 36

Schools and Mystery Schools

I WAS A HIGH SCHOOL dropout. So, when I started to live and work with J-R, he encouraged me (and you haven't been encouraged until you've been encouraged by J-R) to get my G.E.D. as a completion. I decided to take his advice and I'm really glad I did.

I studied for the exam, and I actually got better grades than if had I stayed in high school, because when I was in my teens, I was sort of lost. I was certainly not motivated to study stuff that did not seem relevant to me at the time. So when I came back to the high school studies after gaining life experience, I found the material a lot more meaningful, I became engaged, and I did well on the test.

But back in the day, I left high school and went right into acting. At that point, I might not have been in high school, but I was definitely a student. Acting classes challenged me in different ways than high school classes, but they were no walk in the park.

I'm currently 53 years old. I've had an acting career and been in over 51 films—a lot of them pretty major. I also directed three feature films with John-Roger. Despite all that, at some point I realized the main reason I came down to this Earth, at this particular time, in this dispensation, was for me to be in mystery schools and to meet the Sound Current Master, John-Roger. To have him connect me to the Sound Current and return into the heart of God and to serve.

During a Master of Spiritual Science (M.S.S.) class at Peace Theological Seminary and College of Philosophy (PTS), I realized I was doing just that. I eventually graduated from their Doctorate of Spiritual Science (D.S.S.) program. While I received my certificate of completion in living the spiritual principles, which was an amazing experience, I also found living with the spiritual warrior really deepened my education. In fact, my practical treatise, my final paper for the doctorate program, was titled, "Living with a Spiritual Warrior: A look at living with J-R and my Inner Spiritual Warrior." I also graduated from the University of Santa Monica (USM) and received my certificate of completion, another step in my quest for self- (and Self-) awareness. This "getting an education" was something J-R continually encouraged me to do.

I never went to a regular college and I don't really have a lot of use for degrees. I know they're meaningful for some people, and I don't mean to minimize their value. But too often I've seen people with degrees who couldn't do what the paper implied they could. So I subscribe to John-Roger's idea of the "degree of doing." That is, I respect people for their ability to accomplish, not for having a piece of paper.

So, for me, I graduated from what some people call the School of Hard Knocks. I prefer to think of it as the school of life, or, better yet, the School of John-Roger.

What I've observed is that with the Doctorate in Spiritual Science degree and the Masters in Spiritual Psychology from USM, you don't get the paper until you can demonstrate you can do what it says you can do. When something would come up in my life, John-Roger often asked me if I wanted the information or the experience. In certain ways the information is good for the intellect. But you can be persuaded to many different points of view based on information.

You can't be argued out of your experience; it can't be negated. If you keep telling me that if I go into the kitchen and cook something I may get burned, I would have the information, but I wouldn't know the implications of that. If I'm cooking in the kitchen and I get burned one time, I'll completely understand your warning and I'll never do it again. No matter what you tell me, you can't take away my having been burned such that I'll intentionally do it again.

Spiritual intelligence is also experiential. It's called wisdom. Working with J-R is pure experiential learning.

"*The willingness to do gives the ability to do, and by God that's the truth, but you can't fake it. The willingness to go out there and clean shit out of stables. They asked last night, 'How many want to go do stables,' maybe it was the night before. Zeus raised his hand and said, 'I want to do it,' and some of the others, Jim and some of the others and a girl that was in here said, 'I want to do it.' They went out and had more fun. It was what I hear—somebody said, 'with all this horse shit, there's bound to be a pony some place.' They got all through, and guess who wants to be chosen to go do it again? Same ones. Why? Because they made fun out of it.*"

– JOHN-ROGER, D.S.S., AT A PAT
TRAINING AT WINDERMERE

CHAPTER 37

About Relationships & Loving

WHEN I WAS RESEARCHING THIS book and listening through countless hours of seminars, I realized how annoying I could be. Especially while videotaping J-R, because I was always bugging him to try to get him to tell me things I wanted to know that he didn't want to talk about. Despite how annoying I could be, for me, J-R's bottom line message always was love. Love transcends everything, and with that you get soul transcendence.

In the last month or so of J-R's life, I experienced intense loving for him. I found myself asking why I couldn't love everyone like I loved J-R. I came to learn that loving J-R was spiritual and one of my jobs was learning to find a way to experience that level of loving with everyone. It's almost like I put J-R around each person I meet so I have that relationship with them.

I really do work to share my loving. Most of the time it's easier to share it with my fiancé, Nicole. But as I observed J-R do, I am learning to be loving with anyone and everyone. It's a pure form of loving—nothing romantic or sexual. It's so pure, that it instantly grants the recipient freedom. Of course, the physical body misrepresents that. But, to paraphrase J-R, if anyone asks what Zeus is doing, it's always accurate to say he's working on his bad habits.

The other day, I was listening to a J-R seminar and he mentioned a poem about a man named Abou Ben Adhem, who J-R said was a Traveler. J-R said that this poem was his favorite.

Abou Ben Adhem
By Leigh Hunt
Abou Ben Adhem (may his tribe increase!)
Awoke one night from a deep dream of peace,
And saw, within the moonlight in his room,
Making it rich, and like a lily in bloom,
An angel writing in a book of gold:—

Exceeding peace had made Ben Adhem bold,
And to the presence in the room he said,
"What writest thou?"—The vision raised its head,
And with a look made of all sweet accord,
Answered, "The names of those who love the Lord."

"And is mine one?" said Abou. "Nay, not so,"
Replied the angel. Abou spoke more low,
But cheerly still, and said, "I pray thee, then,
Write me as one that loves his fellow men."

The angel wrote, and vanished. The next night
It came again with a great wakening light,
And showed the names whom love of God had blest
And lo! Ben Adhem's name led all the rest.

I have to say that I think that also describes J-R.

"But thy eternal summer shall not fade,
Nor lose possession of that fair thou ow'st,
Nor shall death brag thou wander'st in his shade,
When in eternal lines to time thou grow'st,
So long as men can breathe, or eyes can see,
So long lives this, and this gives life to thee."

– WILLIAM SHAKESPEARE (SONNET 18: SHALL
I COMPARE THEE TO A SUMMER'S DAY?)

"I was raised by hookers and thieves and I learned to love."

– JESUS GARCIA, D.S.S.

CHAPTER 38

In Life, All Good Things Come to an End

I EXPERIENCED TWO WORLDS WITH J-R.

In one, we'd watch his old seminars together and feel a joy of the loving and Spirit's majesty. It was really interesting because I'd see him wearing a tie or a watch on the video and that would trigger me back to those times when, after the seminar, we would be driving for hours as J-R worked to clear himself from all the garbage he picked during the seminar.

Often, we even had to go to all sorts of practitioners throughout the night, most of whom worked with energetic levels. J-R once told me that a Traveler can't heal himself. They need to go to someone who can identify the problem and verbalize it. J-R once said, "Remember, if you can name something you have dominion over it." But, as the Traveler, when it affected him, he was not permitted to name it. He needed someone outside himself reflecting back to him the conditions that were present in him. Once they identified it, then J-R could work with them to clear it.

This "picking up stuff" was the reason why J-R always had staff around him. They could act as a buffer for him, so if something was coming at him and we could take it on, then, later, he could clear us, where he might not be able to clear himself. So J-R was always clearing the weakest link in the staff.

In the other world, which was the present, J-R's body was preparing for transition. I often checked with J-R to make sure he was okay to keep going until the wheels fell off. He always said, "sure", so we did. We went until the wheels fell off.

But until that would happen, there were plenty of hard and long nights of trying to heal and help J-R, and we would have to call for Michael Hayes or Dr. Ed Wagner for assistance.

This pattern of good days and bad days seemed to be the final stage of training the staff and me to become hard-core spiritual warriors. The qualities of endurance and perseverance were being strengthened and tested. They were tough times but filled with loving for J-R.

Of course, you know the rest.

For me, all I can say is, God bless you, J-R. It's been a helluva ride.

"Energy and persistence conquer all things."

– BENJAMIN FRANKLIN

"You don't have to tap into the memory of something, but you tap into the energy of it."

– JESUS GARCIA, D.S.S.

Epilogue

J-R OFTEN SAID THAT HE would check things out for a period of about two years before he would thoroughly understand them. Interestingly, we just observed the two-year anniversary of J-R's passing and, to be honest, I feel like I am emerging from a long, dark tunnel.

I consciously know now that I came down here to connect to J-R and get initiated into the Sound Current and return home to the heart of God.

At 16 years old, in the Coconut Grove neighborhood of Miami, Florida, I was playing the guitar and singing up to the sky, wishing to feel what true love was. Over time, seeking and questing on my new spiritual path, I often found myself agonizing in complete despair about not knowing what was to come. Although I didn't know it at the time, I was praying to find my teacher, to find John-Roger. Decades later, I would return to Coconut Grove with J-R while I was on staff doing the work of the Traveler. I remember looking over the city from the balcony of a hotel, appreciating that connection after so many years, and attuning to the Light columns that J-R had left behind not too far away at Rama Fox's house, when she hosted home seminars in the '70s. I felt that I had come full circle and my prayer had been answered. And today, I continue that work to the best of my ability.

I recently graduated from the University of Santa Monica, which was a two-year course in Spiritual Psychology. My 2nd-year project was this book, *The Love of a Master*, which I am just now completing.

I've made it my personal ministry to start traveling and sharing what I call the J-R Marathons: eight one-hour J-R seminars in a row and *The Mystical Traveler* movie, the documentary of J-R's life and times. I am also enjoying the inner connections I have with J-R during my Spiritual Counseling sessions with others. Doing this is what is in my heart and my bliss. I find that J-R rides with me on my right side through all these activities and in all these places. I'm finding that folks are wanting to screen *The Wayshower* and *Spiritual Warriors* films. Like Joseph Campbell says, "Follow your bliss and doors will open."

After John-Roger's passing, I began to notice a lot more spiritual experiences that would alter my consciousness. I found myself aware of the many layers in the multi-dimensional realms from the astral, causal, mental, etheric, and soul levels, and above. And I became particularly aware of the traps in the mental and in the causal realms when grieving. I guess there's nothing to really report except telling the story is a very therapeutic way for me to objectify it so I can look at it and acknowledge myself.

As a friend once told me, I needed to cry my tears. I am aware of the different levels of consciousness where the grieving was taking place. This is an interesting experience that allows me to constantly check and verify that while John-Roger physically isn't here, the fact is, he's inside. I am now having those experiences. J-R always said the experiential learning is the key, and I am learning from my experiences.

I nurtured those experiences with J-R when he was alive; taking care of him, through the making of the movies, working with him. I am realizing now that it was really all about becoming strong for when it's time to leave the body. I saw him do it; he did it with style, grace and ease. But for 26 years, I saw J-R go in and out and come back. Those were the experiences I saw.

The key is the Christ. J-R demonstrated the purest love I have ever seen or ever experienced in my lifetime. I am very clear inside of me that I'll never be able to get over his passing. I don't think it's true that a person needs to get over the loss of a loved one. One needs to get *into* it, inside of it. Time heals the emotional part to some extent. But the reality is that there is something missing. It's like those stories where someone loses an arm or a leg and they sometimes still sense the shadow of the "phantom" limb.

I feel J-R constantly around me, even in the physical, and I want to lean over and ask him a question or I want to pick up the phone and give him a call. I guess the thing is that I'm not in a hurry to lose that connection—in fact I now think there's something beautiful about grieving.

It is two years now and I have experienced the Bhandara, the celebration of the passing of J-R, October 22 at 2:49 AM. After two years, there are things being revealed in my consciousness. The loss of J-R physically has really been a catalyst for me to go forward to continue his work. If I could wish anything, I would wish that you, in reading this book, are inspired to seek to connect to the Sound Current and ride back home to the Heart of God while serving your fellow brothers and sisters.

But, ultimately, nothing's changed inside. The connection and the spiritual wisdom and talent I learned from J-R are better than ever.

I realize he left with us the secret and it's what Jesus has said: "The miracles of Jesus were not really miracles in the sense that they were unrepeatable. He said, 'He who believes in me will also do the works that I do; and greater works than these will he do because I

go to the Father.' (John 14:12). Jesus promised this to us. He made us heirs to his kingdom of Light—not the worlds of illusion, but the pure realms of the Spirit. Each one of us will inherit the throne if we follow the Light and the way of the Light, which is the Holy Spirit.'
– Excerpt from John-Roger, *Fulfilling Your Spiritual Promise.*

J-R, you are as alive as ever inside of me. I love you. "For where two or three are gathered together in my name, there am I in the midst of them." (King James Bible, Matthew 18:20).

That's really the bottom line: In the end, J-R left me his love… the love of a Master. And I will continue his work and share the love with myself and others. We can indeed do what J-R did and even greater, because J-R went to the Father.

>   – Jesus Garcia, D.S.S.
>   October 22, 2016
>   Los Angeles, CA

Afterword

I WROTE THIS ARTICLE A few months after the manuscript of the book was complete. I wanted to share it here because it encapsulates some of my experiences not covered in the book.

FOLLOWING IN THE FOOTSTEPS OF A MASTER
J-R Marathon and Mystical Traveler Screenings in Europe, 2017

I went through an intense period of grieving after John-Roger died. There was no manual that could prepare me for this. The dilemma for me has been how to stay in this energy that I'd been experiencing with him for 26 years. But J-R did leave a lot of himself behind in people and places he visited while he was on the planet. He planted Light columns all over. He said we're all conductors of divine energy, so I get lit up by the same energy that J-R left in those places.

So much of my life was traveling alongside J-R and our crew, and going in and out of airports. So as soon as I go to the airport I touch into that energy, and I'm back in the spiritual flow that I experienced with J-R. When I first hooked up with him in 1988, he told me if I stayed with him long enough he'd change my DNA. When I visit these countries where J-R traveled, I'm back doing staff work, and it releases something inside me, in my physical body and also in levels above. I touch into the transformation that he created in me in my DNA.

My ordination and all of my initiations except for one took place on the road—Syria, England, Russia, Lake Tahoe and Las Vegas (which J-R loved). So now I'm traveling the world, meeting other initiates and ministers, doing counseling and showing the Mystical Traveler movie and J-R seminars. I've been traveling on my own dime to distant countries where the staff has been unable to go, to initiate people who otherwise would have had to wait a long time for their initiation. These people are so grateful for the opportunity.

My recent trip was to England, Bulgaria and Switzerland. Being on the road again reinvigorated my relationship with J-R, and I planted Light columns to reinforce what we put there many years ago. It's not just about getting to an airport, into a taxi, etc. It's like walking where Jesus walked when we were in Israel. It's following the footsteps of a Master.

For many years I had dreams of flying in a plane that I couldn't land. I often have them before I travel. When I would ask J-R he used to say that I was soul traveling. I've always loved traveling both in the Spirit and physically, and I'm learning to trust that the physical will pay for itself. In May 2017, I'll begin a tour of Central and South America. I'll be celebrating J-R's birthday with all-day J-R seminars and the Mystical Traveler movie on September 24 at the new location of the Mystic Journey bookstore in Venice, CA, where J-R did book signings, and I'll be introducing my new book, *The Love of a Master*.

However, my last Europe trip started in London where I had ten days to prepare for the J-R Marathon and *Mystical Traveler* screening. Nathalie Franks and Andrew John Clark were amazing servant-leaders. I was able to streamline the process of presenting the movie, and I bought a nice projector so I can now show videos even in an unequipped room. Thank you J-R. I had the ability to stay for a couple of days at a minister's home and then in Airbnb rentals so I was able to travel on the cheap.

On February 11, 2017, about 27 people showed up to the J-R Marathon, with ten hours of J-R seminars and the *Mystical Traveler* movie at the Columbia Hotel where J-R and John had been doing seminars since the '80s. I used a SIM card in my phone to create a hotspot so I could upload video to Facebook Live anywhere I traveled. Very cool.

London was a place for me to really get creative and heal. I found myself reframing and rewriting a lot of the memories of J-R. It became more about finding the subtle energy that he left behind on this planet through Light columns. I tried to go wherever he went to recharge and align with what J-R left there for us to walk into. As I realized this, I found myself having a much better time, and it overcame a lot of my sadness. I felt like I had the space to breathe.

I've had many dreams where I cry in the dream, and I wake up crying in this physical world. I remember J-R saying, "Better to clear the karma there in the Spirit than down here." It was great running into people and telling stories about how they met J-R. New people came and it was an experience of, "when two or more are gathered in my name there I am also." I felt J-R's energy there. I recalled the statement, "You too can do you what I do and even greater because I go to the father." J-R has gone to the father. I'm living my ideal scene in being able to contact the energy and then transmit it to other people.

Bulgaria was uncharted territory for me. John has been there many times and I had heard that J-R traveled through there in 1986 or 1987. Once again I thought, "Here I am in the energy, following not as a memory but walking through the light columns and the energy that J-R has left here."

Hristina and Theodora and other MSIA ministers greeted me and we started with a ministers meeting. Some of these people had never met J-R and yet they carry his energy. For someone like me who had the benefit of so much physical contact with J-R, it puts you in your place to come across people like this.

When we showed the movie *Mystical Traveler*, 80 people attended. They clapped and laughed and loved; some were crying. The way had been prepared. Many of them had taken Insight and I found out that a leader of the Great White Brotherhood, **Master Beinsa Douno,** lived in Bulgaria. I have subtitles built into the Mystical Traveler movie so it can be shown all over the world, and one of the languages is Bulgarian.

Then I was off to Thessaloniki, Greece, driving four hours there and back to initiate someone who had been waiting patiently for an initiator to come to this part of the country. I thoroughly loved it. I thought I would be willing to spend all the money in the world to be able to help someone get connected to J-R and John and the Sound Current; and my thoughts wandered off to how it would feel if I was far away from Los Angeles and all the MSIA initiates and organizations there, and some American dude came all the way to connect with another loved one, another soul for the Travelers and God. It blows my mind that to me this is my ministry, and it hasn't changed much since J-R was alive.

I went from Bulgaria to Switzerland and again there was the same theme of following the energy that J-R has left. It's for us to soak in and activate the Conductor of divine energy inside us into the world and connect with each other.

We had a great screening with the ministers and friends from the area there in Neuchâtel, Switzerland. Veronique Sandoz and friends, along with many friends of MSIA minister Robert Waterman, all shared the loving for John-Roger at the Swiss premiere of the *Mystical Traveler* film. While Switzerland is a combination of German, Italian, and French, Neuchâtel is very French and exquisitely beautiful. By grace and through friends, Nicole and I were gifted a train trip around this magnificent country.

While we were doing all that, I was having massive flashbacks, memories of being there with J-R with John and family, and then J-R and me by ourselves covering the same ground. In 1997, J-R was trying to get me to learn how to see etheric temples that were in the area. I went to the hotel where we stayed in Zermatt for lunch with our friends. There were clear skies and clouds that rode in over the mountains, and I remembered how J-R would say that UFOs sometimes hide behind the clouds and that the etheric temples were right on the mountain peaks. He taught me to look obliquely, not directly, to see into other dimensions. If you stare right at it, you miss it. It felt like J-R was on the trip so we called the trip "The Etheric Temple Tour." We were having fun with it because we had no physical participants—just us and maybe some invisible folks. It was fantastic, a lovely gift to end our journey.

It doesn't matter where we go. Back in the day we were on the road with J-R six months out of the year. When two or more are gathered, especially ministers and initiates, there "He" is inside me. Waiting to board a plane means we're going to work, and J-R and spirit are with me. And the work is everywhere. I just want to thank everybody for your support and thank you most of all, John-Roger, for the inner support that just keeps getting bigger.

Thank you.

"The moment inside of you where you forgive what's happened…it is the moment where you are enlightening yourself."

– JOHN-ROGER, D.S.S.

Resources

IN THIS SECTION, I PRESENT some resources I found particularly valuable in my learning and growing during the years I lived with J-R and beyond.

John-Roger Films
Mystical Traveler (documentary)
The Wayshower (feature)
Spiritual Warriors (feature)

John-Roger Books
J-R wrote a great many books over his lifetime. I don't think there's a bad one in the bunch, but here's a list of the ones I like best:

Passage into Spirit
The Way-Out Book
When Are You Coming Home? (Co-authored with Pauli Sanderson)
Fulfilling Your Spiritual Promise
Spiritual Warrior: The Art of Spiritual Living
Sex, Spirit & You
Relationships
Dream Voyages
The Rest of Your Life (Co-authored with Paul Kaye)

John-Roger Books on Audible.com
Spiritual Warrior: The Art of Spiritual Living
Inner Worlds of Meditation
The Way Out Book
Living the Spiritual Principles of Health and Well-Being
Spiritual Promise

John-Roger Seminars
Over the years, J-R presented literally thousands of seminars. These are some of my favorites, with their MSIA Store order numbers:

Passages to the Realms of Spirit (Nov. '81) - 7037
Are you Experiencing Your Prosperity? (Aug. '80) - 3411
The Blessed Curse (June '83) - 8210
Authentic Empowerment - 7426
Nuclear Radiation from Ground Zero - 7061
Journey to the East – Egypt & Israel – 3924
The Way Out - 7051
The Golden Thread of Divinity - 7466
Breaking the Ties That Bind - 7277
Centering to Find the Soul - 7918
Doubting the Ever-Present Christ - 7196
Humor is the Balm for Karma - 8132
Healing the Hurt - 7292
Christ Has Risen - 7389
Contributions with J-R in Alaska - 8207
Intelligence vs. Intellectualism - 2144

For more information or to order, visit: www.msia.org/store

Websites of Interest

www.soultranscendence.com
www.mysticaltraveler.com
www.SpiritualWarriors.com
www.john-roger.org
www.msia.org
www.pts.org
www.jsugarcia.com
www.mysticaltraveler.com

"If you would be loved, love, and be loveable."

– BENJAMIN FRANKLIN

The 12 Signs of the Traveler

First, the Traveler lives as an ordinary citizen. He could be married, single, divorced, or living with someone outside of marriage. Any "lifestyle" of an ordinary man might also be that of the Traveler. He lives an ordinary life—not a high life or a low life. Ordinariness is the condition just prior to God. When you become ordinary and cease to look upon yourself as unique or separate, you flow with the Spirit as it is present and become one with it and thus with God.

The second sign of a Traveler is that he does nothing to distinguish himself from the people among whom he lives. Some spiritual teachers and masters set themselves apart from their students by wearing specially colored robes, turbans, or other ornaments and paraphernalia. That is a little like moving into a community with all the people you love and then putting a fortress around your house so you can be uniquely separate from the people you love and want to be with. It doesn't make a lot of sense. If you set up your flag of separateness, you become a leader of flagpoles, not a lover among people.

There are reasonable times when leaders must be separate from others, just as there are reasonable times when everyone must be separate from others. There are reasonable times in your life when you must take time for yourself, away from the distractions of others—time to pray, meditate, rest, and revitalize yourself. That's not what I'm talking about. I'm talking about the attitude of, "I'm special and unique and greater than you." That kind of separateness is not a part of the Traveler's expression.

The third sign of a Traveler is that he has never separated his initiates or set one part of the group apart from another or allowed a caste system to evolve. He may delineate what is already present— like saying, "She is on that chair, and he is on the chair over there." That is just identifying choices which have already been made; it is not making those choices. The Traveler will never divide his people by encouraging separate dress, headgear, housing, ornaments, or other methods of separation. The Traveler encourages the experience of oneness in all ways.

The fourth sign of a Traveler is that he does not hide himself in a jungle, on a mountain, or in a cave. Could one who has separated himself and meditated in a remote area for many years become a Traveler later? Sure, if he comes out of the cave and comes down to do "battle" for the Souls of people, to share his love, and to put himself on the line for the salvation of their Souls. The "battleground" for the Soul is where the negative power is most present, and that is in the fields of emotional desire, mental decision, and financial gain. In those levels the negative power sits on the throne. The Traveler comes right into that field of endeavor to demonstrate how the positive power can prevail in the very midst of negativity.

The fifth sign of a Traveler is that he is not interested in founding religions or organizing sects. His work with people cuts across all of humanity regardless of race, creed, color, situation, circumstance or environment. His work encompasses all mankind.

The sixth sign of a Traveler is that he does not promise worldly wealth or success. I don't know how many times I've told people, "I don't promise you anything in the physical world, and when it comes to the spiritual world, there is no need to promise because that is being fulfilled all the time." Promising the spiritual world to you is like promising that you can breathe. It is happening. It is ongoing. You are participating in it right now. There is no need to promise what is already present. Some people attempt to manipulate Spirit into bringing them wealth or power in worldly manifestation. They go to psychics, use Ouija boards, or ask questions of pendulums in an attempt to "get an edge" on life's game. Sometimes they attempt to channel ascended masters, asking for information. The trouble is that the ascended master isn't there to say if the information is right or wrong, so the person gets to manipulate the information and thus manipulate other people who are depending on the information. And if they start to channel contradictory information from the master, there is additional confusion. Inner guidance given by the Traveler will never contradict the outer teachings of the Traveler. There is a oneness of the inner and outer Traveler which precludes contradiction. Some people attempt to manipulate the world around them by the procurement of spiritual charms, amulets, medallions, and so forth. The Traveler will never give any such device as a means to gain worldly success. Things like crosses, stars of David, Hu pendants, pins, and crystal hearts can all be used to reflect back to you the nature of God. Thus, such reminders can have value for you as you use them in a valuable way. They are not magnetized or charged to be used for any type of control, travel, divination or anything paranormal.

The seventh sign of a Traveler is that he does not recall dead spirits or practice any form of occultism. Calling of dead spirits might look like entering into a trance state and calling upon a spirit to speak through you. The Traveler does not practice this type of thing. The Traveler is aware that when a Soul departs from this physical world, its experience here is over, and it has gone to another place to continue its experience on another level. To attempt to bring a Soul back to this level can cause delay spiritually. It is not a loving action or one that is spiritually clear.

The eighth sign of a Traveler is that he is spiritually perfect and can extend spiritual perfection to his initiates by connecting them to the Word of God, which purifies and brings perfection to them. This is not done in the physical level because nothing can be perfect on this physical level except change. The Word of God produces a change perfectly, which is reflected inwardly on the spiritual form, not outwardly on the physical form that is gathered around the spiritual form. The physical form will never be perfect, and because it is not perfect, it is always in a state of change. As soon as you are born, you have the disease of death already in you. By your birth into the physical world, you have set your limitations and have contracted for the end of this form. That which is perfect, Spirit and Soul, does not end with physical death. The perfection is infinite. The imperfect baggage connected to Soul undergoes the process of purification through initiation into the Sound Current. It's not unlike getting the pearl out of a clam. You just have to open it up, reach in there and take the pearl. It is that "pearl of great price" with which we deal. I hear theologians sometimes refer to the Soul as "crippled." That's just nonsense. There is no Soul that is crippled. All Souls are perfect. Anyone who says otherwise hasn't seen the Soul.

The ninth sign of a Traveler is that he comes as a giver, not a receiver. He gives the very essence of life. He gives encouragement and support. He gives the seed of awakening faith and hope, but at the same time he gives these qualities, he destroys them because the experience of reality is the foundation you must stand upon. If you stand on any other quality, you'll fall. If you only have hope and faith without reality, at some point you become discouraged and say, "Where am I going with all this faith and hope? What is it doing for me?" It's like someone continually telling you the check is in the mail, but it never gets to you. You have faith and hope that you'll receive it, but you never do. At some point, you start wondering what's going on. When you get in the car, drive to the person's house, pick up the check, drive to the bank and deposit the check—then you have the reality of the experience.

The tenth sign of a Traveler is that he comes to dispel superstition. I dispel a lot of superstitions by ridicule. People tell me what they are doing and I'll say, "Why on earth would you do that?" They say, "Because I'm hoping this will take place." I say, "You mean you're going down track A hoping that you're going to get to track L? Are you hoping two parallel tracks will intersect each other? They don't! You know they don't. What you are promoting is superstition." If you have two events that are connected and you change one to affect the other, that can be a valid approach. If you have two events that are not connected and you change one in the hopes of affecting the other, you're in trouble. I used to play basketball with a friend of mine, and this fellow was better than I, but he was superstitious. He "had" to stand in a certain place on the court in order to "make" the shot. So it was easy to guard him. If I could make him move off his "spot," even by inches, I could throw his game off. He had another superstition, which was that he had to dribble twice before he shot. So all I had to do was count; he'd dribble once and I'd hit the ball out of his hands. I told him how I could read his pattern. He said, "But if I don't dribble twice, it won't go in." And he had set it up so firmly in his consciousness that it appeared to be so. Was it reality or superstition? Definitely superstition. There is no connection between how many times you dribble a ball and how many times you make the shot. They just don't go together. But they did for him. Eventually, I made his life on the court so miserable that I forced him to learn to vary his game. He had to learn to shoot from other places. And he had to learn to vary the number of times he dribbled before a shot. If you have children and you see them starting to create superstitions, talk to them about it. If you let them continue, what starts out as a relatively harmless pattern can become a compulsion that may lead to an obsession. It can lock into the subconscious and unconscious and create a block to spiritual progression. Once those things lock in, they can take a lot of work to change.

The eleventh sign of a Traveler is that he does not perform miracles for public exhibition. He may do so for the spiritual advancement of an initiate. The initiates experience miracles all the time, because they Live the miracles instead of looking for the miracles. Prior to initiation, neophytes may look for the phenomena of miracles and, although I know there are the small daily miracles of perfect timing, I also suggest strongly that they get free of all superstitions and live their lives to the fullest. When they do that, their timing automatically becomes perfect. Then they do not have to manipulate their world. They can drive to the store, pull up right in front, and have another car pull out so they can park. It's like someone has been saving a place for them. They don't have to sit and create it in their minds or try to figure some other way to do it; it will just happen. That's the phenomenon of spiritual at-tunement.

People say God is closer to you than your next breath. Right! He is the next breath. And you don't even have to wait for the next one. He is entirely present. God is not solely in the future or solely in the past; God is present. When you live in the moment, you are living in God's timing. If you do mental gymnastics, you are living ahead of yourself, and you'll distort the timing. The timing is a lot better if you just move into the flow of the timing Spirit is already bringing forward for you. What about planning ahead? You can plan ahead—in the now. How is that done? You cannot be present in the moment and be planning ahead in your mind at exactly the same time because two things cannot occupy the same space and time. But you can change the focus of your attention very rapidly. You can look at one thing, think of something else, hear something else, and keep your attention on all three by moving it from one to the other so rapidly that it looks like a continuum. It's not; those are all separate actions. As you develop your mind, you can keep more things going at what appears to be the same time. There are people who play chess with fifteen or twenty people at the same time. They just walk along making moves, then circle back and keep it all going. But since this is done in the mind, it is not truly a method of planning ahead and being in the now. Some people have this awareness out of a spiritual form, rather than a mental form. In this way they can plan ahead and still be in the now. These people don't even think. They just become the game. They know the whole process and all the moves before they are even made. But they move through the game in a process of now. They do not make a move before its timing, even if they can see it coming. Do you understand that? You never have to do something prior to the moment you have to do it. Sometimes you think you do, but you don't. You can always wait until the moment thrusts the action upon you. When the right moment appears, you will not be able to deny the action. Prior to the moment, you may think a certain action will be required, but that can always shift before the moment comes present.

The twelfth sign of a Traveler is that he relies solely on the Word of God—not the Word of God as it is printed on a piece of paper or written in a book, but the Word of God as it is given inwardly.

The Traveler gives the Word of God to his initiates so they may do likewise. Then we all get to stand in the same line, eat at the same table, and live the same love. There is no more separation, grief, terror or hurt, because we are all together. No man is an island. No man stands alone. Each man's joy is joy to me. And each man's grief my own, although I do not support the expression of grief in my initiates. Grief is nearly always a response based upon a false expectation. Some people who follow certain religious teachings talk about grief and sorrow experienced relative to the "loss" of Jesus Christ. That's nonsense. Since God and the savior consciousness are truly present, there is no room for sorrow or grief. There is only joy and abundance, no matter what has taken place. The illusion of "loss" holds no power when Spirit is present in your heart. There is always joy in the presence of the Lord. And the presence of the Lord is not a once-in-awhile process. It is a constant, ongoing, moment-to-moment reality. When you focus on the Lord, you find Him present with you. He has never been apart from you; you have just been distracted by other levels. When you focus on the Lord, you come to know Him. When you know God, you can love God. The keys to the knowledge and love of God are within you. You cannot be taught those things, only awakened to them. When you know God, you will know the Traveler because he comes as an emissary or agent of the Supreme God. There is no separation. The Traveler comes to assist you in awakening consciously to the Lord. As you add the strength of consciousness to the intuitive knowledge and love, you can move yourself deeper and higher into awareness of the spiritual realms. Again, my friends let me emphasize that you will know the Traveler by the living love that is present for all humanity. Jesus the Christ said it this way: "By this shall all men know that ye are my disciples, if ye have love one to another." (John 14:34) A teacher is one who lives the loving quality. There is only the teacher or Wayshower now.

You are sophisticated and can go to God directly. God is living love, as you must be the same living love to reach him. God is so large that to explore all the levels of God requires such a loving commitment of time that there is no time to pick on people, backbite, or be depressed. You only have time—eternity. All is present inside of you. God has prepared the table of plenty for you. God has placed Souls of resourcefulness here. We are beyond the scriptures. Mohammed completed scripture. Bahaullah completed scripture. All that remains to do is love. God is dwelling among his chosen people. God is dwelling in the heart. God is greater than the heart. God is all, not a part, yet every part. Love God with all your heart. Love yourself with the same devotion. Love all who come to you as you love God. But practice finding the loving within yourself before you look out. With loving, nothing is impossible. With loving, you can overcome all things. You can overcome your fears, your insecurities, your disturbances, everything. Through the Christ consciousness that is your heritage, you are born anew, resurrected in Spirit.

"Buddha said, "I am the Light of Asia." Christ said, "I am the Light of the world." The Traveler says, "I am the Light of the universe." And the Preceptor says, "I am the Light of all universes." This is not a spiritual promise. It is reality. It is present now, as are all the saints and saviors and masters of all time. You breathe the same air that Bahaullah, Mohammed, Jesus, Solomon, David, Moses, Joseph, Abraham, and all the others breathed. When you attune yourself to the Christ, you tune yourself back into the heritage of this whole line of energy and power. Their love and Light comes right down through you, and the only way you can manifest it is to love. Loving is the glory of God made manifest. As you become one in consciousness with this line of spiritual authority, you experience the greatest joy and peace you can ever imagine.

– Excerpt from John-Roger, D.S.S, *The Path to Mastership*

"Genius without education is like silver in the mine."

– BENJAMIN FRANKLIN

Glossary of Terms

WHILE MANY OF THE FOLLOWING terms were used in *Love of a Master*, other phrases not specifically mentioned have been included as common references by John-Roger or used often within the MSIA community. Most of these definitions are excerpted from the 3-book set, *Fulfilling Your Spiritual Promise* by John-Roger, D.S.S. Other defined terms are taken from *Spiritual Gems* by the Great Master Hazur Baba Sawan Singh.

Affirmation – A positive statement that is repeated to oneself in order to generate an uplifted mindset and positive results.

Akashic Records – The vast spiritual records in which every Soul's entire experiences are recorded.

Ani-Hu – A chant, or spiritual tone, used in MSIA. "Hu" is an ancient Sanskrit name for God, and "Ani" adds the quality of empathy and unity. See also *Spiritual Exercises* and *Tone*.

Ascended Masters – Nonphysical beings of high spiritual development who are part of the spiritual hierarchy. May work out of any realm above the physical realm. See also *Spiritual Hierarchy*.

Astral Realm – The psychic, material realm above the physical realm. The realm of the imagination. Intertwines with the physical as a vibratory rate. See also *Inner Levels/Realms* and *Psychic, Material Realms*.

Astral Travel– Occurs when the consciousness leaves the physical body to travel in the astral realm.

Aura – The electromagnetic energy field that surrounds the human body. Has color and movement.

Aura Balance – A service offered by specially trained MSIA staff members that helps to balance the aura and dispel negativity using a crystal pendulum.

Baruch Bashan (bay-roosh´ bay-shan´)– Hebrew words meaning "the blessings already are." The blessings of Spirit exist in the here and now.

Basic Self – A part of the consciousness that has responsibility for bodily functions; maintains habits and the psychic centers of the physical body. Also known as the *lower self*. Handles prayers from the physical to the high self. See also *Conscious Self* and *High Self*.

Beloved – The Soul; the God within.

Causal Realm– The psychic, material realm above the astral realm and below the mental realm. Intertwines somewhat with the physical realm as a vibratory rate. See also *Inner Levels/Realms* and *Psychic, Material Realms*.

Christ, Office of the – The Christ is a spiritual office, much like the presidency of the United States. Many people have filled that office, Jesus the Christ having filled it more fully than any other being. One of the highest offices in the realms of Light.

Cosmic Mirror – The mirror at the top of the void, which is at the top of the etheric realm, just below the Soul realm. Everything that has not been cleared in the physical, astral, causal, and mental levels is projected onto the cosmic mirror.

Crown Chakra – The psychic center at the top of the head.

Devas – Nonphysical beings from the Devic kingdom that serve humankind by caring for the elements of nature. They support the proper functioning of all natural things on the planet.

Discourses – See *Soul Awareness Discourses.*

Doctor of Spiritual Science (D.S.S.) – a degree program from Peace Theological Seminary & College of Philosophy.

Dream Master – A spiritual master with whom the Mystical Traveler works and who assists one in balancing past actions while dreaming.

Etheric Realm – The psychic, material realm above the mental realm and below the Soul realm. Equated with the unconscious or subconscious level. Sometimes known as the esoteric realm. See also *Inner Levels/Realms* and *Psychic, Material Realms.*

False Self – Can be thought of as the ego, the individualized personality that incorrectly perceives itself to be fundamentally separated from others and God.

Great White Brotherhood – Nonphysical spiritual beings working in service to mankind in the spiritual line of the Christ and Mystical Traveler. They can assist with spiritual clearing and upliftment.

High Self – The self that functions as one's spiritual guardian, directing the conscious self towards those experiences that are for one's greatest spiritual progression. Has knowledge of the destiny pattern agreed upon before embodiment. See also *Basic Self, Conscious Self*, and *Karmic Board*.

Holy Spirit – The positive energy of Light and Sound that comes from the Supreme God. The life force that sustains everything in all creation. Often uses the magnetic Light through which to work on the psychic, material realms. Works only for the highest good. Is the third part of the Trinity or Godhead.

Hu – A tone, or sound, that is an ancient name of the Supreme God in Sanskrit. See also *Spiritual Exercises* and *Tone*.

Initiation – In MSIA, the process of being connected to the Sound Current of God, known as Shabd or Shabda. See also *Initiation Tone, Shabd*, and *Sound Current*.

Initiation Tone – In MSIA, spiritually charged words given to an initiate in a Sound Current initiation. The name of the Lord of the realm into which the person is being initiated. See also *Initiation*.

Inner Levels/Realms – The astral, causal, mental, etheric, and Soul realms that exist within a person's consciousness. See also *Outer Levels/Realms*.

Inner Master – The inner expression of the Mystical Traveler, existing within a person's consciousness.

Insight Seminars – A series of experiential, transformational seminars, designed by John-Roger and Russell Bishop in 1978 to provide people with practical and accessible tools for living a successful life, based on universal truths of loving, acceptance, and personal responsibility.

Institute for Individual and World Peace (IIWP) – A non-profit organization formed in 1982 to study, identify, and present the processes that lead to peace.

John-Roger Foundation – An organization that established an annual global Integrity Day on September 24. Presented International Integrity Awards to such luminaries as Mother Teresa, Bishop Desmond Tutu, Solidarity leader Lech Walesa, Dr. Jonas Salk, and others between 1983 and 1987.

Karma – The law of cause and effect: as you sow, so shall you reap. The responsibility of each person for his or her actions. The law that directs and sometimes dominates a being's physical existence. See also *Reincarnation* and *Wheel of 84*.

Karmic Board – A group of nonphysical spiritual masters who meet with a being before embodiment to assist in the planning of that being's spiritual journey on Earth. The Mystical Traveler has a function in this group.

Light – The energy of Spirit that pervades all realms of existence. Also refers to the Light of the Holy Spirit.

Light, Magnetic – The Light of God that functions in the psychic, material realms. Not as high as the Light of the Holy Spirit, and does not necessarily function for the highest good. See also *Light* and *Holy Spirit.*

Light Masters – Nonphysical spiritual teachers who work on the psychic, material realms to assist people in their spiritual progression.

Line of the Travelers – The line of spiritual energy extending from the Mystical Traveler Consciousness, in which the Mystical Traveler's students function.

Lords of Karma – See *Karmic Board.*

Master of Spiritual Science (M.S.S.) – a degree program from Peace Theological Seminary & College of Philosophy.

Masters of Light – See *Light Masters.*

Melchizedek Priesthood/Order — Spiritual authority emanating from the Christ that originated with the Biblical high priest who met Abraham. The line of energy into which MSIA ordains its ministers. See also *Minister, Ministry,* and *Ordination.*

Mental Realm – The psychic, material realm above the causal realm and below the etheric realm. Relates to the universal mind. See also *Inner Levels/Realms* and *Psychic, Material Realms.*

Minister – A person in MSIA who has been ordained into the Melchizedek priesthood. *Melchizedek Priesthood/Order, Ministry,* and *Ordination.*

Ministry – The spiritually charged focus on service to self, others, community, and the world by an ordained MSIA minister. See also *Melchizedek Priesthood/Order, Minister,* and *Ordination.*

Movement of Spiritual Inner Awareness (MSIA) – An organization founded by John-Roger whose major focus is to bring people into an awareness of Soul Transcendence.

Mystery Schools – Schools in Spirit, in which initiates receive training and instruction. Initiates of the Traveler Consciousness study in mystery schools that are under the Traveler's auspices.

Mystical Traveler Consciousness – An energy from the highest source of Light and Sound whose spiritual directive on Earth is awakening people to the awareness of the Soul. This consciousness always exists on the planet through a physical form.

Negative Realms – See *Psychic, Material Realms.*

New Day Herald – MSIA's bimonthly printed newspaper for many years. Now available only online, except for special issues.

90-Percent Level – That part of a person's existence beyond the physical level; that is, one's existence on the astral, causal, mental, etheric, and Soul realms. See also *10-Percent Level.*

Ocean of Love and Mercy – Another term for Spirit on the Soul level and above. See also *Soul Realm* and *Spirit*.

Ordination – A sacred ceremony to ordain a new minister into the Melchizedek Priesthood with a universal charge to minister to all, regardless of race, creed, color, situation, circumstances, or environment. In the MSIA Ministerial Handbook, John-Roger says, "Once a person is [approved to be] an ordained minister, there are two levels of ordination that take place. One is the fulfilling of the law; the laying on of hands ... those that hold the keys to the Melchizedek Order then communicate to other people a direct line of electric magnetic spiritual energy. The other is the gift of Spirit through the Order of Melchizedek; the Spiritual Blessing. Almost every [minister] has the same wording [at the beginning of their] ministerial ordination. Then the Melchizedek Order stands in and says, 'And Spirit brings its blessings.' AS YOU FULFILL YOUR MINISTRY IT IS THEN THAT SPIRIT DROPS THE BLESSING IN UPON YOU." See also *Melchizedek Priesthood/ Order*, *Minister*, and *Ministry*.

Outer Levels/Realms – The astral, causal, mental, etheric, and Soul realms above the Soul realm also exist outside a person's consciousness, but in a greater way. See also *Inner Levels/Realms*.

PATs – See *Peace Awareness Trainings*.

Peace Awareness Labyrinth & Gardens (PAL&G)– The official name for PRANA since 2002; its grounds feature an embedded stone labyrinth and terraced meditation gardens that are open to the public. See also *PRANA*.

***Peace Awareness Trainings** (PATs)* – A series of weeklong spiritual retreats offered by Peace Theological Seminary & College of Philosophy in various locations around the world.

Peace Theological Seminary & College of Philosophy (PTS) – A private, nondenominational school founded by John-Roger as the educational arm of MSIA to present his teachings of practical spirituality that integrate the physical and spiritual worlds.

Physical Realm – The earth. The psychic, material realm in which a being lives with a physical body. See also *Inner Levels/Realms* and *Psychic, Material Realms*.

Positive Realms – The Soul realm and the 27 levels above the Soul realm. See also *Psychic, Material Realms*.

PRANA – An acronym for "Purple Rose Ashram of the New Age," a group residence and the headquarters of MSIA and PTS since 1974, located in the heart of Los Angeles near downtown. The property was renovated and renamed Peace Awareness Labyrinth & Gardens in 2002. See also *Peace Awareness Labyrinth & Gardens*.

Preceptor Consciousness – A spiritual energy of the highest source, which exists outside creation. It has manifested on the planet in a physical embodiment (such as John-Roger) once every 25,000 to 28,000 years.

Psychic, Material Realms – The five lower, negative realms; namely, the physical, astral, causal, mental, and etheric realms. See also *Positive Realms*.

Reincarnation – the repeated embodiment of a soul onto the physical realm to clear its debts, right any wrongs, and bring balance and harmony. See also *Karma* and *Wheel of 84*.

SATs – See *Soul Awareness Tape* (SAT series).

Satsang – (Sanskrit) A spiritual discourse or sacred gathering, such as when a congregation is addressed by a Master; to contemplate the Master's teachings and engage in the prescribed meditation; association of one's soul with the Shabd or Sound Current inwardly. See also *Seminar, Shabd, and Sound Current.*

Seeding – A form of prayer to God for something that one wants to manifest in the world. It is done by placing a "seed" (donating an amount of money) for the highest good with the source of one's spiritual teachings.

S.E.'s – See *Spiritual Exercises.*

Seminar – Refers to a type of Satsang (sacred discourse) to an assembly of students by John-Roger or John Morton; also, an audiotape, CD, videotape, DVD, or download of a talk either of them has given. See also *Satsang.*

Shabd (or *Shabda*) – Sanskrit name for the Sound Current; the Word of God that manifests itself as Inner Spiritual Sound, as the Soul manifests in the body as consciousness. Also known as the Audible Life Stream. There are five forms of the Shabd within every human being, the secret of which can only be imparted by a True Master. See also *Sound Current* and *Spiritual Exercises.*

Soul – The extension of God individualized within each human being. The basic element of human existence, forever connected to God. The indwelling Christ, the God within.

Soul Awareness Discourses – Booklets that students in MSIA read monthly as their spiritual study, for individual private and personal use only. They are an important part of the Traveler's teachings on the physical level.

Soul Awareness Tapes (SAT series) – Audiotapes, CDs, or mp3s of seminars given by John-Roger, for individual and private study only. They are an important part of the Traveler's teachings on the physical level.

Soul Consciousness – A positive state of being. Once a person is established in Soul consciousness, he or she need no longer be bound or influenced by the lower levels of Light.

Soul Realm – The realm above the etheric realm. The first of the positive realms and the true home of the Soul. The first level where the Soul is consciously aware of its true nature, its pure beingness, its oneness with God.

Soul Transcendence – The process of moving the consciousness beyond the psychic, material realms and into the Soul realm and beyond.

Soul Travel – Traveling in Spirit to realms of consciousness other than the physical realm. Sometimes known as out-of-body experiences. This can be done in one's own inner realms or in the outer realms, the higher spiritual realms. See also *Inner Levels/Realms* and *Outer Levels/Realms.*

Sound Current – The audible energy that flows from God through all realms. The spiritual energy upon which a person rides to return to the heart of God, also known as *Shabd* or *Shabda*. See also *Shabd* and *Spiritual Exercises*.

Spirit – The essence of creation. Infinite and eternal.

Spiritual Exercises (S.E.'s) – The active practice of the Sound Current; the union of the soul with Shabd; applying the current of consciousness to hearing the Sound within; joining the mind and attention to the Sound Current through chanting a spiritual tone such as "Hu," "Ani-Hu," or one's initiation tone. Assists a person in breaking through the illusions of the lower levels and eventually moving into Soul consciousness. See also *Initiation Tone, Shabd* and *Sound Current*.

Spiritual Eye – The area in the center of the head, back from the center of the forehead. Used to see inwardly. Also called the *Third Eye*.

Spiritual Hierarchy – The nonphysical spiritual forces that oversee this planet and the other psychic, material realms.

Spiritual Warrior – a spiritually focused person who expresses with impeccable honesty using the "sword of truth" from their heart and lives a life of health, wealth, happiness, abundance, prosperity, riches, loving, caring, sharing, and touching to others. From a John-Roger audio seminar and book of the same name.

10-Percent Level – The physical level of existence, as contrasted with the 90 percent of a person's existence that is beyond the physical realm. See also *90-Percent Level*.

Third Ear – The unseen spiritual ear by which we listen inwardly and hear the Sound Current of God.

Third Eye – See *Spiritual Eye*.

Tisra Til – The seat or headquarters of the mind and soul in the human body, located in the center of the head, back from the forehead and between the two eyebrows, where the Soul energy gathers. Because the first nine doors (eyes, ears, nose, mouth, and two lower apertures) lead outward, this is also known as the Tenth Door or Gate—the only one that leads within.

Tithing – The spiritual practice of giving 10 percent of one's increase to God by giving it to the source of one's spiritual teachings.

Tone – A spiritual sound such as "Hu," "Ani-Hu," or other specially charged word that is chanted inwardly (and sometimes aloud).

Twaji – Gaze of grace from the Spiritual Master; the gaze of God.

Universal Mind – Located at the highest part of the etheric realm, at the division between the negative and positive realms. Gets its energy from the mental realm. The source of the individual mind.

University of Santa Monica (USM) - A private, non-profit institution that pioneered a Master's in Spiritual Psychology program from 1981 to 2016, and continues to offer Soul-Centered educational courses worldwide. John-Roger was the Founder and Chancellor; John Morton serves as the current Chancellor; Drs. Ron and Mary Hulnick are USM's Co-Directors.

Wheel of 84 – The reincarnation, re-embodiment cycle. See also *Karma* and *Reincarnation*.

Windermere Ranch – MSIA's 142 acres of land in the Santa Ynez mountains overlooking Santa Barbara, CA, originally established by the Institute for Individual and World Peace.

Acknowledgments

THERE ARE A NUMBER OF people I want to acknowledge here, because without them, this book would not exist.

Always first is John-Roger, for reasons way too numerous to mention, but I'll try. J-R, I so appreciate you letting me be with you this lifetime. I'd do it again in a heartbeat. Wherever you go, I'll go. You taught me so much and I'm indebted to you. I always asked you before going to sleep and I'll continue to ask: "Wanna do SEs, J-R?" J-R: "Sure, you first." Jsu: "Take me with you?" J-R: "Okay." I want to continue to work with you forever, John-Roger. I love you.

Nicole Tenaglia, thank you for your loving and holding for me during the really difficult times. We both stood strong for each other looking towards the Lord. Thanks for sitting in the passenger seat and letting me drive you as J-R. I love you and twice on Sundays!

Elda and Delile Hinkins, I met you both years back and we became family immediately. Thank you for your love and kindness over the years and especially after Roger Hinkins, AKA John-Roger, passed. I'm forever grateful to the Hinkins' DNA instilled in my blood. Love you always.

LDM, you supported John-Roger and his personal staff for many years. Personal trips etc. I won't forget. Thank you so much for your endless and bountiful Christmas days with you and your family. I love you.

Zoe Golightly Lumiere, thanks for your endless devotion to J-R, your loyalty and what an amazing ride we had. You are a true soldier and Spiritual Warrior. The mission was "Get J-R out." You never failed. Thank you. Love you.

John Morton, thank you for serving as my example of devotion to our Traveler John-Roger and continuing to show up and hold for the things he stood for. And for being my older brother. Love you.

Laren Bright and Penelope Bright, you are amazing at turning ideas into words. You were there for me in the beginning as my facilitators for J-R home seminars back in 1986. God bless you and I love you.

Nat Sharratt, it was a long ride for you and me. You have stood strong during the fierceness and force of this storm/Paradise journey. You found, like I did, the eye of the storm is where we lived. Love you, brother.

Keith Malinsky, my friend since 1982. You lovingly did a massive job of transcribing hours and hours of mp3s. I really thank you for your friendship. We've come a long way. I love you, my friend.

David Sand, thank you for the many trips together with J-R. I appreciate all of the great images and graphics you captured to document the life of a Great Master and your friendship. Love you.

Leigh Taylor-Young Morton, thank you for your caring and your examples of devotion. Keep smiling and shining.

Nicia Ferrer, my mother. I prayed for you and Granny Rosa Rey to be taken home by J-R, and I'm so glad J-R's got both of you. Love you, Ma and Granny.

Ron Hulnick, thanks for your support days after John-Roger passed. The lunch with the scorpion was a learning. USM was a lab that helped make my broken pieces stronger. Love you.

Mary Hulnick, I will always love your reading of the USM handouts; it truly was a beautiful reminder that it was how I loved learning from grade-school days. USM truly comes from John-Roger's teachings and he chose two masters to run it and demonstrate its love into the world.

Howard Lazar, my dear friend. Thank you for holding and encouraging me to be strong. You helped me through many tough times. Thanks for playing J-R in *The Wayshower*. Love you.

Heidi Banks, thank you for your love and support to me and J-R. Thanks for your help.

Marilyn and Irwin Carasso, thank you forever for your love and support. Thanks for being there. I love you.

Laurie Lerner, I saw you help J-R and staff in many ways for many years. Thank you, Laurie. Love you forever. Raphi too.

Zane Morton, thanks for letting me be your second father. I love you. Thanks for ministering to me son.

Clare Morton, Love you.

Betsy Alexander, we've worked together and I truly learned from you. Thanks for letting me borrow parts of your Glossary from FYSP. I really appreciate it. Thanks for being with John-Roger to the end. You're a Warrior. I love you

Nathalie Franks, thank you for your support and I love you. London calling us forever.

Barbara Weiland, you are amazing and so resourceful and I'll always treasure the work you did for me and J-R on Mystical Traveler. Love you!

Phil Danza, 29 years in the same home with J-R. Thank you for being there for me at Mandeville after John-Roger's passing. I love you always.

Brooke Danza, 29 years living together…amazing. Living with J-R was amazing. Living with the Danzas was easy. Love you.

Prez (Paul, Mark and Vincent), thanks for holding for MSIA and John-Roger and supporting my Ministry. Love you.

Jason Laskay, Love you always. You've served the Boss for many years, Don Jason. J-R's dogs love you forever. You are a good man.

Jan Shepherd, thank you for being there when times were tough. Thanks for serving J-R and for being my Jewish mom. I love you.

Rick Ojeda, thanks for being there for J-R and me. Great times and I appreciate your devotion and dedication to the Master.

Erik Raleigh and Mark Harradine, thank you for being there for J-R and me. Only a J-R staff member knows what that is, and I wanted to say I love you guys.

Ishwar Puri-ji, you and Toshi were there and brought understanding on the inner. You lost your master physical also and I thank you for letting me lean on you for comfort. I do love you for it. We are friends always. I love you.

Toshi Puri, once I saw you we were connected. I truly appreciate you and how you love and support Ishwar.

Nicholas Brown, thanks brother for all you've done for me and John-Roger and the Trips we lead together. Love you very much.

Marc Alhonte, thanks to you for helping, supporting and creating the freedom I needed for my Ministry.

Melba Alhonte, you have been my light for all the trips and for all your support of J-R and me. I love you. Gracias.

Christine Lynch, you and Jim created a home for me to nurture myself in the big Apple. Love you.

Jim Lynch, thank you for holding for me and I love your animals. Love you. Love you.

Katherine and Frank Price, thank you for being there months after J-R's passing. You've always hosted J-R with love and I felt the fellowship and love from the Prices.

Hollie and Robert Holden, thank you for your dinners and welcoming me to your warm home with your wonderful kids. I love you.

Carrie Doubt, my Project Leader, thanks to your commitment and encouragement during USM and outside of USM. You are Light. Love you.

Howard and Jeeni Lawrence, thank you for holding for me and loving me through it all. Thanks for keeping me going to class. Your light nurtured me. I love you.

Pauli and Peter Sanderson, thank you for your light and love. I love you.

Veronique and Babadandan, thank you for being my friends. I truly love you guys. Love you.

Teri Breier, thank you for hand holding and your love for *The Love of a Master*. You are a writing goddess. Love you.

Wayne Alexander, thanks for being there for me.

Jesus Garcia, Dad, I love you. Thanks for being there.

Terry Garcia, my stepmother, I love you always.

Lana Barreira, you nurtured me and took care of me your heart is Brazil.

Paulina Haddad, thanks for your friendship and all you've done for J-R and the kids, I see you.

Juliana Rose, thanks for letting me be me.

Rinaldo and Maritza Porchile, thank you and I love you guys.

UK Ministers, thank you for all your support and love for John-Roger and our trips.

Reymi Urrich, thanks for supporting me and John-Roger's films.

Yoci Touche and Mavi Lopez, thank you for your support and love.

Ozzie, Maravilla, and the rest of the Delgadillo family. I love you and so appreciate your support to John-Roger and my Ministry.

Myles and Olga Abrams, I truly love your friendship.

Angel Harper, thanks for your light and Love. I Love you.

Timothea Stewart, love you always.

Steve Small, you were there in the beginning working with J-R I love you and appreciate your many years of supporting us.

Thank you to all the practitioners that I've witnessed over the years assisting J-R and staff, thank you for the teachings I observed. God bless Baraka Clinic.

Roberta and Bertrand Babinet, thanks you for the many memories with J-R.

Michael and Alisha Hayes, thanks for your support to J-R and staff. Love you always.

Ed Wagner, Thanks for your love and support to J-R and many in MSIA. Love you.

David and Serene Denton, I remember the love and support to J-R and me. Thank you and I love you. God bless.

Bryan Mcmullen, thank you for all your help and support to me.

J-R's Angels: Rodi, Trish, Joan, Nancy, Christina, Shannon, Annie and Terri.

"...the greatest similarity we have of all of these groups that are out of the Sound Current would be the Surat Shabd Yoga out of India, out of Hazur Sawan Singh, who is the great Master that brought it forward through the line of the Sikhs. I have the same spiritual lineage as that."

– John-Roger, D.S.S. (May 30, 1982
Q&A in Gustavus, Alaska)

About the Author

REV. JESUS GARCIA, D.S.S., SPENT 26 years working for and learning from his spiritual teacher and Mystical Traveler, John-Roger, D.S.S., founder of the Los Angeles-based Church of the Movement of Spiritual Inner Awareness (MSIA). Garcia was initiated into the Sound Current of God by John-Roger and ordained as a minister into the order of Melchizedek Priesthood by John Morton, who currently holds the keys to the Mystical Traveler Consciousness.

In creative collaboration with each other, John-Roger (known as J-R) and Garcia—a respected Hollywood cinema veteran—co-produced three feature movies—*Spiritual Warriors*, *The Wayshower*, and *Mystical Traveler*—and four short films. Since J-R's transition in October of 2014, Garcia has continued his ministry of sharing the spiritual teachings of John-Roger through screening *Mystical Traveler*, conducting workshops on Practical Spirituality, and providing spiritual counseling to students and initiates of the Traveler all around the globe.

Previously, as an actor, Garcia appeared on-screen in such popular films as *A Nightmare on Elm Street*, *Along Came Polly*, *We Were Soldiers*, *Spiritual Warriors*, *Collateral Damage*, and *Atlas Shrugged*. *The Love of a Master* is his first book. He resides in Los Angeles, California.

Scott J-R Productions
C/O Jesus Garcia, D.S.S.
1626 Montana Ave Suite 624
Santa Monica, California 90403
www.soultranscendence.com
utah7@mac.com

Made in the USA
Columbia, SC
07 June 2018